SOCIOLOGY IN ACTION

TITLES OF RELATED INTEREST FROM PINE FORGE PRESS

This Book Is Not Required, Rev. ed., by Inge Bell and Bernard McGrane

Sociology for a New Century by York Bradshaw, Joseph Healey, and Rebecca Smith

Exploring Social Issues: Using SPSS for Windows 95 Versions 7.5, 8.0, or Higher by Joseph Healey, John Boli, Earl Babbie, and Fred Halley

Illuminating Social Life: Classical and Contemporary Theory Revisited, 2nd ed., edited by Peter Kivisto

Key Ideas in Sociology by Peter Kivisto

Multiculturalism in the United States: Current Issues, Contemporary Voices by Peter Kivisto and Georganne Rundblad

The Riddles of Human Society by Donald Kraybill and Conrad Kanagy

Sociological Snapshots: Seeing Social Structure and Change in Everyday Life, 3rd ed., by Jack Levin

Sociology Through Active Learning: Student Exercises for Exploring the Discipline by Kathleen McKinney, Frank D. Beck, Barbara S. Heyl

Sociology: Exploring the Architecture of Everyday Life, 3rd ed., by David Newman

Sociology: Exploring the Architecture of Everyday Life (Readings), 3rd ed., by David Newman

Social Prisms: Reflections on Everyday Myths and Paradoxes by Jodi O'Brien

The Social Worlds of Higher Education: Handbook for Teaching in a New Century edited by Bernice Pescosolido and Ronald Aminzade

Enchanting a Disenchanted World: Revolutionizing the Means of Consumption by George Ritzer

Expressing America: A Critique of the Global Credit Card Society by George Ritzer

The McDonaldization of Society, New Century ed., by George Ritzer

Making Societies: The Historical Construction of Our World by William A. Roy

Second Thoughts: Seeing Conventional Wisdom Through the Sociological Eye, 2nd ed., by Janet M. Ruane and Karen A. Cerulo

Shifts in the Social Contract: Understanding Change in American Society by Beth A. Rubin

SOCIOLOGY IN ACTION

Cases for Critical and Sociological Thinking

David S. Hachen Jr.
University of Wisconsin–Madison

PINE FORGE PRESS
Thousand Oaks, California
London ◆ New Delhi

For information:

 Pine Forge Press
A Sage Publications Company
2455 Teller Road
Thousand Oaks, California 91320
E-mail: order@sagepub.com

Sage Publications Ltd.
6 Bonhill Street
London EC2A 4PU
United Kingdom

Sage Publications India Pvt. Ltd.
M-32 Market
Greater Kailash I
New Delhi 110 048 India

Printed in the United States of America

Library of Congress Cataloging-in-Publication Data

Hachen, David S. Jr.
    Sociology in action: Cases for critical and sociological thinking /
by David Hachen.
        p.   cm.
    Includes bibliographical references and index.
        ISBN 0-7619-8663-4
        1. Sociology—Methodology.   2. Sociology—Case studies.
    3. Sociology—Philosophy.   I. Title.
        HM511 .H33   2001
        301'.01—dc21   00-011076

01   02   03   04   05   06   07   7   6   5   4   3   2   1

Publisher: Stephen D. Rutter
Assistant to the Publisher: Ann Makarias
Production Editor: Diana E. Axelsen
Editorial Assistant: Victoria Cheng
Typesetter/Designer: Barbara Burkholder
Indexer: Mary Mortensen
Cover Designer: Ravi Balasuriya

About the Author

David S. Hachen Jr. (Ph.D., University of Wisconsin–Madison) is
Associate Professor of Sociology at the University of Notre Dame.
He has been using decision cases and other active learning pedagogies
in his courses ever since he was a Lilly Teaching Fellow. As a teacher-
scholar and a former Director of Graduate Studies, he has a strong
interest in training the next generation of researchers and educators.
His research and teaching interests are in the areas of social
inequalities and stratification, labor markets, organizations,
and statistics and research methods.

About the Publisher

Pine Forge Press is an educational publisher dedicated to
publishing innovative books and software throughout the social
sciences. On this and any other of our publications, we welcome
your comments and suggestions. Please call or write us at

> **Pine Forge Press**
> A Sage Publications Company
> 31 St. James Avenue, Suite 510
> Boston, MA 02116
> (617) 753-7512
> E-mail: info@pfp.sagepub.com

*Visit our World Wide Web site, your direct link to a multitude of
online resources:*

www. pineforge.com

To my father, who taught me how to think, write, and speak.

CONTENTS

PART I: Doing Sociology

PART II: Decision Cases

FOREWORD

We hardly need another introductory sociology text, so the question is, Why do we need *Sociology in Action*? My answer is quite simple. This is a book that definitely will accomplish what the author intends, provided that those who adopt it require students to use it. This is a book that students will not be able to skim or read occasionally. They will have to use it, reread parts of it, pause and think and discuss and write about what they've read, and apply what they've read to understand and solve problems and issues presented to them in case studies. David Hachen has written a book that will require students to *take* action to understand sociology *in* action. The reasons for this are the two pedagogical techniques around which the book is organized: the use of case studies and the critical inquiry method of teaching and learning. As the author states in the Preface, "In contrast to standard textbooks in which coverage of sociological ideas, theories, and research is the primary objective, this book is designed to teach students how to *use* sociological ideas and knowledge" (pp. xvii-xviii).

To my knowledge, this is the first introductory book in sociology that has a very high potential to develop fundamental skills systematically, skills that every educated person should possess, and to provide an excellent introduction to the discipline of sociology. *Sociology in Action* is designed to contribute explicitly to several general education, liberal arts learning goals: critical thinking, problem solving, and both oral and written communication. As students learn about sociology, they are asked to deconstruct sociologically a variety of case studies through problem solving, critical reasoning, and oral and written communication.

Hachen begins each chapter with a case study and then introduces the reader to a thoughtful, complete, and compelling sociological analysis of the issues and problems the case study presents. In this way, the author models for students what he expects each of them to learn and to be able to do from using his book. Each chapter builds on the preceding one. Each chapter gradually introduces students to key ideas and concepts that are necessary to understand social connections and then asks students to apply these ideas and concepts to a case study at the end of each chapter so they can learn to see through sociological eyes. In this thoughtful, organized way, students are given plenty of opportunity to practice sociological analysis and to sharpen their skills as they learn to see not only the world as a sociologist does, but also how sociology can be used to solve problems that emerge from social connections and interaction. By doing this, students will learn incrementally to do something that they could not do before encountering this text—use critical thinking and problem solving along with sociological knowledge to understand a complex social situation.

The proof of this is in the pudding. If students are asked during the first day of class to analyze and comment on the first case study presented in Chapter 1 and then are asked to do the same assignment again on the last day of class, the results will be dramatic. Using this book, students will leave the introductory course knowing and seeing what they have learned and taken away from it. There will be no guessing on their part. What they learn about sociology will not be a mystery, for students will know at the very beginning that they do not have a sociologist's ability to analyze cases that present real issues and problems. After practice with other cases, following Hachen's model of seeing with a sociological eye, students will gain increasing competency and understanding, and they also will be able to gauge their increasing sophistication with sociological analysis. The best form of learning is when students are able to know what it is they have learned and to be confident about it.

The case study method is long overdue in sociology. Professional programs—nursing, business, medicine, law, engineering—long have used the case method of instruction with great success. Cases present real-world problems and issues that do not have simple, linear answers. They are a good fit with the sociological perspective and with sociological analysis. It is also long overdue that an introductory textbook is designed not only to teach students sociology but also to help them learn some of the fundamental learning goals of a liberal arts education—how to think more clearly and critically, how to problem solve, and how to write and speak more coherently about what they are learning.

In brief, this book has the merit of bringing together in a wonderful ensemble the rudiments of sociological knowledge, critical thinking, and sociological analysis about case examples. In the strange anthropological world of the text as we know it, this is no small accomplishment.

—Dean S. Dorn
California State University, Sacramento

PREFACE

I have created this book for educators who want to use an active learning approach to introduce their students to sociology. As such, this book differs in three important ways from standard introductory books:

1. The book's objective is to help students develop a *skill*—their ability to "read" and analyze situations sociologically.

2. Development of student skills and their "sociological eyesight" is facilitated through practice using *decision cases,* relatively short problem-centered narratives that promote critical thinking.

3. The book's structure promotes the *progressive* and *incremental* development of this skill. Subsequent chapters build on and return to previous material so that as the course proceeds, student competencies are enhanced and expanded.

OBJECTIVE: SKILL DEVELOPMENT

The objective of the book is the development of a *skill*—the ability to "read" and analyze situations sociologically. In contrast to standard textbooks in which coverage of sociological ideas, theories, and research is the primary objective, this book is designed to teach students how to *use* sociological ideas and knowledge. Upon completing a course that uses this book, students should be able to do things they could not have done prior to taking the course. Among the important skills students should acquire are the ability to do the following:

- Identify and describe the social connections (social relationships, groups, networks, organizations) among social actors in a given situation
- Use multiple theoretical perspectives to reframe and see situations from different angles
- Decode the culture in a given situation by analyzing symbols, stories, and worldviews so that situations can be understood from the point of view of the social actors
- Uncover inequalities by examining the distribution of resources and power to see how class, race, and gender differences affect the ability of people to pursue their interests
- Imagine futures by investigating how driving forces can propel social change

These skills are taught through the materials contained in the five chapters in Part I of the book: "Seeing Society," "Using Theory," "Decoding Culture," "Uncovering Inequalities and Power," and "Imagining Futures." In each chapter, core sociological ideas are introduced by showing how they can be used to analyze real situations. Each chapter concludes with a "Sociological Eye Analysis Guide" consisting of questions that students can use to guide themselves through a sociological analysis of a situation using the skills they have acquired in the chapter.

By emphasizing skill development, this book also is designed to enhance four student competencies that all college graduates should possess:

1. *Analysis:* the ability to think clearly and critically, to dissect situations, to develop rigorous arguments for conclusions, and to evaluate evidence for and against claims that are being made.

2. *Perspective:* the ability to investigate situations from different perspectives, to take others' points of view, to compare and contrast different perspectives, and to be cognizant of one's own assumptions.

3. *Problem Solving:* the ability to diagnose a problem, to formulate various solutions and strategies creatively, to link proposed solutions to analyses of the situation, to evaluate alternative courses of action systematically, and to imagine implementation problems.

4. *Communication:* the ability to convey to others ideas, analysis, and arguments; to write, read, speak, and listen effectively; to work with others on collaborative projects; and to vary communication styles based on different types of audiences and settings.

PEDAGOGY: DECISION CASES

Because developing skills requires practice, the pedagogy of this book focuses on creating opportunities for students to do sociology. Practice in doing sociology is facilitated by the use of *decision cases,* relatively short written narratives of some real-life situation in which a person, group of people, organization, or community faces a problem or dilemma. Many educators in professional schools (business, teacher training, and public administration) now use decision cases to develop students' higher-order critical thinking skills. Decision cases challenge students to use acquired knowledge because they involve problem-centered learning. Usually, a social actor in a case has to make a decision and there is uncertainty about how she or he should proceed. Cases typically are written in such a way that the final outcome is unknown and there is uncertainty about what happened and why. As a result, cases are open to multiple interpretations, allowing students to use acquired sociological concepts and theories to develop "readings" of the case. Through practice with decision cases, students learn how to analyze situations they could encounter not in a naive fashion but in a manner informed by a sociological perspective.

Because practice is so important, this book contains a wide variety of decision cases. Included are cases about conflicts, problems, and dilemmas in schools and hospitals, within families and businesses, among friends and within communities. These cases deal with an array of sociological issues, including social inequalities, identities, cultural differences, organizational change, the environment, and sexism and racism. In each of the five chapters in Part I, there are two cases. Each chapter begins with a decision case. The body of the chapter introduces sociological ideas and concepts by using them to analyze the first decision case. The chapter concludes with another decision case so that students can practice the specific skills that they have acquired using that chapter's Sociological Eye Analysis Guide. Part II contains additional decision cases, providing more opportunities for students to practice their skill at reading situations sociologically.

ORGANIZATION: INCREMENTAL LEARNING

The book is structured under the assumption that learning occurs incrementally, with new ideas and skills building on and enhancing previous ideas and skills. In contrast to standard textbooks that organize material by content topics, this book organizes material in terms of a series of skills. The five chapters in Part I are designed to help students acquire progressively higher-order skills. The material in Chapter 1 helps students see situations sociologically by identifying and describing a variety of social connections among social actors. Chapter 2 builds on this skill by showing students how they can use theories to develop multiple readings of social situations and to shift perspectives.

The materials in Chapters 3 through 5 are designed to help students situate cases within various contexts. Chapter 3 looks at the importance of investigating situations from the point of view of the social actors and shows students how to do this by decoding a culture's symbols, stories, and worldviews. Chapter 4 examines the inequalities that often characterize situations. Students learn how to uncover social class, race/ethnic, and gender inequalities and how to use their knowledge of social inequalities to understand the varying power different social actors have. Finally, with the material in Chapter 5, students learn how to imagine future scenarios by examining how the driving forces of demography, technology, and collective action can lead to social change.

The way in which each chapter is organized also highlights for students how subsequent skills build on prior skills. Chapters begin with a brief reading of that chapter's introductory case using the skills that were emphasized in the previous chapters. Then, at the end of the chapter, I summarize the new material by discussing how acquired skills allow students to do something new and different. I also foreshadow material in the next chapter by noting issues that are not addressed with these skills.

The incremental nature of this book allows students to revisit earlier cases and reread them using the new skills that they have acquired in a specific chapter. Through both the ordering of the chapters and the internal structure of each chapter, students can see the progressive series of skills that they are acquiring. Therefore, as students proceed through the course, they will be able to gauge their increasing competence and sophistication at analyzing situations sociologically.

ACKNOWLEDGMENTS

This book project has been many years in the making and would not have been possible without the assistance, advice, and encouragement of many people. The origins of this project can be traced back to a faculty development workshop I attended more than 10 years ago on using decision cases conducted by John Boehrer and Jim Wilkinson from the Kennedy School of Government at Harvard University. My understanding of how to use decision cases was greatly enhanced by Rita Silverman, whom I met at a teaching retreat in 1994. Attendance at a working conference on cases in 1996, organized in part by Rita, exposed me to others who were involved in using and writing decision cases. I also am indebted to the Lilly Endowment for my participation from 1992 to 1993 in the Teaching Fellows Program, through which I learned a great deal about ways to activate student learning. The Institute for Scholarship in the Liberal Arts at the University of Notre Dame also indirectly supported this project with a summer grant that allowed me to create an introduction to sociology course that uses decision cases.

The idea for this book project itself was first broached by Eve Howard, editor at Wadsworth Publishing Company, who gave me the opportunity to pursue this project. But it was Steve Rutter, publisher of Pine Forge Press, who saw the possibilities in the materials I had written and helped me to mold them into an innovative book. I am indebted to Steve and his superb staff for paving new roads by publishing creative learning materials.

Throughout this project, many people have commented on various chapter drafts. I appreciate the comments of the following reviewers:

Dean Dorn, California State University, Sacramento

Myrna Goodman, Sonoma State University

Barbara Heyl, Illinois State University

Anne Martin, Edmonds Community College

Caroline Hodges Persell, New York University

Sally Raskoff, University of Southern California

Steve Sharkey, Alverno College

William Staudenmeier, Eureka College

Mark Winton, University of Central Florida

Susan Wright, Drake University

I also want to express my appreciation to my colleagues in the Department of Sociology, especially Rebecca Bordt, Naomi Cassirer, Lyn Spillman, and Robert Fishman, whose comments on specific chapters were extremely helpful. Barbara Walvoord, Director of the Kaneb Center for Teaching and Learning at the University of Notre Dame, also contributed valuable advice, as did two sociologists in other departments who work with cases, John Foran from the University of California, Santa Barbara, and Paul Starr from Auburn University. I also thank my colleague Joan Aldous, who many years ago challenged me to think about why I was teaching students sociology and who served as my mentor when I was a teaching fellow. Finally, special thanks is owed to the creative case writers who wrote the superb nineteen cases that appear in this book.

This project would not have been possible without the hard work of the many graduate students who served as my research assistants while I was working on this book. Special thanks are due to Volker Frank, Michael Davern, Kerry Rockquemore, David Brunsma, Xiao-qing Wang, Paul Perl, Yuri Chumakov, Ana Laura Rodriguez-Gusta, Eric Stromberg, Michael Gibbons, and Matthew Larner. I also am indebted to my undergraduate students, who have been my "guinea pigs" and who provided very useful feedback on the numerous decision cases I have been using.

This project would not have been possible without all the clerical assistance I received from our department's secretaries, Katie Schlotfeldt, Pat Kipker, and Nancy Mitchell. I also appreciate the "space" my friend and chairperson Richard Williams gave me that allowed me to put aside some of my other responsibilities while I worked on this project.

Above all, I thank my family, Gayle, Aaron, and Seth, for their encouragement, patience, and love.

PART I

Doing Sociology

CHAPTER 1

Seeing Society

Decision Case: "Separate but Safer"

Peter Heywood, alone in his Youth Resources Bureau (YRB) office on a rainy October morning, was finishing his second cup of coffee and rereading the morning headline and editorial, which both read "Separate But Safer." He wondered what he could have done differently to prevent the school committee vote that was taken last night in a crowded auditorium, a vote that upheld a public junior high school practice of separating boys and girls at lunch and recess.

Agency Background

The YRB was established in July 1998 with a state Division of Youth Services delinquency prevention grant written and submitted by the director of the Dewitt–Brownfield United Way. The city of Dewitt was the prime sponsor and grant recipient, but the United Way director supervised the program until it was incorporated. A group of local youth, the United Way director, and five other social agency directors interviewed several applicants before deciding that Peter Heywood, an out-of-town 23-year-old, was best qualified to incorporate the program, hire the staff, and oversee the reduction of local delinquency.

AUTHOR'S NOTE: This case was written by J Forbes Farmer.

Heywood held an M.A. in sociology, had been a camp counselor for six years, and had worked for two years in nonprofit agencies.

Heywood got right to work. With help from the United Way director, he identified a group of incorporators who also would be the Board of Directors. The board members were the Brownfield Juvenile Police Officer, the Dewitt Mental Health Association director, the director of the Dewitt–Brownfield YMCA, the Dewitt District Court judge, a local attorney, the director of Catholic Social Services, the director of Family and Children's Services, and the director of the Drug Counseling Center.

As he worked on the incorporation, Heywood advertised for, interviewed, and hired two outreach workers: Alyson Hart (18 years old) to work with the youth and the youth agency personnel in Dewitt, and Chip McNally (19 years old) to do the same work in Brownfield. At his first meeting with Hart and McNally, Heywood laid out the goals.

> Our mandate and charter is to reduce delinquency in Brownfield and Dewitt. You've got to get to know the youth. Hang out with them. Introduce yourselves to the police, the probation officers, the teachers, guidance counselors, and school officials. I don't want you to get arrested or to be seen by the youth as snitches, but try to be youth advocates and counselors. Organize recreational and other activities. Open up after-school jobs. In our budget, we have the funds to pay half a kid's salary on a reimbursement basis. Find out what the kids' problems and issues are. Let's try to help and keep them out of trouble.

Initial Achievements

Six weeks after the first meeting, Alyson Hart had organized and run a coed street hockey tournament for 13- to 15-year-olds. This was suggested by the Dewitt juvenile police officer and the kids with whom she was hanging around, who spent much of their time playing street hockey in a church parking lot. The tournament drew 12 teams, and the YRB received good publicity. The bureau also received praise from the papers, church groups, and the police in both cities. Hart also befriended five Dewitt elementary school teachers and made arrange-ments for them to attend an educational conference on delinquency prevention. In addition, Hart created 22 afterschool landscaping jobs at the parks and recreation department. All these jobs were filled with referrals from the Dewitt probation officers, the Dewitt juvenile police officer, and some school guidance counselors.

In Brownfield, McNally had focused on working with the Brown-field probation officer, who "gave" him four cases. These probationers spent much of their time at a teen center where McNally hung out with them, listened to their problems, and organized a dance and a car wash to support the center. McNally created 31 afterschool landscap-ing jobs at a local cemetery and at the public beach. The referrals for these jobs came from the Brownfield probation officers and the direc-tor of the teen center. McNally also worked with Heywood to get the Dewitt and Brownfield mayors to proclaim a week in September as "Delinquency Prevention Week."

Heywood's contributions included finalizing the YRB's incorpora-tion, setting up a bookkeeping system, and completing interviews on two local radio stations. He explained the YRB and encouraged refer-rals and afterschool job opportunities for youth. For one of these radio shows, he arranged for the director of the state Division of Youth Ser-vices (the funding source) to join him. He also met with the Dewitt and Brownfield police chiefs and obtained their signatures on staff I.D. cards provided by a bank, the president of which was on the United Way Board of Directors. He also obtained a small grant from the Dewitt School Committee to help defray wages for afterschool jobs for Dewitt youth. Heywood also joined Dewitt probation officers, guid-ance counselors, and teachers at school conferences, where action plans for delinquent youth were determined.

The Discovery

Heywood, McNally, and Hart had forged the YRB into a recogniz-able and trustworthy program. Heywood was feeling quite satisfied one late September afternoon as he finished writing payroll checks for

53 youth. His self-congratulations ended abruptly when McNally walked into the office, collapsed into an easy chair, and related some disturbing news.

> You're not going to believe what some of my Brownfield boys just told me. They're complaining that they're not allowed to have lunch or share recess with the girls at Brownfield Junior High School. In fact, as I understand it, the boys and girls have separate lunch areas and separate recess areas. The lunch rooms are apparently of equal size and each has its own bathroom. The recess areas are different sizes, though. The boys have a large, fenced-in, asphalt area with basketball hoops. The girls have a small, sloped grassy area next to a parking lot that is always full of cars. Man, this is something out of the 50s and 60s. In fact, wasn't all this outlawed by the civil rights legislation 35 years ago?

"It sure was," Heywood responded. "We'd better check out your information and, if true, find out how many students at the school are really concerned about this issue."

Preliminary Action

After verifying the report, Heywood and McNally had the students draw up and distribute a petition that read, "The following students at Brownfield Junior High School respectfully urge the school administration to change its policy of having segregated lunch and recess areas." It was signed by 72 of the 1,040 students in the school. With the petition in hand, Heywood went to see the school principal. Heywood explained the evolution of the petition and the involvement of the YRB in this affair. When he refused to let the principal read the names on the petition, the principal got angry.

> What you're doing here is starting trouble and wasting everyone's time with students we both know are the pot-smoking delinquents in my school. Look, why are you bothering with this? The separate recess areas and lunch areas were created by an old policy written to address problems caused by overcrowding; students eat faster if the sexes are separate and the recreational play is safer if the sexes are kept apart. Many of my students' parents went here under the same policy and they turned out just fine.

Getting nowhere with the principal, Heywood spoke with the superintendent, who also happened to be the principal's father-in-law. Heywood suggested that the segregation policy was illegal, but the superintendent supported it with the same reasons as the principal and suggested that Heywood raise the issue with the school committee.

About two weeks before the school committee hearing, Heywood took the issue to the YRB Board of Directors for their advice. He used a diagram as a visual aid. The District Court judge on the board said, "I expect that the school policy is probably illegal, but if I were the judge in a court where this case came up I'd make sure I was out fishing." After a brief discussion, the YRB board voted to support Heywood's efforts to change the policy. The local attorney on the board suggested that Heywood contact two female lawyers in Cambridge, Massachusetts. Heywood met with the lawyers; one was a law professor at Harvard Law School, and the other worked for the Cambridge Legal Aid Society. The lawyers shook their heads at the diagram and listened in disbelief. They were particularly interested in the discriminatory inequality they saw in the boys' and girls' recess areas. A week before the school committee hearing, Heywood received a legal brief from the lawyers that outlined several legal precedents on sexual segregation.

The School Committee Meeting

Armed with this brief, Heywood stood up in front of a crowded auditorium filled with reporters, TV cameras, and radio microphones. He explained the prepared diagram and slowly and deliberately presented his case to the school committee and the public. He reviewed the history of the YRB involvement with the case and suggested an alternative lunch and recess plan that would solve the segregation problem. Then the school principal presented his case. He admitted that the lunch and recess areas were separate, but he insisted that the lunch system was a more efficient way of feeding the youth in a short period of time. He claimed that integrating the youth at lunch would extend the lunch period and create a longer school day. He also asserted that the recess separation was safer for the girls. "After all," he passionately begged the crowd, "isn't it true that those of you in the audience who have daughters at our school want us to keep them safe from the rowdy boys whom Mr. Heywood represents?" The auditorium filled with a resounding "Yes!" The school board took a quick vote to reaffirm the existing policy.

The next morning, Heywood read the following newspaper editorial.

October 15, 1999

Brownfield Offices
Tel. 432-8756

The Twin City Daily Sentinel

Published at Dewitt, State 00221, 300 Main Street, Tel. 234-5678,

Separate—But Safer

Scott N. Weaver

General Manager–Editor

Robert Westcoat, principal of Brownfield Junior High School, is on firm ground when he chooses student safety over coed factors at the school.

The conflict occurred when 72 of the 1,040 pupils at the school went to the YRB claiming that sexual discrimination exists because there are separate entrances, cafeterias, and recess areas for boys and girls.

The Bureau actually brought the matter up at a School Committee meeting.

Westcoat replied to the charge by pointing out that there are 520 boys and 520 girls crowded into a school built to accommodate 742 pupils.

The boys and girls mix 95 percent of the time, but there are periods of separation to speed traffic flow and avoid confusion. For instance, the school feeds hundreds within

an hour, and some sort of control must be exerted. The location of the lavatories also poses a problem.

The committee wisely took no action.

There comes a time when common sense must prevail. Otherwise, we are led into absurd situations. For example, the Bureau director suggested that one solution to the crowded cafeteria situation might be to have students assigned to the cafeteria by grade and age. But couldn't the eighth graders claim they were being discriminated against because they weren't being allowed to eat with ninth graders? Ridiculous, of course— and yet these split-hair disputes often occur and they waste a lot of time that could be used profitably in other ways. We think the principal's clincher, however, came when he said that elimination of the separation policy would probably mean a longer school day. We have a feeling of what the decision would be if pupils had a choice of boys and girls walking into the cafeteria together or staying in school an extra hour a day.

♦ ♦ ♦

Heywood believed he had done the right thing in pursuing this seg-regation issue, but now he wasn't sure. What had gone wrong? What should he have done differently? What should he do now? He won-dered why the school committee voted the way it did. Were safety and the length of the school days the real reasons?

ACTORS AND ISSUES

Cases such as the "Separate but Safer" case depict situations in which *social actors,* most often people, face a problem or dilemma. The first step in analyzing a case, therefore, is to identify the central characters. In this case, Peter Heywood is clearly a central character. But there are other important social actors, such as Robert Westcoat, the principal of Brownfield Junior High School, and Alyson Hart and Chip McNally, two outreach workers hired by Heywood. There are also collective actors, that is, collections of people, who play an important role in this case, such as the school board that votes to continue the separate lunchrooms policy and YRB's board of directors.

The second step in analyzing a case is to identify the *issue* or issues that are at the center of the case. In the "Separate but Safer" case, the main issue is the school's policy of having separate lunchrooms for boys and girls. There is also the issue of what should be done to change this policy and the issue of how Peter Heywood could have been more effective in his attempt to reverse the policy.

The issues in a case usually pose *problems* or *dilemmas* for the cen-tral characters. Peter, after hearing about the separation policy, sees it as a problem. The principal has to deal with the protests over the pol-icy. The school board must reach a decision about whether to keep the policy. These problems and dilemmas propel the actors into *action.* Peter learns about the separate lunchrooms, calls a meeting of his board of directors, contacts lawyers, confronts the princi-pal, organizes a petition drive, and speaks in front of the school board.

After identifying the key actors, their actions, the central issues, and the problems the various actors face, you should have a good sense of what the case is about and be able to formulate intelligent questions about the case. Why does this junior high have a separate eating rooms policy? Why did Peter decide to challenge this policy? Why did the school board and the school's principal resist any changes? How could Peter have been more effective in getting the school board to reconsider the separation policy?

How would you go about answering these questions? When most people encounter a new situation, they begin their analysis by trying to get inside the key actors' heads. The idea is that if you can uncover the motivations, views, and personality of the actors, then you will be able to understand why each of them behaved the way they did. For example, after reading this case, you may have thought of Peter as a reformer and social activist who dislikes injustices. Peter appears to be an organizing, "gung-ho" type of person who reacts quickly to what he sees as a wrong that needs to be righted. In contrast, you may have thought of the principal, Robert Westcoat, as a conservative, narrow-minded, set-in-his-ways administrator who wants to preserve the status quo. With these "personas," you could then formulate accounts of why Peter was so adamantly opposed to the policy and why Robert was so resistant to Peter's attempt to change it.

This route in analyzing cases usually leads to people taking sides. When confronted with contrasting views, it seems only natural to ask "Whose views are correct?" and "With whose motivations do I identify?" After reading this "Separate but Safer" case, maybe you sided with Peter because you too felt that the separation policy was unfair. Or maybe you sided with Robert because you felt that a change would lead to other problems such as a longer school day. Once people begin taking sides, they tend to see the situation in black and white terms: *Either* Peter is right and Robert is wrong, *or* Robert is right and Peter is wrong.

But the fact that two people—Peter and Robert—confronted by the same issue—the separate lunch rooms policy—have different readings of the situation should make you proceed with more caution and not jump to conclusions. Why? Because the different views imply that there is probably some ambiguity in this case. It seems that reasonable people disagree about whether the school should continue the policy. Seeing the situation from *both* Peter's *and* Robert's points of view reveals that this case is more complex than it initially appeared to be. There are gray areas in between the contrasting black and white positions.

To prevent ourselves from taking sides hastily, we need to recognize that Peter's and Robert's stands on the separation issue are not just the result of their different personalities, motivations, and attitudes. Peter and Robert also are affected by the larger contexts in which they are acting. Peter is a director of a social service agency working with juvenile delinquents. Robert is the principal of a junior high school. Where each of them stands on the issue of separate lunchrooms has as much to do with what is going on around them as it does with what is going on inside their heads.

But to understand the surroundings of the characters, you have to switch gears. Instead of looking at people and their personalities, motivations, views, and behaviors, you need to refocus your attention on the *connections* among people. You probably noticed right away some important connections in this case, such as Peter's connections to various members of the community through their membership on YRB's board of directors or Robert's ties to the superintendent. But, for most of us, the skill of seeing social connections and then using our knowledge of connections to understand situations is underdeveloped. The remainder of this book is designed to help you develop this skill so that you are better equipped to analyze real social situations.

THE SOCIOLOGICAL "EYE"

What will help you develop your ability to see social connections? You may have already guessed my answer to this question—sociology. The ideas, theories, research, and insights of sociologists are much more than a body of knowledge that has been compiled over many years. That body of knowledge can help you develop your own "sociological eye" (Collins 1998). When sociologists look at a situation, they often see things that other people do not notice. So let's begin to put sociological knowledge into action by helping you develop your sociological eye!

Like others, sociologists also begin reading situations by identifying social actors, issues, problems/dilemmas, and actions. But instead of turning next to internal motivations and personalities, sociologists take a different route. They look for the social connections in a given situation. As you read the case "Separate but Safer," what connections did you notice? Peter Heywood, the YRB director, forges connections left and right. Through the hiring of Chip McNally and Alyson Hart, he creates connections to two subordinates. And through Chip and Alyson's activities, connections are formed with teachers, juvenile delinquents, probation officers, police chiefs, and many others. Did you notice other connections? What about work connections and organizational connections? Through YRB's board of directors, there are connections between directors of social service agencies and others in the community. The YRB itself is connected to the United Way. There are also family connections. The principal is the superintendent's son-in-law. And, of course, there are connections among students through friendships, although they are not discussed in the case.

The remainder of this chapter is designed to help you identify social connections in situations so that you can better understand such situations. **Social connections** are forms of social organization that shape human actions and interactions. **Sociology** can be viewed as the study of social connections and the social interactions that occur in society. This chapter will help you see social connections by exploring four important social connectors: *social relationships, social groups, social networks,* and *organizations.*

SOCIAL RELATIONSHIPS

The first type of social connections you need to be aware of are the social relationships between the key actors in the case and other persons. You detect **social relationships** by looking for enduring social interactions between two or more social actors. We usually refer to these relationships in terms of the people who are connected. Peter Heywood is Chip and Alyson's supervisor. Alyson is friends with some elementary school teachers. The principal, Robert Westcoat, is the superintendent's son-in-law. But you also can think about social relationships as connections between positions. The Peter–Chip and Peter–Alyson relationships are *supervisor–subordinate relationships,* the Alyson–teacher relationship is a *friendship relationship,* and the relationship between the principal and the superintendent is a *kinship relationship* involving a husband–wife relationship and a daughter–father relationship.

When sociologists look at social relationships, they first look at the *positions* that are connected through a relationship and then at the people who occupy those positions and how occupancy affects what they can do. There is a special word for social positions—**status.** In this case, many statuses are evident. When I reread the case before writing this section, I highlighted all the statuses I could find. Here is my list: social service agency director, grant recipient, job applicant, outreach worker, mayor, attorney, probation officer, guidance counselor, juvenile delinquent, police officer, student, teacher, parent, principal, superintendent, reporter, school board member. Did you find any statuses that I didn't notice?

One way you can tell whether you have identified a status is by imagining whether different people could fill that position. In this case, for example, the director of the YRB is Peter Heywood, but there were other people who applied for this job and who could have been selected. This means that when we talk about a status like parent, student, director, or friend, we are not talking about specific people. Rather, we are talking about a social position within a social relationship, just like we talk about the catcher position in the game of baseball independently of who just happens to be the catcher on a specific baseball team.

But how do sociologists talk about statuses and positions apart from the people who are in these statuses? We do this by mapping out the content of a status by examining the status's **role**—the behaviors expected of someone when he or she occupies a particular status. What are the behaviors expected, for example, of a friend, a principal, a student, a parent? We all have some ideas about these expected behaviors as a result of watching people who are friends and observing principals administrating school, parents parenting, and students learning. But to obtain a better sense of a role, focus on the *expected behaviors* that a person in a status is supposed to exhibit *toward* the person who occupies the other position within the relationship. For example, what is a teacher expected to do when she relates to the students whom she is educating?

One way to develop a list of expected role behaviors is to identify the *dos and don'ts* of a role. Sociologists call these dos and don'ts **norms**—the shared rules and expectations that guide behavior (Biddle 1979). Consider, for example, the role of "director of a social service agency." What are some of the dos and don'ts governing being a director? To get some ideas, look at Peter's activities and then try to describe them in a general way. For example, Peter obtained a grant, so one of the things directors do is to write grant proposals and seek external funding for their organization. Peter also held meetings with his board, people in the community, and radio stations. These activities indicate that part of a director's role is working with a board of directors and obtaining support for the director's agency.

People and Social Relationships

Once you are clear about the norms governing behavior in a role, you can imagine an ideal person who, when occupying that role, perfectly complies with all the role expectations. Of course, there are no such ideal people. All of us from time to time make mistakes while in a role. Students sometimes come unprepared to class. Parents on occasion ignore a child's needs, and teachers at times present material unclearly or grade unfairly. People's actual role behaviors do not always correspond to **role expectations,** the behaviors expected according to the role's norms.

How is this gap between actual and expected behavior decreased? Consider the different ways people in Dewitt and Brownfield attempt to curb *juvenile delinquency,* that is, young people's behaviors that are viewed by others as inappropriate. One way to discourage such behaviors is through incentives, including both negative incentives (punishments) and positive ones (rewards). For example, when delinquency is dealt with through arrests and punishment, negative incentives are being used. In this case, we see that some teens are on probation, indicating that their freedoms have been restricted. But positive incentives are also being used. Teens are being given after-school jobs, places to hang out, and activities such as street hockey in which they can be involved. Notice also that the incentives being used to change behavior in this community are not just material incentives like money and consumer goods. Nonmaterial incentives, such as granting privileges, showing approval, restricting freedoms, and ostracizing, can be very powerful forces. Because incentives are so important in social relationships, you often can discover a role's content (the dos and the don'ts) by looking at which behaviors are rewarded and which are punished.

Another way in which the gap between expected and actual behavior is decreased is through what sociologists and psychologists call **socialization,** the process of learning how to behave in expected ways within roles (Bush and Simmons 1990). When parents raise children, they do much more than just feed, clothe, and provide shelter. They also teach children how they are supposed to behave around others. Although socialization is most intense during childhood, socialization continues throughout our lives and is especially important when someone takes on a new role. During such *role transitions*—moves from one role to another role—people may not know how to behave, and, therefore, they may need to learn, somehow, what is expected of them in the new role (Turner 1990).

There are many ways in which people are socialized. Within families, parents socialize children. In schools, teachers socialize students. Peer groups play an important role in adolescent socialization, as does the mass media and the role models portrayed through it. Job training programs often teach people not only skills but also norms. In this case, the YRB socializes troubled teens who are making the difficult transition from childhood to adulthood.

In the "Separate but Safer" case, we see not only the YRB, but also the junior high school, acting as a socializing agent. One of the things schools teach children is how they are expected to behave as young men and women. Sociologists refer to this as *gender role socialization* (Renzetti and Curran 1995). A **gender role** is the expected behaviors that are socially linked to each gender, that is, to men and to women. During the past 20 years, the content of gender roles has undergone changes, and there is controversy over what men and women are expected to do as men and women. Although at one time people expected women to stay at home, be subservient to men, raise children, and be beautiful, today many people question this view of femininity. Similarly, although at one time men were expected to be the breadwinners, protect women and children, be strong, and be active outside the home within the community, today many people have different views of masculinity.

Brownfield Junior High does not have a curriculum and classes designed to teach boys and girls how to behave as boys and girls. However, through their actions, principals, teachers, and counselors often convey to students expectations about gender roles. Consider the principal's response at the school board meeting to Peter Heywood's speech. Talking to the parents, Robert Westcoat states that his job is to keep their daughters safe from the rowdy boys. The principal used a **stereotype**; that is, he attributed a set of characteristics to all members of some specific group or social category of people. In this case, he stereotyped girls as people who need to be protected and boys as rowdy to justify the separation policy. In turn, these stereotypes reinforce specific views of gender roles (e.g., women are passive, whereas men are active agents), socializing children to think of themselves in these ways.

In fact, you can view the policy of separate lunchrooms as contributing to gender role socialization and stereotypes. Research has shown that stereotypes tend to be undermined when there is interaction between those who hold the stereotypes, especially if the interaction entails cooperation and not competition (Sherif et al. 1961). Why? Because through interaction people see that the stereotypes are exaggerations. So by decreasing interaction between boys and girls through the separate lunchrooms and recess areas policy, the school is contributing, albeit unintentionally, to the perpetuation of gendered stereotypes.

Role Problems

By now, you should realize how important roles within social relationships are. The roles people occupy affect what they do. Within roles, people are encouraged and in some cases even forced to conform to role expectations. When analyzing any situation, it is important, therefore, to map out the various social relationships by looking at roles, norms, incentives, and socialization processes.

However, such a mapping can convey an overly idealized picture of social relationships and roles. To obtain a more realistic understanding, you need to explore the *problems* that people encounter as they occupy roles. Perhaps the biggest problem is **role conflict,** the incompatibility between two or more different roles that a person occupies. Role conflict often occurs when people wear many different hats. Consider, for example, Peter Heywood. He is director of the YRB, supervisor of his workers, a community activist, and probably many other things. For the most part, the expectations in each of these roles are compatible. Peter can be director, supervisor, activist, and friend, although probably not at the same time.

The problem occurs because acting out the role of community activist could undermine his ability to be YRB's director. In fact, one could argue that the "Separate but Safer" case is a story of someone overstepping the boundaries of his role. As YRB director, Peter is supposed to develop and implement programs for youth that will help reduce juvenile delinquency. When he pushed the YRB board of directors to become involved in the separation policy controversy, Peter engaged in behaviors that went beyond the role expectations of the

YRB director. Peter as a private citizen could have sought to change school policy. But by organizing dissension to the policy as YRB's director, Peter conflated two roles and created role conflict. In the end, this role conflict could undermine Peter's ability to perform his central role, the role of YRB director.

What do people do when faced with role conflicts? To decrease role conflict, people initially attempt to compartmentalize their roles by performing each role at different times and in different places (Merton 1968). If this does not work, they try to prioritize roles, giving some roles precedence over others. Prioritizing even may require giving up some roles to reduce role conflict.

What do you think Peter should have done to prevent the role conflict he experienced? Should he have given up his role as community activist, letting others take on that role? Do you think the protest would have been successful if Peter had not played the lead role in the protest? Do you think there will be any fallout from this role conflict? Will Peter's ability to be YRB director become more difficult? Or do you think that Peter was really acting in accordance with his YRB role because that role should include being an advocate for youth within the community? Maybe this is a situation not so much of role conflict but of ambiguity about what the role of YRB director entails. *Role ambiguity* frequently occurs when a status is relatively new or when a status is changing. In this case, because the YRB has just been created, there is probably some ambiguity about what its director should and should not be doing.

GROUPS

The second type of social connection you need to investigate in a case is the social group. **Social groups** can be identified by looking for two or more social actors who have in common some trait that connects them and provides the basis for their interaction. When attempting to identify groups, the key thing to look for is the common trait.

What are some of the groups with a common trait that you saw in the "Separate but Equal" case? Early on in the case, we learn how

Peter identified a group of incorporators that would become the YRB's board of directors, an important group in this case. There is also the group of juvenile delinquents, as well as specific groups of delinquents, often referred to as *gangs,* although this case does not talk about specific gangs. There are the teachers at the various schools and the group of administrators who manage the schools. There is the school board as well as the group of people who attended the school board meeting. There is the group of 72 students who signed the petition. Groups are everywhere in this case, although at first glance this case seems to be more about individuals. In fact, this case can be read as a case about *grouping* because the central issue is whether to group students at lunch time based on their gender.

What makes each of the groups in this case a group? The answer is that everyone in a group has something in common with everyone else in the group. In some cases, this common trait is a role, for example, all the school administrators occupy administrative positions. In other cases, it is a behavior, as in the case of juvenile delinquents. In still other cases, the common trait is membership in an organization, as in the case of YRB's board of directors.

Connecting people through groups creates what sociologists call *homogeneous* social entities, in which everyone within the group is similar in some important way. Of course, within any group there are differences. The members of YRB's board of directors are all voting members, although some are directors of social service agencies, others judges and lawyers, and still others police officers. But this within-group *heterogeneity,* that is, differences within the group, does not imply that the board is not a group. A group is a group because of the common feature that all group members share, even if there are other features that they do not share. This commonality is important in groups (Michener and DeLamanter 1994) because it

- is related to the *purposes* or *goals* of the group,
- provides the basis for *interaction* within the group,

- generates *norms* that promote behaviors that are consistent with that trait, and

- provides the basis for a group *identity* through which group members consciously think of themselves as belonging to a group.

Consider again YRB's board of directors. The common trait is being on this board. This feature is related to the purpose of this group, which is to make decisions about YRB's policies and its use of resources. Board membership obviously provides the basis for inter-action within the group. Norms exist in the form of procedures for debating issues (e.g., Robert's Rules of Order). And although each board member has other roles (which are part of the reason he or she is on YRB's board), when at board meetings members are supposed to act on behalf of YRB and identify with YRB's mission.

Groups come in all sizes. Large groups are quite different from small groups. In large groups, such as the entire student body at Brownfield Junior High, it is difficult for everyone to know everyone else. As such, responsibility becomes more diffuse as others think someone else will pick up the slack and do what the group needs done. On the other hand, large groups are more stable. If one person leaves a small study group of three people, it may be difficult for the remaining two people to continue the group. But if one person leaves a larger study group of 10 people, he or she might not be missed.

Groups also come in different "shapes." One important distinction made by sociologists is between primary and secondary groups (Dunphy 1972). In a *primary group,* people interact with each other in an intimate, face-to-face, and personable manner. Friendship and family groups are examples of primary groups. People "join" and stay in primary groups for intrinsic reasons, that is, for the benefits they receive just from interaction with other group members. In contrast, *secondary groups* are larger and more impersonal groups that are ori-ented toward a specific task or objective. YRB's board of directors, the school board, and even the group of people at the school board meeting are secondary groups. People join secondary groups for instrumental reasons, that is, for what the group does for them. Some sociologists have argued that primary groups create stronger social bonds among people than do secondary groups (Cooley [1902] 1964; Cooley [1909] 1962). People come and go from secondary groups, leaving when they are no longer instrumental in helping them attain their personal goals. In contrast, primary groups have more holding power.

Groups also vary in how important they are to us. Think about the various groups to which a juvenile delinquent in this town might belong. He may be a member of a gang, a student at the junior high, one of the workers at a pizza parlor, a member of a street hockey team, and one of the group of young people who are on parole. Which group do you think would be most important to such a person? Although we do not know the answer to this question, and the answer would probably vary from person to person, one would expect that the gang could be an important group. If it turned out to be the case, then the gang would be what sociologists call this person's **reference group,** a social group that serves as a point of reference for a person's decisions and judgments.

Often, our reference groups are groups to which we currently belong. For example, my reference groups are my colleagues at the university where I work and other sociologists. I wonder what my reference groups will think of a new line of research I am developing or, for that matter, this book that I have published. But sometimes our reference groups are groups we do not belong to but to which we aspire to join. Such groups are important in the process of *anticipatory socialization,* a process that occurs prior to entering a group or role. Through this process, people learn what is expected of them by emulating the behaviors of those in their reference group. In this case, an example of anticipatory socialization is YRB's relations with juvenile delinquents. It seems that one of YRB's goals is to change the reference groups of juvenile delinquents and thereby socialize these young people into different social groups and relationships.

Understanding who someone's reference groups are is often very important in explaining his or her behavior. Consider the difference between Peter Heywood and Robert Westcoat. What do you think are Peter's reference groups? Most likely they are groups involved in the provision of social services such as social workers and administrators of social service agencies. For people in these groups, issues of fairness and equity are very important. In contrast, the principal's reference group seems to be the school board and the parents. With those groups in mind, Robert Westcoat sees nothing wrong with the separation policy. In fact, he views it as the safest and most efficient way to arrange lunch time at his school.

Social Identities

Connections formed through groups and social relationships play a very important role in our lives. Not only do we behave differently when in different roles, but our sense of who we are develops as we take on different roles. The very hats we wear change who we are and what we think of ourselves. This fact has led *social psychologists,* those who study the social causes of human behavior, to focus on the self and the formation of identities.

The core idea behind much of social psychology is the idea that the self develops through social interactions with others. How does this occur? According to Charles Cooley (1864–1929), one of the first social psychologists, this occurs through us imagining how others see us. Cooley ([1902] 1964) calls this the **looking-glass self,** our sense of ourselves derived from how we think others view us. How do we develop ideas about how others think of us? Through social feedback.

Consider some young man in Brownsville who is viewed by others in town as a juvenile delinquent. Maybe when he was younger he joked around a lot, trying to get attention because he was not a very popular kid. As other kids laughed at his jokes, he was encouraged to engage in such behavior. Eventually, the jokes became pranks, and the pranks became mischievous acts. The young man began to think of himself as a prankster. As others labeled him a "troublemaker," he began to see himself as someone who causes trouble. Through such social feedback, a *self-fulfilling prophecy* occurred as the way others viewed this young man led him to act in that way.

Another pioneer of social psychology, George Herbert Mead (1863–1931), also emphasized how interactions with others shape ourselves. Mead thought of the self as having two parts, the *me* and the *I*. The I, which we are all born with, is the active, creative, doing self. It is the self as subject. The me, on the other hand, takes time to develop. It is the reflective self, the self as object. This me self develops as children take on the roles of others, pretending through game playing to be those whom they admire (e.g., a parent, a firefighter, a teacher). Through such game playing and role taking, young children obtain a sense of what others expect of them when in various roles (Mead [1934] 1962). As a child internalizes others' expectations, they begin to think of themselves as that type of person. Instead of saying "My teacher wants me to cross my *t*s," a child begins to say "I need to remember to cross my *t*s better."

An implication of Mead's and Cooley's ideas is that people do not have just one self, but multiple selves. Just think about Peter Heywood. If you could ask Peter who he is, what do you think he would say? Would he tell you he is director of the YRB, a new person in town, a young man, a sociologist, a camp counselor, a friend, a supervisor, a social activist? Would Robert Westcoat tell you about his administrative self, his family self, his involvement in the community?

To capture this idea of multiple selves, social psychologists study people's *identities*, the categories people use to characterize who they are and to situate themselves relative to others (McCall and Simmons 1978; Stryker 1980). Identities are constructed by observing ourselves and people's reactions to our behaviors. Through social interactions, we construct mental pictures of ourselves. These pictures do not portray physical features like hair color and height. Rather, these mental pictures capture behavioral features, the actions we would carry out if we were to enact the identity. In our heads, we have multiple pictures, but this does not mean we flip from identity to identity. Rather, as research has shown, people construct *identity hierarchies* in which they rank their identities in terms of their **salience,** the likelihood that a person will enact an identity (Stryker and Serpe 1981).

Why are some identities more salient than others? There are a number of factors that can push an identity higher up in an identity hierarchy (Michener and DeLamanter 1994). When we invest more resources (time, effort, money) in constructing an identity, that identity tends to be more salient. When we get rewarded for enacting an identity, either through extrinsic or intrinsic rewards, that identity is likely to be more salient. Finally, the more our self-esteem is tied up with an identity, the greater an identity's salience. We rank higher in our identity hierarchies those things at which we are better.

Because our salient identities are so important to us, we seek out situations in which we can enact our identities, and we try as best as we can to avoid situations in which we cannot be who we want to be. Sometimes, however, when our situation changes, it becomes difficult to enact a salient identity. The result is an identity crisis such as the empty nest syndrome, experienced by some parents when their children leave home.

Gender Identities

A very important identity is our **gender identity,** a person's sense of self as either masculine or feminine. People usually adopt the gender identity that corresponds to their sex because of socialization and sanctions associated with gender roles. But how salient gender identities are in our identity hierarchies depends on our actions and interactions with others.

Gender identities are reinforced by **gendering,** the process of differentiating the sexes based on traits and activities that people believe are associated with either men or women. Consider, for example, clothing styles. When parents dress their baby boys in blue and their baby girls in pink, they are engaged in gendering. That is why we now think of blue as a masculine color and pink as a feminine one.

Gender identities are formed through gendering. Gendering processes begin at birth. Parents react to their sons and daughters differently. Crying boys receive attention, whereas girls learn to gesture or pull at mom's clothing when they want something (Fagot 1985). Parents dress girls and boys differently. What you find in girls' and boys' rooms tends to be quite different: dolls versus action figures, miniature kitchen materials versus athletic equipment (Rheingold and Cook 1985). Gendering also occurs among peers (Maccoby and Jacklin 1987). Studies of play patterns show how boys and girls create gendered boundaries (Thorne 1986, 1993). Boys' play areas tend to be large and encompass playing fields and courts, whereas girls' areas are usually near a building or along a sidewalk. Boys patrol their area to prevent girls from "polluting" it, and boys that hang out in girl areas are teased.

One of the most gendered places is schools. Some sociologists even refer to the learning of gender in schools as the second "hidden" curriculum (Best 1983), a curriculum that can be more important than the three Rs—reading, writing, and arithmetic. Within schools, children often are asked to line up in sex-segregated lines, and sometimes classroom activities are organized by sex (e.g., academic contests between teams arranged by sex). Gender messages are evident in textbooks, as well as in extracurricular activities such as sports. And gendering continues after school. Mass media and advertising contain messages about what it is to be a woman and a man (Wolf 1990). In the world of work, *gender displays*—language and rituals characteristic of one sex—signal that the workplace is for that sex only. Men tell dirty jokes, use sexual language, and discuss sports. Women bring gender into workplaces through gossiping about boyfriends and teasing men.

Given the pervasiveness of gendering in society, it is important whenever we analyze a social situation to identify gender roles, gender stereotypes, and gendering and to describe how gender identities are constructed. In fact, the "Separate but Safer" case can be read as a

case of contrasting views about gendering in schools. For the principal, superintendent, many parents, and probably most students, the
separation of boys and girls is seen as an expedient way to solve the
overcrowding problem. Little thought is given by these people to how
this separation could be affecting gender identities. In contrast, Peter
Heywood probably sees in the separate lunchrooms and recess areas
not just differential treatment of the sexes but a gendering process
that reinforces gender identities and makes them more salient in students' lives.

Of course there is nothing wrong with having a gender identity; in
fact, we would think there was something wrong if someone did not
have a gender identity. What Peter may be questioning, however, is
why people arrange their social worlds in such a way as to make gender an overarching identity, a master identity. Today, for example, we
would label an employer a discriminator if, when making hiring decisions, he takes into account a person's sex. School counselors who
encourage girls to take home economics classes and boys to take science and math classes are considered prejudiced. Gender identities
are seen as part of ourselves, but we do not wish to be defined just by
our gender identity.

In part, then, the controversy in this case is over how detrimental
the sex segregation policies are at Brownfield Junior High. To the
extent that you see the separation as one more contributor to the
gendering of social life that makes gender identities very salient, you
are likely to see this policy as problematic. On the other hand, if you
either are unaware of the effects this policy could be having on gender
identities or believe it will have little effect on identities, then you are
likely to view the policy as a reasonable way of dealing with overcrowding.

NETWORKS

Reading social situations requires looking beyond the most obvious
social connectors—social relationships and groups. Often, people are

connected to others in more indirect ways, through intermediaries and third parties. This is why sociologists also pay attention to **social networks,** sets of social ties among social actors. When identifying social networks, there are two things you need to identify: the *social actors* who are connected through a network (sometimes referred to as network *nodes*) and the *social ties* that create linkages between pairs of actors. You can think of a network like a connect-the-dots image. Each dot (node) is a social actor, and the lines connecting the dots are social ties. But how do you know which dots are connected to which other dots? What creates a social tie?

You can identify social ties by looking for flows of resources between social actors. Here are some "resources" that often flow between people within networks (Knoke and Kuklinski 1982; Wasserman and Faust 1994; Wellman 1983). In a social situation, look for each of these "flows" and you will begin to see the social network.

- *Personal Evaluations:* Look at who likes whom, who is friends with whom, who avoids whom, and who dislikes or hates whom. Friendship networks, social cliques at a church, and prestige hierarchies within communities are all examples of networks created by personal evaluations.
- *Transfers of Material Resources:* Look at how money, capital, commodities, services, and other valuable material resources flow. Focus on exchanges in which *A* gives *B* something in exchange for *B* giving *A* something. Examples include who contributes to a local charity, whom banks lend to and where they borrow from, and buying and selling in markets.
- *Information:* Who talks to whom? Who communicates with whom? Through networks, messages are sent and received, creating information networks. Information networks are important in spreading gossip, learning about job openings, and diffusing innovations.

- *Movement of People:* Look for the flows of people between places, organizations, or occupations. For example, some accounting firms recruit a large number of their new accountants from specific business schools. Occupations often are linked by the flow of people such as the recruitment of principals from teachers.

- *Formal Roles:* Look at the rules and regulations that prescribe who can tell who what to do. Command hierarchies in organizations depicted in organizational charts are examples of such networks.

- *Kinship:* Look for who is related to whom either by descent or by marriage.

Once you have begun to see the social ties that connect actors and form a network, you can explore the shape and character of that network. Here are some things to look for in networks:

- How *dense* is the network? In dense networks, the ratio of the actual number of ties to the number of all possible ties is quite high. Almost everyone is connected to everyone else. In contrast, in sparse networks, there are few connections between the many social actors. Networks also can have regions in which density is high. These often are called *cliques,* in which everyone is directly and strongly linked to everyone else.

- Are there social actors who occupy a *central* role in the network? In some networks, there are social actors who are tied to many others, but those others are not tied to each other. An example is a hub network in which everyone except the central actor must go through the central node to connect to anyone else. Centrality gives social actors a great deal of power because other actors must go through them to reach other nodes in the network.

- How *strong* are the ties within the network? Some ties are more important than others. Indicators of the importance of a tie are how often it is used (frequency), how long it has been used (duration), and how intensely it is used (e.g., how much information flows through the channel).

- Where are there *structural holes* (the absence of ties) between social actors? Often when looking at a network, we focus on the social ties connecting people. But the absence of ties also can be very important (Burt 1992). Structural holes create opportunities for social actors to bridge gaps within a network by forming connections between two previously unconnected networks.

Seeing networks and their "shapes" is not easy. When you first read "Separate but Safer" you probably did not notice social networks at work. The case seems to be about people in different roles and groups with different views about the school separation policy. But if you take a closer look at this case, you will notice some important networks. This is often the case with networks. They are initially hidden. All we see are some of the nodes in the network, the tip of the iceberg. Only by thinking about how the nodes are connected to other nodes can you begin to see social networks. So let's explore how you could use these ideas about networks to help you better understand the "Separate but Safer" case.

The first networks I thought about in this case are *friendship networks* among students. We all know from our own schooling experiences how important social cliques can be. I am sure that at Brownsville Junior High there were numerous friendship cliques, connecting together some students and at the same time isolating other students. There also appear to be networks connecting juvenile delinquents.

Although the case is really not about friendship networks, analyzing such networks could be helpful in understanding one of the puzzles of this case—why so few students signed the protest petition. As reported in the case, 72 students out of 1,040 signed the petition requesting a change in the separation policy. Why did fewer than 10 percent of the students sign the petition? Are students apathetic? Did they refuse to sign because they either did not care about or did not support the attempt to change the school's policy? Answering these questions would require further research. But there is another possible reason for why so few students signed the petition. Maybe the petition was distributed through social networks that reached only a limited number of students. In this case, the petition started out among those involved with the YRB, students who are considered juvenile delinquents. The failure to obtain more petition signers could have been the result of a limited distribution network consisting of only those who are friends of the YRB crowd.

The second type of network I noticed in this case are *resource networks*. Consider the YRB's board of directors. As noted earlier, this is a group, but it is also the tip of the iceberg of an extended resource network. Why did Peter seek to have on this board people from such a wide variety of local organizations? In part, the answer is because through their network ties they could provide important resources that the YRB needs. Businesses, voluntary associations, and social service agencies often use boards of directors to build resource networks. Recognizing this, some social scientists study what are called *interlocking directorates,* that is, board members sitting on multiple boards, and how such connections create networks that allow organizations to obtain resources and coordinate their activities (Galaskiewicz and Wasserman 1981).

This case contains a number of illustrative examples of how resource networks are used. As you may recall, a bank generously provided YRB's staff with I.D. cards because its president is on the United Way board of directors, and the United Way president is connected to the YRB board. You also may remember that a local attorney on YRB's board is the person who put Heywood in touch with two lawyers who wrote a legal brief outlining precedents concerning sex segregation.

The final type of network that I noticed are *information networks.* Heywood learns about the separation policy through an information network that ties him to students in the school through his two outreach workers. In all likelihood, problem youth were identified in this community through an information network consisting of police and probation officers.

What Do Networks Do?

Why are networks so important in our lives? How do student networks and the networks Peter Heywood formed affect what they can and will do?

To answer such questions, you need to look at what goes on in a network. Networks do many things. Here are five things that can occur through a social network.

- *Diffusion:* Networks can facilitate the diffusion of ideas and influence. A good example is rumors. Although we do not hear about any rumors in this case, we can imagine how rumors about Peter Heywood and the YRB teens could have spread among parents.
- *Exchanges:* Through networks, people make exchanges with others. Nobody is totally self-sufficient. People exchange with others to obtain things they need to do what they want to do. Peter needed help in finding jobs for some of the youth, and through the networks created by his board he found city jobs. Therefore, the YRB was able to employ some teens, and the city received needed labor. The point is that, through networks, people make exchanges to obtain resources they need (Cook and Whitmeyer 1992). This is why it is important when mapping out a network to look at where resources are located within the network. If strategic resources are located in only a few places in a network, others within the network will be dependent on those social actors. In the extreme, you can have networks with monopolies in which only one social actor controls an important resource that others within the network need.
- *Social Support:* Social networks can provide social support. When people move to a new town or country, they often have a

difficult time because they have lost their *support network,* that is, social ties that can provide assistance and information in times of need. Kinship networks often provide social support (Marks and McLanahan 1993), and the loss of kinship networks following geographical mobility can mean the loss of support networks. Support networks can be very important in finding a job (Granovetter 1995) and, for those who are really having a difficult time, finding shelter.

- *Exclusion:* Becoming connected to a network can open doors, whereas exclusion from a network can perpetuate inequalities. The most obvious case of such exclusion are "old boy" networks in which men, who have traditionally dominated a given line of work, inform only other men of hiring and promotion opportunities. Because networks are created through social ties, the presence of a tie can include people, but the absence of a social tie can exclude. Looking at networks requires, therefore, looking at who is included and who is excluded through the network. The clearest cases of exclusionary networks are social cliques and exclusive clubs such as country clubs.

Why do people create exclusionary networks? In part, it may be due to prejudicial attitudes that lead people to form ties only with those who are similar to themselves. But it also can be because those in the network want to protect something that they have by preventing others from having access to it through their network.

Although each of these network functions is evident in this case, it is probably the inclusion/exclusion logic of networks that is most important. In a way, this case can be read as a case of "disconnection" from important networks. As a relatively new person in this community, Peter Heywood is not a part of the already existing friendship, resource, information, and kinship networks. As YRB's director, Peter realizes this, and that is why he seeks to build social ties to people in the community such as other directors of social service agencies, police officers, teachers, youth, and even the school board. But he is still not part of the social networks that are important within the educational community—the networks connecting teachers, parents, school administrators, and students. As such, Peter appears to those within these networks as an outsider. Even his approach to the problem—the petition, confronting the principal, getting outside legal opinions—is indicative of someone who is not included within existing social networks. Because he is not part of these networks, Peter is seen as someone who is "rocking the boat" instead of someone who is trying to influence opinions.

According to this network reading of the case, Peter should not have been the focal point of the debate over the school's policy. He needed someone with strong social ties within the community and the school system to raise the issue, such as a school board member, an involved parent, or maybe even a respected teacher. Even though Peter and the YRB staff are the ones that believe that the school policy is wrong, because they are disconnected from important community networks, they are not the ones who can succeed in changing this policy. They either must rely on other people who are more connected to fight this battle or must first cultivate their social networks so that they can have the information, resources, and support they need to change the school's policy.

ORGANIZATIONS

The final social connector you need to look for in social situations are organizations. Through **organizations**, people are connected by a coordinated division of labor designed to attain a goal or set of goals. You can begin to notice organizations by looking for objectives and goals that people attempt to accomplish together, often because they are unable to achieve them by themselves.

What are some of the organizations that are evident in the "Separate but Safer" case? Of course, there is the YRB, a newly formed organization whose goal is to reduce delinquency in Brownfield and Dewitt. There is also the United Way, a funding organization whose purpose is to obtain resources and then distribute them to local community organizations. There is Brownfield Junior High School, whose purpose is to educate students. The case also mentions a teen center, numerous social service agencies, and the *Twin City Daily Sentinel*, the local newspaper that reports news and attempts to influence opinions through editorials.

Each of these organizations has specific *ends*, conveyed through their goals, purposes, and objectives. But to do what they want to do, each organization creates the *means* for achieving its ends by connecting people together. Establishing means to ends is not an easy task. Typically, those who run organizations encounter three problems:

1. *Uncertainty:* People running organizations often face uncertainties about such things as attracting customers, what competitors will do, where they will obtain quality supplies, and whether workers will do the work. With uncertainty, it is difficult to make plans, to predict what will happen in the future, and to calculate the costs and benefits of alternative courses of action (Albrow 1970).

2. *Coordination:* Within organizations, different people perform different tasks to realize an organization's goal. But if the left hand does not know what the right hand is doing, success is unlikely. Somehow, tasks and activities need to be coordinated. Otherwise, bottlenecks and inefficiencies are likely to occur (Blau and Meyer 1987).

3. *Legitimation:* In organizations, commands are issued and work is directed. But what gives a person the right to command others? When are people more likely to comply with orders? To increase compliance, directors and managers attempt to legitimize authority so that those who are being asked to obey commands will view the exercise of authority as fair and just (Gouldner 1954).

Those running an organization spend a good deal of their time thinking about and dealing with uncertainties, coordination problems, and legitimation issues. Consider Principal Westcoat. He claims there are uncertainties about how boys and girls would behave if they ate and had recess together. He also argues that coordination problems justify the separation policy. Without distinct lunchrooms, he believes that there would be confusion and bottlenecks leading to longer lunch hours and school days. And Westcoat faces legitimation problems as he tries to justify the separation policy and ensure that students comply with its rules.

How does the principal deal with these problems of uncertainty, coordination, and legitimacy? Like many others who run organizations, the principal creates rules and policies, and then he enforces these rules. This is a typical response of those who run organizations. Faced with uncertainty, coordination, and legitimacy problems, those in charge of an organization establish *bureaucratic* structures.

Initially, you may not have thought of the separate lunchrooms policy and this junior high school as examples of bureaucracy. When people think about bureaucracies, they think of large governmental organizations bogged down with inefficiencies, ineptness, and red tape. But as Max Weber (1946) realized many years ago, bureaucratic practices are everywhere. Why? Because, he argued, bureaucracies are designed to solve problems related to uncertainty, coordination, and legitimation. Let us see how bureaucracies are supposed to do this.

According to Weber, bureaucracies have six important qualities. As you read about each of these characteristics, think about whether Brownfield Junior High School has these traits.

Positions separate from people. In a bureaucracy, people have clear and delimited responsibilities, often conveyed in their job descriptions. They know what is expected of them. People are hired into positions; they do not create their own jobs, nor do they own them. With clear expectations, uncertainties are decreased.

Division of labor. In bureaucracies, complicated tasks are broken down into subtasks, which are then assigned to different positions. The clas-

sic example is an automobile assembly line. But you also see divisions
of labor in sports teams (the different positions), the post office (carri-
ers, letter sorters, haulers), and many other organizations. A division
of labor decreases uncertainties by clarifying who is responsible for
which tasks. However, dividing up work also creates the need for coordination among those doing different tasks.

Hierarchy of authority. In bureaucracies, there are supervisors, not just
for those who do the basic work, but also for those who supervise others. The result is that every position is under the supervision of a higher
one. Hierarchies facilitate coordination through supervision. They
also legitimize authority. Supervisors exercise authority not because of
who they are, but because of their position as supervisors. And because
they are themselves supervised, they are not above the law, so to speak.
They, too, are subject to authority.

Rules and regulations. Perhaps the most important and most noticed
aspect of bureaucracies is the presence of lots of rules governing what
people should and should not do. Rules are important because they
provide clear standards and expectations, thereby decreasing uncertainty. Rules, through their stipulations, contain guidelines about how
tasks are to be coordinated, solving to some extent coordination problems. Rules also legitimize the exercise of authority. Without rules, the
personal exercise of authority can be very arbitrary. Bosses can assign
the worst jobs to those they dislike and save the good jobs for their
friends. Rules curtail this capricious exercise of authority and, in so doing, increase the likelihood that subordinates will comply with commands. In bureaucracies, you have the rule of law instead of the rule of
people.

Impersonality. In bureaucracies, decisions are not supposed to be made
based on personal considerations. Rather, a bureaucrat is supposed to
act rationally, choosing the best means to a given end. This impersonality and formalism are seen in hiring and firing decisions, promotions, dealings with clients and customers, and supervisor–subordinate

relations. Bureaucratic formalism encourages equitable treatment through due process procedures designed to ensure that people are treated fairly. This is in marked contrast to patronage systems in which people use organizations to benefit themselves, their family members, and their friends.

Qualifications and careers. Finally, bureaucracies are places in which people are promoted based on their qualifications and achievements, not on who they know. As a result, people can have careers in bureaucracies as they move up the hierarchy to positions with more responsibilities and authority.

Are these traits evident at Brownfield Junior High? Does having these traits decrease uncertainty, increase coordination, and establish legitimacy at this school? As with most schools, there are lots of rules (often found in student handbooks) that decrease uncertainties by conveying to students, parents, and teachers what is expected. A division of labor, such as different classes in which different subjects are taught, different tracks for those with different academic abilities, and separate lunch rooms, is supposed to coordinate activities. With an authority hierarchy connecting students, teachers, vice principals, a principal, a superintendent, and a school board, those in charge are held accountable for their actions. School rules are designed to coordinate the variety of activities that go on in the school and legitimize the authority teachers have to tell students what to do. Combined with impersonality in such things as grading and class assignment and the ability to move into higher-level classes based on student achievement, bureaucratized schools attempt to advance learning by creating a more certain, better coordinated, and fairer learning environment.

However, if you were to look just at how an organization deals with uncertainty, coordination, and legitimation problems, you would miss something very important about bureaucracies. Bureaucracies can and frequently do create problems. Bureaucracies often dehumanize activities. People feel alienated from each other and their work as they go about doing the same thing over and over again. Rules decrease choice, creating routinization and monotony. Then people react by trying to get around the rules. They may create their own *informal organization* bypassing the formal, bureaucratic order. They may even openly resist by disobeying the rules. Bureaucracies also promote rigidities. Rules, clear responsibilities, hierarchy, and formalization create an incentive for people to do just what they are supposed to do. Rules, which are intended to be means to an organization's ends, become ends in themselves (Merton and Rossi 1957). People follow them methodically and unthinkingly.

Perhaps the biggest problem with bureaucracies is their inability to change with the times. Bureaucracies are like preprogrammed machines. They are "hard-wired" to do specific things in the same way over and over. The positive result is a consistent product or service. But the negative result is their inability to change. When customers or clients want something new and different, their wishes are likely to be misread or ignored.

Bureaucracies are also powerful tools that can be misused by those who control them (Michels [1911] 1949). Instead of using the bureaucratic machinery to achieve organizational goals and satisfy customer needs, those in control can use the organization to advance their own interests. Finally, the rules within bureaucracies can themselves be unfair. If the rules seem to favor some and not others, and if the rules are imposed on some people by other people, organizational members may abide by the rules only grudgingly (Gouldner 1954).

Which of these problems do you think are likely to be found at Brownfield Junior High? In all likelihood, some students, as well as some teachers, are alienated and bored. With lots of rules, students and teachers may act in a rigid fashion. But probably the biggest problem at this school is the bureaucracy's resistance to change. Even though there have been changes in people's views about the role of women and male–female interaction, this school seems unwilling to change with the times. Administrators see school rules and policies as the tried-and-true way of doing things. Consider the principal's reaction to protests about the separate lunchroom policy. He notes that this practice has been around for awhile and claims that if it worked for these students' parents, why should the practice be changed?

What all this means is that when studying the connections forged by organizations, you should look at them from *two* points of view. First, you need to examine organizational connections from the point of view of those who created and run the organization; you need to be aware of how managers have structured activities to accomplish objectives and deal with uncertainty, coordination problems, and legitimation issues. But then you need to look at the organization from the point of view of others who either are part of the organization (e.g., employees, students) or are served by the organization (e.g., customers, clients, parents). How are they affected by the organizational structures established by those who manage the organization?

Looking at organizations from both perspectives can help you develop multiple readings of social situations, a skill that you will develop more with the material in the next chapter. Although the "Separate but Safer" case can be read as a case of administrators trying to run a school efficiently, it also can be read as a case of an organization curtailing beneficial interactions between girls and boys and treating girls differently than boys.

In fact, the conflict in this case between Peter Heywood and the school board could be traced to these different readings of the case. Therefore, looking at organizations from multiple angles can help you understand organizational conflicts.

SOCIOLOGICAL EYE ANALYSIS GUIDE

Now that you better understand the various ways in which social actors can be connected to others, you are in a position to use your sociological "eye" to read social situations. Although your sociological eyesight may not yet be 20–20, I am sure that you are beginning to see things more clearly from a sociological point of view.

Practice at identifying social connections will enhance your socio-logical eyesight and lead to new insights into situations.

As you have seen in this chapter, identifying key actors, the central issues, the problems and dilemmas faced by the actors, and important behaviors is only the first step in analyzing a situation. To gain a *sociological* understanding of a situation, you also must look for and describe the social connections that connect various social actors. This chapter was designed to help you "see" social connections by looking for four important connectors: social relationships, groups, networks, and organizations. You should now be able to use your understanding of these connectors to describe the connections that exist in any situation.

Before you can analyze a situation you need to *describe* the situation adequately by noting who is connected to whom, and how. But this is only the beginning. You then need to use your knowledge of social connections to help you develop *explanations* for what occurred in the case.

Developing explanations is a difficult skill to learn, and the remainder of this book is designed to give you the tools you will need to develop a variety of different types of explanations. Already you have seen in my analysis of the "Separate but Safer" case some explanations. I noted how this case could be read as a case of role conflict and ambiguity, a case of gendering, a case of disconnection from networks, and a case of bureaucracy and its problems. Each of these readings could be used to develop explanations for why Peter Heywood was unsuccessful in changing the school separation policy.

In the next chapter, I discuss in greater detail how you can develop explanations by using sociological theories. But for now, what is important is your ability to see social connections in real situations. To help you map out social connections, I have created the following Sociological Eye Analysis Guide. Use this checklist to guide yourself through your reading of the "Why Can't Things

Stay as They Are?" case, other cases in this book, or even situations you know about from your personal experiences.

Actors and Issues

❏ What are the names of the key social actors in this situation? Briefly describe each actor and the role she or he plays in the case. Are any of these social actors collective actors?

❏ What is the central issue in the situation? What changes have occurred or are being proposed? What is the issue about which reasonable people seem to disagree?

❏ What are the problems or dilemmas faced by the key actors? How are these problems and dilemmas related to the central issues of the case? What have the central actors done (or not done) to deal with the problems and resolve the dilemmas?

❏ In sum, what is the case about? Describe the situation in terms of the actors, issues, problems/dilemmas, and actions. Formulate questions you would like to answer through an analysis of the situation.

Social Relationships

❏ What social relationships are evident in the situation? Which statuses are connected through a relationship to which other statuses?

❏ How would you characterize each of the statuses you identified? What are the norms (the dos and don'ts) of the various roles?

❏ Are there any indications that role behavior does not match role expectations? What rewards and punishments are used to increase role compliance? How are people socialized into roles?

❏ Are role transitions occurring in the case? If so, how would you characterize the transition, and how are people dealing with it?

❏ Are there any role conflicts? If so, which roles are incompatible, and what are individuals doing to resolve the conflict? Is there any evidence of role ambiguity?

Groups

❏ What groups can you identify in this situation? Who is a member of which group or groups?

❏ How would you characterize each of the groups you identified? Are they large or small groups, primary or secondary groups? What are the reference groups of the various key actors in this case?

❏ How would you describe the identity hierarchies of the various social actors in this case? What are the most salient identities?

❏ Are there any indications that gendering is taking place in this situation? Are gender roles prevalent in this case, and, if so, what are the gender role expectations? How salient are gender identities? Do any of the key actors use gender stereotypes, and, if so, what are the stereotypes that they use?

Networks

❏ How many networks connect people who are involved in this case? Who is connected by each network? What flows through each of these networks (information, material resources, personal evaluations, people, authority, kinship)?

❏ Are the networks dense or sparse? Are there central actors in the network? Are there places where ties between actors do not exist? How strong are the social ties within the networks?

❏ What role are these networks playing in the situation? Are they diffusing ideas and information, facilitating exchanges, providing social support, and/or excluding people?

Organizations

☐ What organizations could be affecting what is going on in this situation?

☐ Are those organizations more or less bureaucratized? For each organization, how would you characterize the relationship between people and positions, the division of labor, the hierarchy of authority, the rules and regulations, the level of impersonality and formalism, and the criteria used in hiring and for promotions?

☐ What problems do these organizations face? How do they deal with uncertainties? How do they attempt to gain legitimacy? What do they do to coordinate activities?

☐ From the point of view of the people in this case, what problems are they experiencing when dealing with these organizations?

Decision Case: "Why Can't Things Stay as They Are?"

The staff room was noisy and the tension elevated as the principal took his seat at the far end of the long table. He glanced around the room without smiling, nodding acknowledgment to individual staff members, and waited for the din of voices to fade. As 26 pairs of eyes turned in his direction, he opened the meeting by saying, "Thanks very much for coming today. I know that this is short notice, but I felt that this new business could not wait until the next regular meeting to be discussed."

Roslyn Varon whispered a comment into Janet Tigard's ear that made Janet smile. Neil Horvath nudged Art Metzger with his elbow. Julie Wilson whispered under her breath, to no one in particular, "This is it, folks."

Claus Braverman, the principal of Sherwood Forest Elementary School, fingered the sheaf of papers on the table in front of him. This was hard for him, and he had considered various ways of approaching it. In the end, he had decided that his best option was to lay the cards directly on the table and respond thoughtfully to what came next. This was, after all, not of his own doing; he was not the person responsible for the new policy statements about goals and objectives and about school reforms coming from the school board office. He had not even been a member of the Committee to Restructure Schools that had been meeting for the past two years and that had put together these plans for how schools in the district were to change to meet the challenges of the twenty-first century. He was just the guy in the hot seat, the one on whom the responsibilities for implementation fell, who had to see to it that the changes were going to be made in his school.

AUTHOR'S NOTE: Reprinted by permission of the publisher, from S. Wasserman, *Getting Down to Cases: Learning to Teach With Case Studies* (New York: Teachers College Press, © 1993 by Teachers College, Columbia University, pp. 75-81. All rights reserved).

"As you all know," he began,

> the Committee to Restructure Schools took its plans for school im-
> provement to the school board meeting last night. I was there, so I can
> tell you from personal experience that the meeting was lengthy and
> heated. The proposed changes were not unanimously endorsed. But
> they were supported by the majority of the board, with only two dis-
> senting votes. There was, however, unanimous agreement among the
> board members and the public that we needed to make major changes
> in our school programs to help prepare children to live productively and
> responsibly in the next century.

Braverman had everyone's attention now. The teachers were told
that the plans for change were inevitable. How they would be implemented in each school in this district, however, was the principal's
decision. That meant Claus Braverman had some options with respect
to how the school went about planning for change and what some of
the timelines were going to be for those changes to be put into effect. It
also meant that he and the staff were to be involved in developing specific strategies for change.

Braverman had brought with him copies of the new goal and objective statements, including those changes that were required to be
implemented by the end of the school year. He distributed copies to
each staff member, saying,

> I think it would be a good idea if each of you read through the policy
> statements and became familiar with the goals and objectives part.
> Then, I suggest we focus the rest of this afternoon's discussion on how
> we, as a staff, might most comfortably, and with a minimum of disrup-
> tion to children, move to make these changes in our classroom pro-
> grams. With respect to the restructuring changes mandated by the
> board—that's on pages three and four of the document—I'd like to
> leave that part for a subsequent meeting. But you should take notice
> that the plan calls for an ungraded primary program, an intermediate
> program that will incorporate those grades now defined as 4 through 8,
> and a graduation program that will include Grades 9 through 12. But
> that latter program is not our immediate concern. Now, won't you take
> a few minutes and read through pages one and two of the proposal?

The room fell silent, except for the rustle of papers, as teachers read through the policy statements that had become, as of last evening, school board policy:

◆ ◆ ◆

Policy Statement for School Restructuring

The primary goal of our school programs is to prepare children to live as "educated citizens" in the twenty-first century. This means that school programs will be dedicated to enabling learners to develop their individual potential and to helping them develop the knowledge, skills, and attitudes required to live productively in the world of the future.

Educated citizens are:

- Thoughtful, critical thinkers
- Creative, flexible, self-initiating, and have a positive sense of self
- Capable of choosing responsibly and wisely
- Skilled and have the ability to make positive contributions to our society
- Cooperative, respectful of others, tolerant of differences, and principled

To meet these goals, classroom practice should emphasize the following:

1. Students' active participation in the learning process
2. Learning activities that are reflective of individual differences
3. Learning activities that encourage student discussions with one another in the examination of subject-related issues
4. Evaluation practices that are learner-focused and provide for self-evaluation and meeting individual learning needs
5. Student assessment that encourages informed choices and allows for examination of student work over a period of time

"I'll begin by taking your questions. Then, I hope we can proceed to suggestions for what we do next to get these ideas into your day-to-day classroom lives. Yes, Effie?"

Effie Thibadeau, a veteran kindergarten teacher two years from retirement, made the first of what was going to be a stream of negative remarks. "You know, Claus, I've been at Sherwood Forest longer than anybody here." Effie liked to begin her comments at staff meetings by directing everyone's attention both to her seniority and her senior position on the staff:

> I've seen recommendations for change come and go. I was here 20 years ago when all the children were going to learn to read with the Initial Teaching Alphabet. That bombed out quickly and those plans hit the dust. Who here has even *heard* of the Initial Teaching Alphabet! I was here 10 years ago when Madeline Hunter's direct instruction plans were laid on for all elementary teachers in the district. That, too, came and went. Now here's another new plan. I predict this too will die in two or three years' time. So why should we either get excited about it, or even interested in putting it into operation? I'm getting too old for this, Claus. If I'm going to be asked to make changes in what I'm doing in my kindergarten, just for the sake of some committee that's never even been in my classroom, I'm going to take early retirement. The heck with it.

Braverman had anticipated that Effie would be among the first of the teachers to speak against what needed to be done. Effie was an extremely conservative and traditional teacher who had taught very much the same way today as she had when she first became a teacher. The kindergarten equipment might be more modern, but Effie's teaching style was strictly medieval. Claus would be glad to raise a glass at her retirement dinner. He was tired of teachers like Effie, who were so stuck in their ways and so unwilling and unready to meet the changing demands of the profession and of society. He nevertheless responded to her concerns without malice. "Why am I not surprised at your response, Effie?" he said with a smile.

And I do take your point about other changes that have come and gone. But there's something in the air in this district and in this land that suggests that these school reforms are not going to be as fleeting as what was done in the past.

Several other teachers voiced questions about the policy statements, which Braverman fielded. As Braverman read the teachers' faces, however, he saw that his responses did not seem to alleviate their concerns. Their troubled looks indicated that his answers had not satisfied them.

Ruth Anne Potter was new to the Sherwood Forest staff. She had come in October, fresh from her teacher-training program, to replace Bernice Chadwick, who had been transferred to the district office. Ruth Anne was young, inexperienced, and very anxious. She was easily intimidated and rarely spoke at staff meetings. But this time was one of the exceptions: "I hope you won't think it's silly for me to ask this, Mr. Braverman, but I'd like to get some clarification on some of these points." Her voice sounded like cracking ice, but she pressed on in acknowledgment of Claus Braverman's suggestion that she continue.

As I look at some of these goals and objectives, I'm wondering how what I do in the classroom is going to be any different. I mean, look at what the first statement says: Children should be thoughtful, critical thinkers. Look at the third: Children should be capable of choosing responsibly and wisely. Well, that's exactly what I believe in and exactly what I'm doing in my classroom. So how am I supposed to change? Isn't this what we've all been doing all the time? How is this going to be different?

Braverman smiled weakly at Ruth Anne and thought about what a good response to her question might be. He decided to be tactful, rather than confrontational. "I take your point Ruth Anne. I guess the answer to your question is, 'How can we do more, and maybe a better job of what we've been doing all along.'"

Ruth Anne, impressed with her courage to voice her opinion, smiled and sat back in her chair. The principal, it seemed to her, had just given her his tacit approval to continue to do just as she had done all term. She would not have to worry about changing what she did in the classroom to accommodate to the new school board policy. She was safe!

At 4:30, Claus Braverman signaled that they ought to bring the meeting to a close and continue the discussion the following Monday. There were major issues at stake here, and these issues would not be resolved in a day. It would be a better idea if the staff continued to think about them, and to keep the discussion ongoing, until some specific plans could be made.

After chatting individually with several of his staff, Claus Braverman picked up his books and the extra copies of the new policy statements and left the staff room, heading back to his office. In his own heart of hearts, he cheered the new proposals for bringing what he considered much-needed change to the schools. The children in these classrooms would be entering the job market in the twenty-first century. The skills they would need were going to be different. The world would be far more complex with the population increasing significantly and the nature of jobs and work changing dramatically. Unless teachers were prepared to face the changing needs of society and to help children become equipped to live in that uncertain future, schools would indeed become obsolete. Already, existing technology had far outpaced the individual classroom teacher's ability to present curriculum in meaningful, exciting, and knowledgeable ways. How could teachers justify spending endless hours drilling the multiplication tables when pocket calculators cost $4.95 and were in each child's pencil case?

His eye caught the last glimpse of Ruth Anne Potter's blue scarf as she pushed through the exit door to the parking lot. Ah, Ruth Anne, he mused to himself, thinking about what she had said about what she was doing in her classroom. He was hard put not to smile at the discrepancy between what she *thought* she was doing and what she was actually doing. Her anxiety about having to change was palpable; he could almost smell her fear.

As he walked past her first-grade classroom, he could see evidence of her program, even in the absence of any living being. Desks in rows, so that children were isolated from one another and could not talk or work cooperatively together; red-and-white Valentines, all cut from the same pattern, all virtually identical, on the bulletin board. If there was independent thinking going on in this classroom, he'd eat his knife and fork. If children were learning to make their own decisions, he'd eat his spoon, too.

He recalled with distress the three times he had spent an hour in Ruth Anne's class in the past three months. They were painful visits for an administrator who believed in children's thinking, creativity, and independent decision making, but he thought it was a good idea to give Ruth Anne some space. She was new, anxious, and very inexperienced. He hoped that given time, and a climate in which change was encouraged and supported, she would grow professionally, take some risks, and break out of the narrow and restrictive educational practices she was using.

Ruth Anne was a teacher who liked to be in control of all classroom decisions. "Let's open our books for reading now," she'd say, and when children responded obediently, she thought that was involving them actively in learning. When she asked, "Now, would you like the story of *The Little Engine That Could* or *The Boy and the Flute*?" she believed that was allowing the children to be independent decision makers.

All of Ruth Anne's worksheets required children to give single, correct answers, which she then graded as "right or wrong." Ruth Anne thought that asking children to determine the right answers to questions such as "What color was the wagon?" was an activity that required children to think.

In her classroom discussions, she also relied heavily on interactions that called for children to give the single correct answers to her lower-order questions. "How many cupcakes did Mother bake?" and "What was Tom's sister's name?" were the kinds of questions she emphasized in her teaching, and when children could respond by recall of simple facts, she thought she was providing for individual differences.

To Claus Braverman, teachers like Ruth Anne were preparing children to live in the past. She was teaching obedience, conformity, and passivity, rather than thoughtfulness, creativity, flexibility, and independent decision making. And in all of that, the big irony was that Ruth Anne thought she was doing all the right things. She would not have to change her ways. She was already doing all that the new policy statements required!

Claus Braverman opened his office door, put down his books and papers, sat down in his swivel chair, and put his face in his hands. Whatever he was going to do with Ruth Anne, that job would not be easy.

CHAPTER 2

Using Theory

Decision Case: "The Towering Dilemma"

Late in 1994, Deborah Liggett faced a towering dilemma. Deborah was superintendent of Devils Tower National Monument in northeastern Wyoming, and for almost two years, she and her coworkers had been trying to find a way to manage the conflicting uses of the monument. To many casual tourists, Devils Tower is best known as the backdrop for the popular 1970s film *Close Encounters of the Third Kind*. Rising 867 feet above the surrounding landscape, Devils Tower is thought by geologists to be an isolated monolith from an ancient volcanic core. Established as the nation's first national monument in 1906, Devils Tower now attracts nearly 500,000 people annually to camp, picnic, hike, climb—and pray.

"We've known for a long time that climbing on the tower was offensive to American Indians," stated Deborah. "Devils Tower is the only area [in the Park system] where the most significant issue is traditional cultural use in conflict with recreational use." In 1992, the National

AUTHOR'S NOTE: This case was written by Steve Simmons and Tammy Dunrud. It is part of the database of cases available through the Clearinghouse for Decision Case Education at the University of Minnesota.

53

Park Service (NPS) began an environmental assessment that led to development of a management plan to "preserve and protect the monument's natural and cultural resources for present and future generations." Key to this effort was a need to increase understanding between two of the monument's principal users—rock climbers and American Indians—each of whom saw Devils Tower very differently.

Indian Perceptions and Use

For American Indian tribes in the Northern Plains region, the explanation for the origin and significance of Devils Tower is much different from that of modern geologists. Traditional tribal cultures of the region regard Devils Tower as having a supernatural origin. For example, the Crow people believe that Devils Tower was "put there by the Great Spirit for a special reason, because it was different from other rocks." Another narrative attributes the origin of Devils Tower to an encounter between seven small girls and a large bear. When the bear chased the girls and was about to overtake them, the girls jumped onto a flat rock and prayed for the rock to help them. The rock responded by elongating upwards, taking the girls out of the reach of the bear. In its frustration, the bear clawed at the sides of the rock, creating the cracks that are a characteristic feature of the tower today.

The Lakota Sioux maintain that their people have an ancient and sacred relationship with Devils Tower and the nearby Black Hills, which they believe was their place of creation. One Lakota wrote, "Those who use the butte to pray become stronger. They gain knowledge from the spirits that helps us preserve our Lakota culture and way of life." Because of its cultural significance, Devils Tower is considered eligible for listing on the National Register of Traditional Cultural Property.

Thus, to American Indians, the tower long has been regarded as a spiritual place and a pilgrimage destination. People from as many as 20 tribes gather at the site annually for prayer offerings, spiritual dances, vision quests, and sweat lodge ceremonies. One of the monument's archaeological sites is a shelter made of stone and wood, which is thought to have been used long ago for such vision quests and ceremonies.

Rock Climber Perceptions and Use

For climbers, Devils Tower is one of the premier destinations in North America. Since it was first climbed in 1893, the fame of Devils Tower as a technical climbing site has grown. The director of a national climbers advocacy organization once stated, "It [Devils Tower] is nationally, if not internationally, significant. It is recognized as one of the premier crack climbing areas in America." Records of climbs have been kept since 1937 and show that in recent years more than 6,000 climbers have scaled the tower annually. There are almost 220 climbing routes charted. Climbing involves teamwork and individual effort, and some even describe it as a "spiritual" experience. Climbing also calls for individual courage and self-confidence. The climbing "season" at Devils Tower usually runs from spring through early fall, although climbs have been made in all months of the year. About two thirds of the climbers choose routes that do not reach the summit, emphasizing that it is the technical challenge, not necessarily the destination, that is important to many climbers. Eighty percent of the climbs occur on only 23 of the routes. In 1994, there were seven commercial climbing guide companies operating in the monument under NPS licenses that depended on climbing activities at the monument for their economic well-being.

Controversy

As the number of climbers grew, Indians in the region became increasingly angry at what they considered desecration of the tower by climbers, as seen in the words of one Indian woman from South Dakota:

A group of elders would be telling the children about honor and respect, and we could hear the climbers [on the tower] being very loud, using real profane English, real vulgar language. And the children are looking up and saying, "How come he gets to say things like that when you're telling us to respect the tower?"

Some also disapproved of the climbers' practice of driving metal bolts and pitons into the tower to assist with climbing. They felt that this practice, which had grown as new climbing routes were established in the 1980s and 1990s, also adversely affected the spiritual quality of the site. Approximately 600 bolts and several hundred pitons had been driven into the rock by the mid-1990s.

Environmental Concerns

Naturalists consider Devils Tower National Monument part of a significant ecoregion, where mountain and plains species of plants and animals coexist. More than 450 plant species, 200 vertebrate species, and 550 insect species have been documented, including falcons, white-tailed deer, and prairie dogs. Some expressed concern that increasing use of the tower by climbers would destroy or disrupt the natural qualities of the tower. Although the tower was not known to be a habitat for endangered species in 1994, there were concerns that larger numbers of climbers and climbing routes would destroy vegetation, increase erosion, and lessen the tower's capacity to serve as suitable wildlife habitat. Of special concern was the negative effect that climbing could have on nesting raptors.

Management Plant Alternatives

In response to the many climbing issues at Devils Tower, the NPS prepared a Draft Climbing Management Plan. This plan presented six management alternatives:

1. Allow unlimited climbing and bolting year-round.
2. Continue current monument climbing management policies and restrictions.

3. Phase in a voluntary closure of the tower to climbing during June, a time that was deemed significant because of use of the tower by Indians for ceremonies around the summer solstice. The June closure would become fully implemented in 1997. Regulated new bolting would be allowed. Close climbing routes within 50 meters of nesting raptors.

4. Impose voluntary June closure to climbing in 1995 with a ban on new bolt placements (replacement of existing bolts or pitons would be permitted). Climbing routes would be closed within 50 meters of nesting raptors.

5. Mandate a June closure of the tower to climbing, beginning in 1995, with no new or replacement bolting permitted.

6. Indefinitely close the tower to all climbing year-round, beginning in 1995. All bolts would be removed from the tower, and trails to and on the tower would be rehabilitated to a more natural condition.

Approximately 1,200 copies of the plan were distributed to the public for comment during the period from July through November 1994. A total of 286 letters and two petitions were received. During the public comment period, six public meetings also were held within the region and comments recorded. Substantive public comments from these letters and meetings are summarized in Exhibit 2.1.

The Decision

As 1994 drew to a close, Deborah Liggett had to decide what policy alternative the NPS would adopt.

Exhibit 2.1. Selected (Paraphrased) Responses Received by the National Park Service During the Public Comment Period Following Release of the Draft Climbing Management Plan in July 1994

A. Area of Closure and Scope of Closure of the Tower

- There are no alternatives to climbing at Devils Tower because there is no way to walk to the top. This is the only place in the region where this type of climbing is possible.

- Conflicts between climbers and Indians will decrease without climbing restrictions if there is an education program. A cross-cultural education program should be tried before imposing any closures.

- A June closure will lead to more conflict between climbers and Indians, not less.

- Any closure should be for everyone.

- If June is closed, there should be specific language in the plan ensuring that the tower is open for the other 11 months in the future.

- Close the tower during a winter month, not June.

- An option should have been given to close the tower for two to six months (not just one).

- Shorten the closure period. The June closure should be intermittent, only a few days per week.

- Any climbing closure should be exempted for Indians who climb for spiritual purposes.

- A voluntary closure with a threat of mandatory closure is not an equitable attempt at mediating the competing interests. A voluntary closure is not voluntary if there is a threat that it will become mandatory.

B. Bolting and Pitons

- The final plan should make it clear that noncompliance with bolting restrictions would lead to tighter restrictions.
- The National Park Service is making sport climbing more dangerous by restricting bolting. Bolting is needed to make new climbing routes safe.
- For climbers' safety, the replacement of existing bolts (and fixed pitons) should continue.
- Climbers are still predrilling holes in the tower. This is an illegal activity now, although holes predrilled before summer of 1994 were legal.
- There has been insufficient damage to the rock to warrant banning bolting. . . . There is no documented evidence that bolting affects the rock.
- Asphalting the Tower Trail was done for tourist convenience. It affects the tower more than bolts do.

C. Wildlife Considerations

- There is no basis for claiming that limiting March and April climbing levels will protect raptors.
- Significant evidence suggests that raptors need only a 100-foot radius of protection. There is no basis for establishing a 50-meter limit. Raptor closures should be based on the visibility of climbers, not fixed distances.
- A raptor expert should determine if 50 or 100 meters is enough. Fifty meters should be a minimum. . . . Expand the closure distance if needed.
- None of the birds nesting at the tower is rare or endangered, so the degree of protection proposed is excessive.
- Peregrine falcons should be reintroduced to the tower.

D. Cultural Perspectives and Significance

- There is no archaeological evidence that the tower was a sacred site in historic times. The sacred nature of the tower is of modern origin. Rock climber use is older than Indian ceremonial use at the tower.

- Climbing does not desecrate sacred ground.

- There is nothing sacred about Devils Tower—it is only an extinct volcano.

- Devils Tower is culturally significant not only to Indians, but climbers too. Some alternatives in the plan ignore the rights of climbers.

- People like watching climbers on the tower. It is a positive, not negative, impact.

- Closure will affect small businesses in the region adversely. The economic effect (of a closure) is downplayed along with the impact to climbing guides and outfitters.

- Devils Tower is a place to pray, not for sightseeing or sporting events.

- The Devils Tower area should be designated a historic district.

- Indians should perform their ceremonies during the winter when there are few tourists and fewer climbers.

- The National Park Service should give the Indians someplace else to worship.

- Closure in deference to one ethnic group will lead to closures for other ethnic groups.

- The 1868 Treaty is still intact through the precepts of U.S. Treaty law. Devils Tower National Monument is Indian land.

- You can't close public land for religious purposes. Closure is un-constitutional and sets a legal precedent challenging the First Amendment.

⬚ REVIEW: SOCIAL CONNECTIONS

In this chapter, you will learn how to analyze a situation from multiple perspectives with sociological theories. As you already know, to examine a situation, you first need to understand what the situation is about and identify the important social connections. So let us begin the analysis of the "Towering Dilemma" case by reviewing what you learned in Chapter 1 about how to describe a case sociologically.

First, what is this case about? Who are the key actors, and what is the central issue? Clearly, the major actor in this case is Deborah Liggett, who works for the NPS as the superintendent of Devils Tower National Monument. The other important actors are collective actors, the various groups that have an interest in how Devils Tower is used: American Indians, rock climbers, and naturalists. The central issue in this case is whether rock climbing should be restricted, and if so, how and how much. The actors face problems and dilemmas pertaining to this issue. Rock climbers' access could be restricted. Native Americans' spiritual use is adversely affected by rock climbing. Naturalists are concerned about environmental damage resulting from overuse. Therefore, Deborah Liggett faces a dilemma as she tries to reconcile the competing and at times conflicting uses of Devils Tower.

Second, what are the important social connections (social relationships, groups, networks, and organizations) that are evident in this case? Who is connected to whom, and how are they connected?

In terms of social relationships, the most important one is between Deborah as superintendent and the various groups that use Devils Tower. This is a relationship between a regulator and those who are regulated, in this case, users of a public facility. In the role of regulator, Deborah, on behalf of the NPS, has the right to determine who uses the monument and under what conditions. You may recall that her office licenses climbing guide companies that operate in the monument. There are also social relationships within the various groups, such as between elders and children among Native Americans, and between guides and rock climbers.

Groups are clearly important in this case. Besides the three collective actors that are groups—rock climbers, American Indians, and naturalists—there are the rock climber guides, teams of rock climbers, groups of Native Americans visiting the monument, and those who attended each of the six public meetings.

Social networks are harder to detect in this case. Within each of the groups there are probably information networks through which people are kept informed about developments. Probably the increasing use of Devils Tower by climbers occurred in part as word spread through climbing networks about how great a place Devils Tower is for climbing. Kinship and tribal networks among Native Americans probably spread the word about the problems at Devils Tower, and I am sure there are networks among naturalists as well. Networks were probably also instrumental in getting people to attend public meetings, sign petitions, and write letters.

Finally, the most important organization in this case is the NPS, a governmental agency that protects, preserves, and manages national parks, monuments, and other public sites. Other organizations mentioned in the case are the guide companies and a national climbers advocacy organization.

From this description of the various connectors in this case, how would you describe this situation sociologically? In a way, this case seems to be a case in which connections exist *within* groups but not as much *between* groups. The groups are brought together, so to speak, not because of social connections but because they all use Devils Tower. The only connections between the key social actors are between Deborah and each of the groups. As the regulator, she interacts with each of them. And now, because of conflicts between the groups, she has to decide how to reconcile the competing uses. To develop an understanding of this conflict and ideas about how it could be resolved, you will need to examine the interrelationships among the three groups in the absence of social connections between them. The remainder of this chapter shows you how to do this by using sociological theories.

 ## SOCIOLOGICAL THEORY

One of the most striking aspects of this case is the different perspectives that people have on the conflict. Consider the responses the NPS received during public hearings, as detailed in Exhibit 2.1. Some view this as a case of infringement on the rights of climbers to climb, whereas others see this as yet another case of the lack of respect for American Indian practices and beliefs. Still others talk about the inability of people to work out a compromise, whereas others highlight the need to protect natural resources that cannot protect themselves. I am sure that as you read this case and began to react to it that you too saw it from a particular perspective, a perspective that informed how you thought the conflict could be resolved.

We cannot help but view social situations from certain *perspectives*. Because we want to make sense of events, we use perspectives to guide our thinking. However, often we are not very aware of what our perspective is and how it differs from other perspectives. People have a tendency to look at events from only one perspective, a perspective that they take for granted. And from that perspective, other people's points of view can appear ridiculous or inappropriate, leading us to dismiss them without much reflection. But fully understanding the complexity of social life requires shifting perspectives from time to time. The ability to *reframe,* to examine social connections from different perspectives, is an important and useful skill. How can you become more aware of the perspectives you use to understand social situations? How can you develop the skill of reframing so that you can see social situations from alternative perspectives? What would help you to see "The Towering Dilemma" case differently?

One way to begin to develop your reframing skill is to listen carefully to other people's readings of a situation. Students, when first exposed to decision case discussions, are surprised when they hear widely different reactions to a case. But as they explore why others have *different* views of the *same* situation, they begin to see how readings of a case, including their own reading, are based on certain assumptions. By comparing the assumptions that they bring to the case with the assumptions others hold, they learn how they can shift perspective by using different assumptions.

Understanding assumptions and employing them to develop perspectives is exactly what sociologists do when they use sociological theories. **Theories,** sets of concepts and propositions that people use to develop explanations of observable phenomena, often seem quite abstract and removed from real situations. Yet, as you will see, the reason sociologists "do" social theory is to help them understand real social situations. Here are three ways in which theories can help guide your research on and thinking about social realities:

1. *Posing Questions:* With theories, you can pose questions that focus attention on certain aspects of a case or situation. For example, questions about "The Towering Dilemma" case could direct your attention to the relationships within and between the various groups in the case, toward the NPS and what it does, toward who benefits and who loses under various proposals, toward the trade-offs that exist, and toward the cultural views of Native Americans and the climbers. As you thought about the case, what were some of the important questions you had?

2. *Developing Explanations:* With theories, you can develop explanations, that is, answers to your questions. These answers are claims about why, according to some theory, you think specific events in the case occurred. The explanations that you develop from theories are tentative answers or what scientists call **hypotheses,** unverified statements about the causes of some (social) phenomena. With this case, as you shall see, you could use a number of different theories to explain why there are conflicts between American Indians and climbers. To see which of these

explanations of the conflict are valid, you would have to do research. The information gathered through research could provide evidence, either for or against, your tentative answers.

3. *Formulating Action Plans:* Theories also can help you to formulate solutions or plans of action that someone could take in a
given situation. Explanations derived from using theory form
the basis for developing such solutions. For example, if you analyzed the conflict in "The Towering Dilemma" case as being
caused by a lack of understanding of another group's culture and
values, then you would propose educating people. If, on the
other hand, your explanation focused on social inequalities,
then you would propose changes that would create a more equal
situation. How you read a situation affects how you react to the
situation and what you think you would do if you were in that
situation.

To use a theory to pose questions, develop explanations, and formulate action plans, you must first understand it. How can you learn
theory? One way is to read social theorists. In their writings, theorists
seek to define their concepts carefully, state their core propositions,
and articulate their key assumptions. I strongly encourage you to read
social theory. At first, it may seem quite dry, abstract, and esoteric. But
as you begin to understand a theorist and acquire another way of
looking at social realities, you will become excited about the new perspective on the world you have gained from reading social theory.

You will know that you understand a theorist when you have a
good picture in your mind of the core *image* that guides that theorist's
way of seeing and thinking about society. Images and the metaphors
they convey are powerful tools that can help you understand the different ways you can think about social situations (Morgan 1980).
Metaphors are based on assertions of the form "A is (or is like) B." For
example, consider the claim "My best friend is a saint." The image
contained in this metaphor is the image of a saint. It is used to understand the behavior of my best friend by focusing attention on certain

aspects of his behavior—his kindness, doing of good deeds, and compassion. Similarly, theories have core images that focus attention on specific aspects of social connections. The five theories that I explore in the rest of this chapter can be "pictured" using five different images of social connections:

- As *bonds* that unite
- As *integrators* of parts into a whole
- As conflictive *tugs-of-war*
- As *exchanges* among rational actors
- As emergent *webs* of interaction

In what follows, I examine each of these images, drawing out the key ideas and theoretical assumptions and seeing how each perspective can be used to understand the conflicts in "The Towering Dilemma."

SOCIAL CONNECTIONS AS BONDS

A society is more than just the people who are living in some geographically defined area. Something seems to hold people in a society together, preventing it from coming apart at the seams and disintegrating into many pieces. What creates *order* among a diverse set of elements? What is missing when there is disorder and chaos?

These are the types of questions that are central to the theoretical framework that views social connections as *bonds*. The image is a powerful one. The components of society—people—are like atoms. There are different types of people, just like there are different types of atoms. Atoms are bonded to other atoms, creating molecules and compounds. It takes a good deal of effort to create these bonds, so once they are created it is difficult to separate the elements. If the bonds are broken, there is usually an explosion, just like when chemical bonds are broken and energy is released. The atoms go flying off in all directions. Eventually, most of them are attracted to other atoms, leading to new and possibly different bonds.

The bonds that connect people are not chemical bonds, although sometimes we use a chemical analogy, like when we say that there is a real chemistry between two lovers. Rather, the bonds among people are social connections formed through social relationships, group affiliations, networks, and organizational memberships. Connections forge bonds, and it is these bonds that hold society together. From this theoretical framework, much of what goes on in our social worlds concerns bonding, and sociologists who use this framework view the need to form bonds as the central driving force in society.

The first social theorist to develop this image was Emile Durkheim (1858–1917). In his attempt to understand the changes occurring as a result of the Industrial Revolution, Durkheim ([1895] 1964) distinguished between two types of bonds, or what he called solidarity—mechanical and organic solidarity. Durkheim argued that **mechanical solidarity,** social bonds among persons based on shared moral sentiments, were more prevalent in preindustrial societies. In these societies, powerful moral and religious systems united people, and traditions played an important role in people's everyday lives. There was a strong *collective conscience* that demanded mechanical conformity to traditional norms.

According to Durkheim, the Industrial Revolution undermined mechanical solidarity. With new technologies came new occupations and a greater *division of labor,* or specialized types of work. With all these differences, it became less likely that people shared moral sentiments. People now thought and acted in different ways. According to Durkheim, this did not mean that social bonds had disappeared, but only that they had changed. Instead of solidarity being based on shared moral sentiments, Durkheim saw people with common interests and tastes creating bonds by forming groups and associations, such as occupational associations, professions, labor unions, and political parties. These social bonds seemed to emerge "organically" out of the daily lives of people, instead of being imposed on people mechanically by some central authority. Therefore, Durkheim referred to these bonds as **organic solidarity**, social bonds based on a complex division of labor that connects members of industrialized societies.

Organic solidarity not only connects people who share a common interest, but it also connects those who are engaged in different activities. How? According to Durkheim, the increased complexity of industrial societies entails greater interdependence. In preindustrial societies, small communities and sometimes even households could meet most of their needs on their own. But in industrial societies, with their greater differentiation, self-sufficiency was no longer possible. Increased interdependence creates bonds of *dependence*, a much different type of solidarity than mechanical forms.

Durkheim realized that social bonds, whether they be mechanical or organic, are not permanent and can be broken. When this occurs, you have **anomie**, a condition of normlessness in a society or in a group. Durkheim expected that anomic behavior, such as antisocial behaviors and criminal activity, would be greater during transition periods. During those periods, when one type of social connection is being replaced by other forms of connection, people become disconnected. Disconnected people, Durkheim thought, are more susceptible to extreme ideas, allowing cults and radical movements to grow. According to Durkheim, anomie also is seen in stable societies within segments of a population in which social bonds are weak. This is the idea behind one of Durkheim's more famous works, *Suicide* (Durkheim [1897] 1966). In that study, Durkheim showed that rates of most types of suicide are higher among groups characterized by weak social bonds.

Now that you are familiar with Durkheim's ideas and the image of social connections as bonds, how would you use these ideas to analyze a social situation? Here are three things you would want to do when using this theoretical perspective:

1. Identify the *social bonds* that are connecting the various social actors.

2. Characterize each bond in terms of whether it is based on *mechanical* or *organic solidarity*. Is the bond the result of shared moral sentiments, or is it maintained more because of common interests and tastes?

3. Note behaviors that are indicative of *anomie*. To what extent is this anomie the result of weak or nonexistent social bonds? Why are these social bonds not as strong as other social bonds that are evident in the situation?

Case Application

How can you use Durkheim's theory and his conceptual distinction between two forms of solidarity to understand "The Towering Dilemma" case? What types of social bonds did you see in that case? Right away, you probably noticed how the bonds among Native Americans seemed to be based more on mechanical solidarity, that is, shared moral sentiments having to do with respect for the land and elders. On the other hand, organic solidarity seems to bond the members of the other groups in the case. The climbers have a common hobby that brings them together. The naturalists have a common interest in protecting the natural environment. There are also tourists who want to enjoy nature's beauty and the tour guides who are trying to make a living by arranging climbing expeditions.

In fact, you could read this case as a case of the problems that often occur in societies based on organic solidarity. Bonds form among people who have common interests and who seek to pursue the activities related to those interests. As long as the interests of the various groups overlap and there is interdependence, everything is fine. For example, the interests of climbers and the tour guides overlap. Tour guides benefit by having climbers to take on climbs, and climbers benefit by having tour guide companies that can arrange climbs. So there are bonds both within and between each of these groups. But when it comes to the use of Devils Tower, for which there are multiple uses, organic solidarity can lead to conflicts between groups whose land uses are, to some extent, incompatible.

You could wish the conflict away by hoping for some form of mechanical solidarity that would provide a collective conscience among all those who use Devils Tower. But in modern societies in which freedom and individual choice are valued, the imposition of shared moral sentiments is very difficult. In the absence of a collective conscience, and with strong bonds within groups and little interdependence between groups, fragmentation is likely. This is exactly what seems to be occurring in "The Towering Dilemma." Using the image of social connections as bonds, the conflicts in this case can be explained as either the result of (1) the lack of mechanical solidarity among all those who want to use Devils Tower or (2) the absence of bonds between groups that have high internal levels of solidarity.

From this theoretical perspective, what is the solution to these problems? If you see social connections as bonds, you will tend to see problems as resulting from the absence of social bonds and the solutions as having to do with creating bonds. As long as there are no bonds connecting American Indians, climbers, and naturalists, conflicts over the use of Devils Tower will continue. But what could create bonds between these three groups that have quite different uses of this rock? It is hard to imagine some collective conscience emerging from shared moral sentiments. Instead, it is more likely that bonds would be created through interdependence. For example, suppose climbers began to see that some of their actions are destroying the rock and making it more difficult for them to use it in the future. Then they may recognize that the naturalists' attempts to preserve the rock also could benefit climbers by curbing abuses of the rock. Interdependence is also conceivable between naturalists and Native Americans, although it is more difficult to see how climbers and Native Americans could form these types of bonds.

SOCIAL CONNECTIONS AS INTEGRATORS

Societies and the organizations and institutions within them attempt to survive. How does a society survive over time? What must be done in an organization for it to stay alive and grow? How does a whole society composed of many different parts keep on going?

These are the questions that lie at the core of the theoretical framework that views social connections as *integrators* of parts into a whole. This image draws on an analogy to living organisms. Societies are like living bodies. A body has parts (the heart, lungs, kidneys) that perform various functions (pumping blood, absorbing oxygen, eliminating waste) that allow the whole body to survive and grow. The parts are structured in such a way so that each can perform its function. If a part's structure changes (e.g., an artery becomes blocked), it is likely to malfunction. And because parts are interconnected, one part's malfunction can lead to another part's malfunction and potentially to the death of the living organism.

Similarly, a society is a whole social system, composed of parts that perform specific **social functions,** that is, activities that are necessary for the survival of the entire society or social entity. Families raise and socialize children. The economy produces goods and services and distributes resources. Governments set goals and marshal resources for their attainment. These parts of society are able to perform their functions because of the way in which they are organized and structured. **Social structures,** organizing principles of a social system that generate relatively stable patterns of behavior, create the framework in which people act and interact as they go about performing important social functions. For example, there are various family structures, such as the nuclear family and the extended family forms, and there are different governmental structures, such as parliamentary systems, totalitarian structures, and monarchies.

But a society and other social systems is more than just a collection of parts that are structured in such a way so that they can perform important social functions. What makes a collection of parts a whole system is the *integration* of the parts. To survive, whole systems must be in **equilibrium,** a state of balance among the parts of a whole. For example, in an organization, if the activities of the sales division are not "in sync" with those of the marketing and manufacturing division, serious problems can occur. Orders may be placed that cannot be filled. Customers may ask for an advertised product that is not yet available. Without integration, without the parts of social system being in sync, strains are likely to occur, potentially leading to the death of the social organism.

The major social theorist who articulated and used this image was Talcott Parsons (1902–1979). In his numerous books and essays, Parsons developed **structural functionalism,** the theoretical framework that examines how social entities survive through the functioning of their parts. Parsons (1966), when analyzing social systems, began with the whole system, attempting to decipher its needs and, therefore, the functions that had to be performed if that social system was to survive. He then proceeded to identify the parts and their social structures that enabled that social system to perform those functions. Other structural functionalists, especially anthropologists studying unfamiliar cultures, often begin by noticing various structures such as rituals and social rules and then analyzing the society to determine what function these regularized behavioral patterns played in the larger social system (Malinowski 1966; Radcliffe-Brown 1964).

Parsons (1968) also used this image of integrated wholes to understand social change. He claimed that societies and other social systems evolve by becoming more differentiated into various parts, each part having its own function. For example, in preindustrial societies, institutions such as religion and the family had multiple functions. Religions often transmitted core values and established order in society through church-based legal systems; the family was an arena in which children were socialized and a place in which goods were produced. But as societies evolved, the legal functions of the church were taken over by secular courts, and the production function that occurred within families shifted to the economy and its factories.

Now that you are familiar with the core ideas of structural functionalism, how could you use this image when analyzing social situations? Here are four things you would want to do when viewing social connections as integrators of wholes into parts:

1. Look for and identify *social systems,* that is, social entities or wholes that are attempting to survive.

2. Distinguish the various *needs* of the social system and identify the *functions* that must be performed to meet these needs.

3. Look for the *parts* of the social system that perform each of these functions. Note how each part is organized or *structured* so that it can perform its function.

4. Examine the extent to which the parts are in *equilibrium* (in sync) so that they are compatible with each other and working together to enhance the whole's survival.

Case Application

How can you use this theoretical perspective to help you develop another perspective on "The Towering Dilemma"? First, what social systems are evident in this case? Maybe you identified the NPS as an important social system. To achieve its goal of preserving and protecting the monument's natural and cultural resources for present and future generations, it must perform various functions. It must employ and train personnel who understand the park's resources and how to use them without destroying them. It must set and prioritize goals, which in this case means developing a land use plan for Devils Tower. It must coordinate and integrate the various uses of the land so that all those who want to use the park can do so. Finally, it must transmit important values about the natural and cultural resources by educating the public about the land and the other natural resources.

From this perspective, the problem in this case is that there are many constituencies putting demands on the NPS, making it difficult for it to function smoothly. NPS is not a social system existing in a vacuum. It is an open system embedded within a larger social system that has many parts: the climbers who climb the rock, the tour guides who provide services to climbers, Native American tribes that use the tower for religious purposes, local residents who make a living off the tourist trade, naturalists, and, of course, the NPS.

The problem is that although these are all entities within the "socioecosystem" surrounding the park, they are not an integrated whole. Why? For many of these parts, their activities are not geared toward the survival of the whole but toward their own specific objectives. Climbers are organized to mount expeditions; Native Americans are organized to hold spiritual events. What we have then is a collection of parts that are not in sync. The conflicts and tensions that are evident in this case are the result of imbalances. From this perspective, the challenge is to create a whole social system in which each part performs an important function and the parts work together to ensure the survival of the park for future generations.

How can this social system be brought into balance? First, the various functions of the park must be identified. Clearly, there are many functions: to provide a relaxing place for people, to provide a challenging rock formation for climbing enthusiasts, to be a spiritual place for those who want to worship and pray. Then, structures must be created to allow these functions to occur. Such structures may take the form of rules and regulations, as well as amenities that allow for various activities. For example, there must be rules about where people can walk, and there must be maintained trails that allow people to hike through the area. Similarly, there must be rules governing the use of climbing equipment and facilities that allow climbers to exercise their climbing skills. Finally, performance of specific functions must not impede the performance of other functions, and, whenever possible, performing one function should enhance other uses of the land.

Analyzing this case with this image of connections as integrators of wholes into parts raises an important issue about this theoretical framework. What happens when social entities are not fully wholes composed of functioning parts? In this case, it is difficult to speak of a whole social system comprised of the various groups that use Devils Tower. Instead, the parts appear to be more like conflicting parties. What is functional for the climbers is dysfunctional for Native Americans, and what is functional for Native Americans is dysfunctional for the climbers. It seems more reasonable to dispense with the idea of an overarching social system and to focus instead on the parts and their conflicting relationships.

As we see in the next section, this is the approach taken when you view connections as conflictual tugs-of-war. It may be that, in this case, a conflict approach is more appropriate, and that a structural–functionalist reading is really a misreading of the situation. Even if one reached this conclusion after examining this case from both of these perspectives, it is important to compare contrasting views of the situation. Looking at this case from a systems perspective forces you to identify the various functions and uses of Devils Tower and to think about how this park could be restructured so that these functions can be performed.

SOCIAL CONNECTIONS AS CONFLICTIVE TUGS-OF-WAR

Within all arenas of social life, we see conflicts: in schools and workplaces, in families and religious congregations, in national and local politics, and between countries. We may wish that conflicts would disappear, but the reality is that conflicts are very much a part of all societies. Why is conflict so ubiquitous? When are conflicts more likely to occur?

These are the questions that lie at the heart of the perspective that views connections as conflictive *tugs-of-war.* In the tug-of-war game, two teams oppose each other, each trying to drag the other team across the dividing line. Connected by a rope, each team pulls in the opposite direction. Without the rope, there is no game and no conflict.

The image of connections as conflictive tugs-of-wars focuses attention not just on disagreements between people but also on the object of contention. The rope in the tug-of-war game connects the conflicting parties and is the object over which they are fighting. What are these objects over which people come into conflict?

For people to do the things they want to do, they need *resources*. However, valuable resources are often not in abundant supply. They may be naturally scarce, or they may be scarce because certain individuals, groups, or organizations possess them and people must go to them to acquire those resources. Farmers need seed and fertilizer, but there are only a few seed and fertilizer companies. An aspiring electrical engineer needs knowledge of how circuits work, but there are only a handful of good schools where she can acquire this knowledge. The scarcity and uneven distribution of resources in society make resources objects of contention, like the rope in tug-of-war. People become connected to each other as they battle to possess valuable resources.

The first sociologist to use this image was Karl Marx (1818–1883). Like Durkheim, Marx was trying to understand the profound changes that were occurring during the Industrial Revolution. But whereas Durkheim saw changes in the social bonds that connect people, Marx saw changes in the forms of conflict. In preindustrial, feudal societies, conflicts were over slavery. People owned the most valued resource of all, other people. Political revolutions like the French Revolution (1789–1799) and the American Civil War (1861–1865) sought to abolish slavery and end conflicts over ownership of people. But as Marx and Engels ([1847] 1972) observed, the abolition of slavery did not end social conflicts. On the contrary, new conflicts appeared, especially those between workers and employers (Hobsbawm 1975).

Marx (Marx [1867] 1967; Marx and Engels [1847] 1972) saw conflict as rooted in economics and, in particular, in a new economic system, **capitalism.** He thought that it was very important to look at a society's **mode of production,** the economic system through which people produce useful goods and services. To produce useful things, people use **means of production,** resources such as people, land, tools and equipment, factories and buildings, and knowledge and skills.

Modes of production differ in terms of who owns the means of production. Under slavery, the important resource owned by masters was other people, the slaves. Capitalism, in contrast, is a mode of production in which means of production such as land, tools, equipment, factories, and even knowledge and information are privately owned. The tug-of-war over control of such resources is fought between two social classes, capitalists or the *bourgeoisie,* who privately own factories and other productive enterprises, and workers or the *proletariat,* nonowners who therefore must sell to capitalists their ability to labor in exchange for wages. The result is social connections between two social classes in which capitalist owners employ workers who are nonowners. This employment relationship generates both inequalities and conflicts. Owners exploit workers by paying them less than the value of their labor. Through laboring, workers generate surpluses (profits). But because they do not own the means of production, they do not receive these profits; instead, capitalists receive them. As a result, conflicts emerge as capitalists seek to protect their right to privately own means of production and accumulate profits, and workers attempt to gain control of the means of production and a share of the surplus through higher wages.

Although Marx used this image to understand economic and class conflict, the ideas contained in this theoretical framework can be used to understand other types of conflict. According to this view, there are three important things you need to do when trying to understand social conflicts:

1. Identify the valuable *resources* over which there is a conflict. If it is not evident what the valued resources are, look at the *interests* of the actors in the case. What do they need in order to accomplish what they want to do?

2. Examine the *ownership* of these resources. Who has control over how these resources are distributed and who can use them? What do people have to do in order to gain access to these resources?

3. Investigate *inequalities* by looking at who benefits and who loses through the use of these resources. Are some people better off and others worse off? Is one person's gain the result of another person's loss?

Case Application

How can you use this theoretical framework to help you obtain another perspective on the conflicts in "The Towering Dilemma"? First, what is the valued resource over which there is a conflict? Obviously, the answer is Devils Tower. Although this rock is not used to produce useful goods and services, it is of value to climbers, American Indians, and naturalists. Climbers have an interest in using the rock to enhance their climbing skills. American Indians want to use it for their spiritual ceremonies. Naturalists have an interest in preserving the wildlife that inhabits the land. The conflicts between climbers and American Indians and between climbers and the naturalists occur because there are competing interests over the use of a scarce resource.

In terms of ownership, although the federal government technically owns the land, there are some who claim that Indians really own it based on past treaties. Even if the government technically owns the land, it owns it so that the public can use it. So the issue of ownership in this case is more the issue of who has the right to use the land. Notice that, in this case, people make claims about these rights. Climbers claim that they have the right to use the rock because it is public land and you cannot close off use of public land for religious reasons. Native Americans claim they have rights because their ancestors used the land for generations; past use is used to justify claims to future use. Naturalists claim that the rights of wildlife cannot be ignored, given that plants and animals need this resource to survive, whereas humans use the resource for either recreation or spiritual enhancement. In sum, the conflicts are rooted in conflicts over ownership and use.

Finally, it is important to note how this conflict generates inequalities. The problem seems to be that one group's gain is another group's loss. Climbers' use interferes with Indian uses and seems to have some adverse effects on wildlife. Indian use would curtail use by climbers. The conflict appears to be a *zero-sum conflict,* that is, a conflict in which one group's gain is another group's loss. In this case, climbers are gaining, and both Native Americans and naturalists are losing. The result is resistance by the latter two groups and demands for changes in the rules governing climbing on Devils Tower.

What will it take to resolve this conflict? From the perspective of social connections as tugs-of-war, conflicts are resolved when aggrieved parties gain control of the valued resources they need to live their lives. So, in this case, those who are worse off under the current situation, the American Indians, need to become better off. Allowing Native Americans undisturbed use of the rock during special times will restrict climbers' use and therefore make them worse off. But they will still be better off than if they were entirely denied use of Devils Tower. Giving Indians more ownership rights should decrease the current inequalities and create a more equitable situation.

SOCIAL CONNECTIONS AS EXCHANGES AMONG RATIONAL ACTORS

Driven by needs, wants, and desires, people spend a good deal of their time figuring out how to get where they want to go. But how do people know what is the best *means* for attaining their *ends*? And given that few people are self-sufficient, how do people acquire the means that will allow them to satisfy their needs, wants, and desires?

These are the sorts of questions that lie at the heart of the image of connections as *exchanges* among rational actors. With this image, attention is focused on individuals with needs and wants who attempt to make rational decisions about the best means to use to attain their objectives and who then enter into exchanges with other rational actors to obtain those means. This is a very modern way of looking at situations, one in which individuals are viewed as *rational actors* whose behaviors are based on the weighing of the costs and benefits of alternative courses of action (Coleman and Fararo 1992). **Rational action** permeates modern societies in large part because of the prevalence of markets in which people make exchanges based on the rational calculations of costs and benefits.

The first sociologist to analyze the importance of rationality in modern societies was Max Weber (1864–1920). Like Durkheim and Marx, Weber was trying to understand the profound changes brought about by the Industrial Revolution. But whereas Durkheim focused on changes in social bonding and Marx on changes in the types of conflict, Weber saw changes in the bases of action, in the *meanings* that lie behind people's actions (Weber 1947). In preindustrial societies, he argued, people tend to base their actions on **traditions,** customs and beliefs that are passed down from generation to generation. People do things because that is the way it has always been done. In contrast, in modern societies, people have choices and make decisions. People try to act rationally by choosing the most effective means of accomplishing a specific goal (Weber [1904-5] 1958). But what does it mean to make rational choices? How do people attempt to increase the odds that a decision that they have made is a good one?

There are three important components to rational decision making:

- *Ends or Goals:* States of affairs that people are trying to attain through their actions.
- *Means or Alternative Courses of Action:* The set of possible choices a person could make that could lead to the attainment of his or her goals.

- *Calculation:* The process of weighing the costs and benefits of each alternative to determine which course of action has the highest net benefit.

According to this theoretical model, rational actors weigh the costs and benefits of alternative means for attaining a goal and then choose the course of action that they think will yield the greatest benefits for the least cost.

Once a decision is made, a rational actor bases her actions on that decision by paying the costs to receive the benefits. Often, this entails entering into exchanges with other social actors who have needed resources. Through exchanges, people receive benefits. But to receive these benefits, they must pay some costs, whether it be in the form of money, time, or some other sacrifice. Markets, therefore, epitomize rational action. In markets, rational actors interact. Buyers calculate to whom it is best to sell, and sellers try to find the best buyers. Through market exchanges, individuals acquire the resources (means) they need to do what they want to do (their goals).

Now that you better understand this perspective, how could you use this image to help you read social situations? Here are three things you could do if you were to look at social connections as exchanges among rational actors:

1. Identify the various *social actors* in a situation and the different goals each is trying to attain through his or her actions.

2. Examine for each social actor the *costs* and *benefits* of the courses of action they could take to reach their goals. This analysis will tell you why some actors are pleased with the current situation (because they are able to take that course of action that yields the highest net benefit) and why other people are aggrieved (because their net benefits are minimal).

3. Look at how the *exchanges* between social actors are allowing exchange partners to acquire the means to obtain their goals.

Case Application

Let us see how this perspective can be used to develop another per-spective on "The Towering Dilemma." First, it is quite clear that there are various actors with quite different goals. Climbers want unlimited use of Devils Tower. Native Americans want to hold undisturbed spir-itual events. Naturalists want to preserve and protect wildlife. Much of the debate in the case concerns the alternative means that could be used to obtain each of these ends. Climbers argue that there are few alternatives to Devils Tower because it is one of the best climbing sites in North America. For climbers, the costs of going somewhere else are so high that the net benefit of doing so is minimal. Native Americans also see the other alternatives as being too costly. Devils Tower has a special significance to them, and holding their worship activities else-where would not have the same benefit. From this perspective, the real problem in this case is that the best means to each group's ends is a use of Devils Tower, which for the other group is a significant cost. If climbers are allowed unlimited use (their optimal choice), American Indians pay a high cost (in terms of interference with their worship). If American Indians have exclusive use of the rock (their optimal choice), climbers pay a high cost in their inability to use a premier climbing site. Instead of an exchange occurring in which each party benefits while paying some costs, a conflict results.

There are in this case some exchanges occurring that are mutually benefiting the parties involved. Guide companies are taking climbers on climbs in exchange for money, and these companies also have entered into an exchange with the NPS whereby they receive licenses, and the NPS receives from fees funds that it uses to maintain and enhance park services.

Given this analysis of the case as a situation in which one group's benefit raises the costs for the other group, what could be done to resolve the conflicts? From this perspective, the solution is to find a *compromise* whereby each group accepts less than its preferred alter-native (with maximal net benefits) but the solution still yields signifi-cant positive net benefits for all parties. The challenge is to find such a compromise. To come up with such a solution would require analyzing the costs and benefits for each social actor of the six management alternatives presented in the case. Which alternative do you think would yield the greatest total net benefit for *all* the parties?

 ## SOCIAL CONNECTIONS AS WEBS OF INTERACTION

When thinking about society, we tend to focus on the highly visible events. Imagine, for example, a reporter covering the Devils Tower story. She probably would have focused on the public hearings and the heated debates over the proposals. But by focusing on highly visible and public events, she would have missed something very important in this case—the everyday interactions among people. How do people interact with each other on a daily basis? What do people do as they go about learning in schools, working in workplaces, shopping at stores, praying at their places of worship, or visiting new places? How is society constructed through the everyday interactions of people?

These are the sorts of questions that lead sociologists to employ an image of social connections as *webs* of interaction. The less visible worlds of everyday interaction are constructed much like a spider builds its web. The spider starts out weaving a thread, which is then connected to another thread. After awhile, a pattern emerges with threads intersecting other threads to form nodes. Eventually, an elaborate, complex, and often beautiful web with many different sections emerges.

Likewise, people form webs as they interact with each other every day. Such human webs also have patterns. You can see who talks with whom, who defers to whom, who looks up to whom, and much, much more. As in the spider's web, from a single node there can be many connections and affiliations.

One of the first sociologists to use this image of society as a web of interaction was Georg Simmel (1858–1918). A keen observer of everyday interactions in many different settings, Simmel was struck

by the numerous associations and groups within which people interact (Simmel 1955, 1971). Simmel sought to understand the patterns
and forms of social associations and interaction, what he called
sociation. Through his observations and historical studies, he noted
different forms of sociation: superordination–subordination; relations of antagonism and conflict; functional interdependence;
in-group/out-group relations; and representation. These forms differ
from each other in terms of how people within these different webs
interact. For example, the way in which a supervisor interacts with a
subordinate at work is different from the way in which a student president interacts with the students whom she represents, and from the
way in which those who are part of a clique interact with those whom
they consider to be outsiders.

Simmel was also one of the first sociologists to stress that forms of
sociation are social constructions, created by people and maintained
over time through social interactions. Simmel, therefore, is often
considered to be one of the founders of the **social construction
of reality** paradigm, the framework that focuses on the process
through which people create their social worlds through social interaction. This approach argues that reality is not as fixed as we sometimes think. Although there are real social worlds filled with organizations, networks, social relationships, and groups, these connections
do not exist independently of the people who are connected by them.
Through their social interactions, people are constantly shaping their
social worlds (Berger and Luckmann [1966] 1990). For Simmel, society is not constructed from the top down but built from the bottom up
through everyday interactions.

How do people build their social worlds, their webs of social interaction? Unlike spiders who build webs from silk, people build
their webs through the use of symbols and the meanings symbols
convey. This idea lies at the core of *symbolic interactionism,* a theoretical paradigm sociologists use to examine how people construct
social connections through the use of symbols and meanings.

I already touched on the importance of meanings in social interaction in the last section. As you recall, according to Weber, meanings are very important. To understand what people do and how they interact with others, you need to look at the subjective meanings that lie behind people's actions.

But how do you know what people mean by their actions? According to symbolic interactionists, meanings are seen through symbols. Symbols—such as the language people use, the way they present themselves, the clothing they wear, and the body language they employ—convey meaning to other people about who they are and what they think and feel. But, most important, symbols can serve as signals, conveying to others how we think they should behave. When a parent stares at her teenager, she is sending a signal that her daughter better get her act together or face the consequences. When your friend changes the subject during a conversation, he is indicating that he does not want to discuss that touchy matter anymore. Through the use of symbols, people convey meanings to others and thereby construct their social worlds.

Now that you are familiar with this image of social connections, let us see how you could use it to analyze a social situation. When you think about social connections as webs, there are three things you need to do:

1. Identify and categorize the *forms of sociation*. Look for how people are interacting in a given setting, and note whether the patterns of interaction are more like interaction between superiors and subordinates, between combatants, between insiders and outsiders, between interdependent people, or between representatives and those whom they represent.

2. Examine how the patterns of interaction between social actors have been *constructed* over time. When did the parties begin to interact and why? How has the pattern of interaction evolved?

Were there any pivotal events that solidified a pattern of interaction?

3. Look for *symbols* and decipher the *meanings* these symbols are
   designed to convey. How do the symbols people use define the
   situation? How aware are various social actors of the symbols
   others use and the meanings others attach to them?

Case Application

Let us see how you could use this theoretical framework to read
"The Towering Dilemma." First, what patterns of interaction or
forms of sociation did you see in this case? Clearly, the one that stands
out the most is the combatant pattern that characterized the interactions between climbers and American Indians, as well as between naturalists and the climbers. But there are also other very interesting
forms of sociation. The interactions between NPS personnel and the
various other parties in the case are those between a regulator and
those whose behaviors are regulated. But this regulator is also a representative, so it seeks input when proposing regulations from those
whom it both represents and regulates.

Therefore, it would be important in understanding this case to
examine how the combatant pattern of interaction, as well as the regulator–regulated form of sociation, evolved over time. From this case,
we know very little about the past, but it is likely that these patterns
are relatively new. Climbing only recently has become a popular
"sport," and the cultural revival among Native Americans is a relatively recent phenomenon. Probably as Devils Tower saw more and
more use by both Native Americans and climbers, everyday interactions between these two parties increased. As the story in the case
about the Indian children reveals, such interactions from time to time
were not very pleasant. Native Americans were probably appalled
by the behaviors of some of the climbers, and climbers probably
wondered what American Indians were doing. Individual encounters probably became stories conveyed within each group. These

stories then reinforced the negative views about members of the other group.

Finally, to understand these patterns of interaction, it would be very important to look at the symbols and the meanings that lie behind people's actions. For Native Americans, Devils Tower is itself a symbol, conveying meanings that are a very important part of tribal culture and religion. The rituals and pilgrimages to the rock are also very symbolic. But climbers also have their symbols and language, conveyed through their tools and the technical terms about climbing that they use. What is important to note is that these symbols are shared within each group, but not shared between groups. Within each group, symbols send signals and convey meanings. But because the symbols and the underlying meanings found within one group are foreign to the other group, they are easily misunderstood or treated as meaningless. Climbers think that there is nothing sacred about Devils Tower, whereas American Indians have little understanding of why climbers find climbing so meaningful.

From this perspective, the solution to this case requires changing the patterns of interaction between combative parties. The conflict of the use of Devils Tower has been exacerbated by the misunderstandings each group has of the other group's meanings behind their actions. The conflicting parties have constructed a web of association that makes it very difficult for anyone to see the other side of the issue. Even if, somehow, new regulations could be devised that would allow American Indians and climbers to use the rock, the existing animosities could lead to new conflicts that could undermine the accord.

According to this reading of the case, what is needed is a cross-cultural educational program through which people can learn about other people's points of view and put themselves in the others' shoes, so to speak. The expectation is that as the combatants come to see the meanings that inform other people's actions, they will gain respect for them and realize how their own actions have been insensitive. Increased understanding of the "other" could even lead to support for regulations that they had previously opposed.

SOCIOLOGICAL EYE ANALYSIS GUIDE

Theories are wonderful things. As you have seen, they can open your eyes to perspectives you never may have entertained. With theories and the images that they contain, you can go beyond merely describing a situation. You can develop explanations. Theories also can help you pose interesting questions and come up with novel solutions based on your theoretical explanations.

But, most important, with theories you can become cognizant of the assumptions that *you* initially used when analyzing a case. Any analysis of a situation is based on assumptions, but often people are unaware of their own assumptions. People tend to be so comfortable with their own perspective that they assume that their perspective is the only one. But by comparing and contrasting different readings, as I have done with the "Towering Dilemma" case, you can learn what perspective you are taking, what its assumptions are, and how to shift perspectives and look at the situation from a different angle. These are valuable skills that, with practice, can help you to gain perspective on a situation. By reframing and thinking about the important social connections in a case in different ways—as bonds, as integrators, as tugs-of-war, as exchanges, and as webs—you, as a social observer, can develop a fuller understanding of a case.

But there is more to understanding a case than just seeing it from multiple perspectives. Cases occur in a context. The social actors in a case bring to the situation their own perspectives. They frequently differ in their ability to pursue their interests. They are affected by social forces that are often beyond their individual control. In subsequent chapters, you will learn how to put cases in context by examining culture, power and inequalities, and driving forces. But for now, what is important is your ability to reframe and analyze situations from multiple theoretical perspectives. So with the following Sociological Eye Analysis Guide, practice using each of the five images to analyze the "Changing a Hospital's

Culture" case at the end of this chapter, other cases in Part II, or, for that matter, situations you have encountered personally.

Social Connections as Bonds

❏ What are the important social bonds in this case? What types of social connections (social relationships, groups, networks, organizations) are created through these bonds? Who is connected through these bonds?

❏ How would you characterize these bonds? Are they based on shared moral sentiments (mechanical solidarity)? Or are they based on common interests and tastes (organic solidarity)?

❏ Are there any behaviors that you would characterize as anomic? Do those exhibiting such behaviors have weak social bonds to others? Why are their social bonds weak?

❏ How could bonds be strengthened to address the problems in this case?

Social Connections as Integrators

❏ What are the various social systems that are present in this situation, that is, the social wholes that are composed of parts?

❏ How would you characterize the various needs of each social system? What functions need to be performed for each of these systems to survive?

❏ Which parts perform which functions? Are some parts performing more than one function? How is each part structured so that it can perform its function(s)?

❏ Is the system in equilibrium? Are the parts compatible with each other? Are they working together?

❏ What could be done to make the parts of the system more in sync with each other? Is there a need to break up a part that is performing too many functions?

Social Connections as Conflictive Tugs-of-War

❏ What are the valuable resources in this case over which there are conflicts? Who are the various social actors in this case, and what are their interests? What resources do they need to realize their interests?

❏ Who owns the important resources? How are these resources distributed? Who controls their distribution? What do nonowners have to do to gain access to the resources that they need?

❏ Who benefits and who loses through the use of these resources? Are some people in this case better off and others worse off?

❏ How could ownership and control of resources be redistributed so that those who are worse off would become better off?

Social Connections as Exchanges

❏ Who are the central social actors in this situation? What are their goals or ends that they are trying to achieve through their actions?

❏ For each social actor, what are the costs and benefits of the various courses of action that they took or could take in this case? Will they (or did they) receive a net benefit, or will they (or did they) have a net loss?

❏ What exchanges are people entering into to acquire the means that they need to attain their ends?

❏ Are there compromises that could be made so that all social actors receive a net benefit?

Social Connections as Webs

❏ What are the important forms of sociation that are evident in this situation? How would you characterize each of these forms (superior–subordinate, combatants, insider–outside, interdependence, representation)?

❐ How were these patterns of association constructed over time? When did the interaction begin? How has it evolved? What events solidified the pattern?

❐ What symbols are used to define and construct these patterns of association? How aware are others of these symbols and the meanings others attach to them?

❐ Are there patterns of association that are inhibiting interaction? Are there misunderstandings about the meanings behind actions that are preventing interaction? How could these misunderstandings be decreased? How could patterns of association be changed so as to enhance social interaction?

Decision Case: "Changing a Hospital's Culture"

When Carl Fisher became executive director of the Medical College of Virginia (MCV) Hospitals in 1986, he knew there was no quick fix for the nagging financial problems that threatened to erode the quality of patient care and research programs at the 125-year-old public institution. But pressure to control costs, combined with the hospital's relatively low number of patients whose insurance coverage would support the full cost of care, made it crucial to take some quick steps.

Fisher brought considerable experience in hospital management to his new position at MCV. A nurse by training, he held a master's degree in nursing administration and had attended Yale's program in hospital administration. Before coming to MCV, he had served as chief operating officer at the University of Cincinnati Hospitals and then as executive director at the University of Arkansas Hospital. At MCV, he would be assuming the reins of an institution with a long and distinguished history, but a rocky recent past and a somewhat troubled future.

Formally established as a public teaching hospital in 1861, MCV had by the mid-1980s grown into a sprawling complex comprising some 60 buildings and 950 beds—more than three times the number of any other local hospital—and a staff of 4,500 employees. Its emergency ward was considered the biggest and best in the Southeast, and its skilled medical staff made it a magnet for people seeking highly specialized treatment.

When Fisher first arrived at MCV, the hospital was operating in the black. However, he saw an increasingly grim fiscal outlook as he cast

AUTHOR'S NOTE: This abridged version *(C16-90-1017.3)* of the case was prepared by David Hachen based on the case *Changing a Hospital's Culture: The Guest Relations Program at Medical College of Virginia Hospitals (C16-90-1017.0)* written by Philip Holland and Esther Scott under the supervision of Marc Roberts, Professor of Political Economy and Health Policy, and Howard Husock, Director, Case Program, Kennedy School of Government. Copyright © 1990 and © 2000 by the President and Fellows of Harvard College. Reprinted by permission of the Kennedy School of Government Case Program, Harvard University (www.ksgcase.harvard.edu).

an eye over the next few years. All told, about 84 percent of the hospital's reimbursements for patient services was fixed by state and federal government reimbursement formulas. That left approximately 16 percent, or $60 million, in revenues that came from privately insured patients whose treatment was reimbursed according to what the hospital actually charged for services rendered (known as "charge-based" revenues). Of some $15 million in profits, about $10.6 million came from such charge-based payments.

Fisher intended to implement measures to contain rising costs. But although these measures would curb MCV's "expense growth" somewhat, they would hardly provide the infusion of funds that Fisher saw as necessary to maintain the institution's reputation as a leading light in medicine. The lack of funds would prevent MCV from attracting top professionals to the staff of the medical center. The potential weakening of MCV's position was particularly troubling in view of what Fisher saw as the "cutthroat competition" that characterized the Richmond area hospital scene.

MCV, Fisher reasoned, had to take part in that competition for "patient dollars." Specifically, he concluded, it needed to do more to attract the "well-insured patients" whom other hospitals had been skimming. It was the privately insured patient who had a minor ailment that did not require special care—or a long hospitalization—and who usually chose to go to a community hospital for treatment whom Fisher hoped to lure to MCV. To do this, he planned to launch marketing initiatives aimed at familiarizing the local population with MCV, particularly the private physicians who could bring "paying" patients to the hospital. While that got under way, however, Fisher concluded that MCV would need a guest relations program as well. Fisher saw "guest relations" as a way to make MCV more competitive in the local market.

Jeffrey Yarmel, director of professional services at the hospital, recalls that Fisher was "appalled" by existing guest relations at MCV. Patients wrote to Fisher to complain of errors in billing, long waits for service, or the elusiveness of physicians ("I didn't see my doctor once!"

was a common complaint, says Fisher). Fisher hoped that improved guest relations would alleviate such problems and help counteract the public perception of MCV—a perception that many believed deterred patients from choosing MCV when they needed hospitalization. MCV was the only facility in southeastern Virginia that routinely provided indigent care, and it was widely viewed, in the words of one hospital staff member, as the place "where poor people go." Thanks largely to news stories, MCV also was seen as an unsafe place, where victims of crime, and criminals, were sent for treatment.

That sense of danger was compounded by the fact that MCV was located on the edge of downtown Richmond, near the city offices and the governor's mansion, a busy area during the day but quiet and deserted at night; the shopping and residential neighborhoods it bordered were mostly black and often run-down. Also, the hospital complex itself was dauntingly big and confusing, a block-long maze of small and large buildings, some connected by walkways and tunnels.

Fisher was eager to start on a guest relations program and began setting things in motion in his first year at MCV by hiring a coordinator, Dana Jenkins. Over the next couple of years, Jenkins, with the aid of the consultant and in-house staff, introduced MCV employees to the concept and practice of guest relations. Through "think tank" sessions with informal leaders in the hospital, the concept of guest relations was expanded to include intrahospital issues, such as lack of support from certain departments (e.g., housekeeping and transportation) and the chronic issue of inadequate parking. She also sponsored a contest at the hospital to name the new program: the winning entry was "Make Caring Visible," later modified to "Making Caring Visible," to avoid the implication that caring was not in fact happening at MCV.

With the aid of the consultant, Jenkins pulled together the material she had gathered from the think tanks into an "overview presentation" for all employees. Over a period of about a month and a half, some 144 sessions were conducted, each three and a half hours long, before groups of 60 employees at a time. To underscore the importance of guest relations, a chief administrator—including Fisher himself—conducted the first 45 minutes of each presentation. Each session consisted of slide presentations that reviewed the material culled from the think tanks and then focused on 16 "House Rules" that formed the core of MCV's guest relations policy (see Exhibit 2.2). By the end of 1987, all 4,500 employees at MCV had attended the overviews.

The doctors at MCV, however, did not sit in on the three-and-a-half-hour overview sessions with the rest of the hospital staff. Instead, they were invited to attend voluntary 90-minute presentations, which were held in September 1987 and conducted with the aid of a physician. This arrangement in part grew out of scheduling problems—rotations of interns and residents were changing just as the overview sessions began in May—but it also reflected the autonomy of physicians at the hospital. The doctors—faculty members who were on the attending staff at MCV, as well as interns and residents—were employees of the medical school, not the hospital, and they were answerable to the dean, not to the executive director. Day-to-day supervision of physicians at MCV was the responsibility of neither the dean nor the executive director, but of the chairs of the academic departments of the medical school. Therefore, physician participation in the overviews tended to reflect the attitude of the individual department chairperson and, consequently, attendance was spotty.

Once the presentations were concluded, a variety of follow-up programs ensued. To reward staff members for good guest relations behavior, Fisher and Jenkins instituted a program whereby either patients or fellow employees could report the good actions of an employee. Employees who won three pins (awarded by patients) were eligible for election as "employee of the month," and those elected were feted at a breakfast in their honor.

At the end of this series of guest relations initiatives, both staff and patient responses seemed on the whole positive: Surveys conducted before and after the overviews indicated a 17 percent improvement in patient satisfaction, whereas employees gave the overviews a 94 percent positive rating. But despite upbeat comments, the guest relations

Exhibit 2.2. House Rules

HOUSE RULES

1. Break the ice.
Make eye contact. . . smile. . .
introduce yourself. . . call people by
name. . . extend a few words of
concern.

2. Does someone look confused?
Stop and try to help.

3. Courtesy.
Kind gestures, polite words. . . make
people feel special.

4. Explain what you're doing.
People are always less anxious when
they know what's happening.

5. Anticipate.
You'll often know what people want
before they have to ask. . **Act.**

6. Respond quickly.
When people are worried or sick,
every minute is an hour.

7. Privacy and confidentiality.
Watch what you say and where you
say it. . . **Show respect.** . . Knock as
you enter.

8. Handle with care.
Slow down. . . give. . . imagine you're
on the receiving end.

9. Dignity.
That patient could be your child,
your spouse, your parent. Give
choices, close curtains. . . See the
person.

10. Take initiative.
Just because it's "Not your job"
doesn't mean you can't **help or find
someone who can.**

11. Treat patients as adults.
Your words and tone should not
insult.

12. Listen.
If a person complains, don't be
defensive.

13. Help each other
and you help a patient.

14. Keep it quiet.
Noise annoys! It also shows a lack
of consideration.

15. Phone skill.
When you're on the phone, our
reputation's on the line. . . sound
pleasant. . . be helpful. . . listen with
understanding.

16. Look the part.
You're part of a long proud medical
tradition.

program also had generated considerable hostility, chiefly among
nurses and most particularly among nurse managers, some of whom
regarded the program at best as a "frill" and at worst as a disruptive

force in their already stressful work environment. To some, it challenged their most fundamental views of their mission and MCV's; to others, it failed to address the most serious issues facing the hospital as it struggled to upgrade its image in the public eye.

Nurses made up by far the largest single employee group at MCV—1,500 out of the total of 4,500 employees at the hospital. Although almost half had been at MCV for less than five years, a significant number had worked there for 10 years and more. Because it paid a significantly lower differential for evening and weekend shifts—90 cents, compared to $4 to $5 at other local hospitals—MCV had suffered a steady attrition in its nursing staff during 1987; by the winter of 1987–1988, 15 percent of its nursing slots were vacant. Those who stayed on often cited MCV's challenging setting as its chief drawing card, as well as their commitment to caring for the poor. To some of them, at least, the guest relations program was an affront to their dedication of purpose. Their reaction, recalls Lu Kratsch, a member of the nursing education staff, was, "This is what we're already doing." "We go into nursing in the first place," says one MCV nurse, "to care for people."

Many of the nurses viewed the guest relations program as an effort, in the words of one nurse manager, "to make us nice," as part of MCV's drive "to attract private clients for money." Nurses were particularly sensitive to what they saw as "just another ploy to get paying patients," says Kratsch, because many of them took "pride in [providing] indigent care." Their concern that MCV might be heading, in the words of Dana Jenkins, toward a "two-tiered" system of care that would "turn us into a VIP hospital" was exacerbated by plans to increase the number of private suites at MCV.

But, by all accounts, what offended many nurses and other MCV employees the most about a program that they saw as a "train to smile" campaign was that physicians had not been required to participate; "physician avoidance" of the program "sent a very bad message" to employees who had been given no choice about participating. The doctors' indifference was particularly irksome because they were

viewed by many as the hospital's most serious guest relations problem. Physicians openly discussed medical cases in the halls and in
public areas at MCV, some said, and frequently lost their tempers or
behaved arrogantly with employees. Moreover, resentment brewed
because although doctors were exempt from the overviews, supervisors at MCV had to struggle to free up nurses to attend the long sessions, at a time when summer vacations and staff shortages made it
hard to provide necessary personnel on each ward.

However, the nurses were not entirely critical of the guest relations
activities at MCV. They cited the orientation program for new employees as a "good reminder" of the importance of courtesy and acknowledged that in the high-stress environment of a big hospital like MCV
"nurses can get tunnel vision." They were particularly enthusiastic
about the ongoing "Harmony Program," a "professional renewal"
program for nurses that emphasized stress management.

Many of the critics of the guest relations program readily acknowledged that MCV's image had suffered in recent years. However, guest
relations was, in the words of one, "a drop in the bucket," a "Band-Aid,
not a solution." They pointed to more serious problems that, they felt,
needed addressing. Security, for instance, both at the hospital
entrance and on the wards, was an ongoing issue at MCV. Basic services were problematic as well. Housekeeping services continued to
be "awful," according to one nurse; toilets were "filthy," trash was not
collected promptly. The laboratories and pharmacies were slow to
process orders. Even modest amenities were sometimes lacking, such
as soft drinks on the wards for patients. There was sentiment that
essential systems such as the emergency room (which accounted for
almost half of the hospital's admissions) needed more attention than
guest relations.

In view of these and other perceived failings, the guest relations
program was regarded as "a joke" by some at MCV, "not a high prior-
ity" by others, particularly by nurse managers who also saw it as an
ephemeral effort by "a flash in the pan management" that would be
gone, like other administrations before it, in a few years. This "cynical"

view did not escape the notice of senior management. The attitude of the nurses was crucial because of their highly visible role in the activity of the hospital. "If they're happy," they thought, "others are [too]."

For Fisher, the question was how to make nurses happy and keep the hospital fiscally healthy. Guest relations, he argues, fit in well with the ethic nurses claimed to work by. "Market share is *not* the emphasis [of the program]," he maintains. "Patient-centered care *is*." Fisher was aware of the resistance the program had met. "The toughest challenge in implementing [guest relations]," he reflects, "has been getting employees to buy in."

Even tougher challenges lay ahead. With the hospital-wide intro-duction to guest relations completed, Fisher believed he needed to press on with the program and begin laying plans that would involve the individual departments at MCV in making guest relations part of the day-to-day life of the hospital. He would choose his next steps against the backdrop of a steadily worsening fiscal picture: By the end of fiscal 1989, the excess of revenues over expenses had shrunk from almost $20 million in Fisher's first year at MCV to just under $4 million.

CHAPTER 3

Decoding Culture

Decision Case: "Perfection or Bust!"

Design Inc., a successful commercial art studio, is the brainchild of its founder/owner, Bill Klee. Its motto, which hangs on a hand-lettered sign in the reception area, is also Klee's personal motto: "Perfection or Bust!"

Design Inc. was started by Klee in 1979. "I'm not interested in launching just another commercial art studio," Klee told his industry colleagues. "I want to found an academy, where talented young artists and designers can perfect their skills. To work at Design Inc. will be a privilege, because I'm not offering people jobs, I'm offering them a unique educational experience!"

And because Klee, a well-known figure in the industry, had a reputation as a perfectionist, his aspirations were taken seriously in most quarters.

Klee's approach to potential staff members was highly unorthodox. Instead of promising recruits high salaries and tempting bonus

---

AUTHOR'S NOTE: This case appears in G. Morgan, *Creative Organizational Theory*, pp. 299-300, copyright 1989 by Sage Publications. Reprinted by permission of the publisher.

packages, he stressed the rigors of the job, as he did to one lettering specialist:

> You won't make as much money with us as you would somewhere else, and you won't be working in a fancy office with a high-fashion receptionist and inch-thick carpeting. But you will be doing the most satisfying job you've ever done in your life, because I demand perfection, and I know that you won't settle for anything less yourself!

The lettering expert, duly impressed, accepted Klee's offer some days later, and, over the next several months, other promising recruits followed his lead. In this way, Klee was able to put together in short order a talented and enthusiastic team of graphic artists and designers.

Potential clients were treated to a similar sales pitch. "We have no frills at this studio," Klee told one prospect, sitting him down in an uncomfortable, hard-backed chair in his austere office.

> If you want luxury, or if you want someone to hold your hand, then go someplace else. But if you want quality, the best commercial art work in this city, if not in this whole country, then you've come to the right place.

In a matter of months, Design Inc. had carved itself a prosperous niche in the commercial art industry. The staff, enthusiastic to start with, became even more entranced by Klee's vision of perfection as time went on. True, they weren't making as much as their colleagues in more orthodox firms, but they had an ideal to pursue, and their intangible rewards went far beyond mere money. At least this is what most of them argued when socializing with their better-paid colleagues. Sometimes, these conversations became quite acrimonious, and some long-standing friendships actually suffered. Employees of other firms did not take kindly to the idea that they were content with mediocrity. On the other hand, the employees of Design Inc. were not pleased when the superiority of their work was called into question by outsiders, especially as its superiority was difficult to demonstrate in any absolute fashion. "Who says your work is so great?" became a common question, to which the common reply evolved: "Our work must be better because we take it more seriously."

As time went on, it became increasingly common for the employees of Design Inc. to spend much of their leisure time together, discussing work-related matters and reaffirming, within the family circle as it were, their commitment to excellence within their field. Many of Klee's turns of phrase—"no compromise with mediocrity," "the best or bust," "perfection is our only concern"—became part of most staff members' vocabulary.

It isn't surprising that Design Inc. employees worked long hours, coming in early and leaving late. Klee was everywhere at once, advising on layout, suggesting new creative approaches for one piece of work, consulting on the choice of color and typeface for another. Things that would be done three or four times at another studio—reviewing artwork, for example—might be done as many as a dozen times or more at Design Inc., as workers agonized to get every last detail of a project right. No stone was left unturned in the staff's pursuit of excellence. These hours cut even more into the social lives of the employees, throwing them more and more into each others' company.

About 18 months after Design Inc. was established, its top layout artist, forced to choose between his career at Design Inc. and his family, left the firm for another job. His departure was handled smoothly, a party being held to send him off.

Klee stepped into his position until a replacement could be found. Advertisements were put in the paper, and the word was passed along the industry grapevine. In line with the all-for-one-and-one-for-all philosophy of Design Inc., it was decided that every staff member should have a say in the selection of the new recruit. After all, as Klee put it, "We'll probably be spending more time with whomever we hire than with our families!" Everyone agreed that the new recruit would have to be enthusiastic about Design Inc.'s training mission and would have to demonstrate an unswerving commitment to perfection in his or her work.

A large number of qualified people applied, but somehow none of them seemed exactly to fit the bill. One had a young family and expressed doubt about his ability to work every weekend if need be. A second was passed over because one employee felt that she wasn't a team player. Another was rejected because several staff members felt he just didn't have the right attitude. After several months, all the candidates had been interviewed, and all had been rejected for one reason or another.

During this time, Klee, because of his additional responsibilities, had begun to neglect his training mission. The studio continued to function, but as a business and not as an academy. Everyone agreed, however, that this situation was temporary. Design Inc. would become a training ground again as soon as it got a new layout person.

In his private moments, Klee occasionally wondered if his studio was quite what he had wanted it to be. It seemed to him that something of his dream had been lost. He did not have a great deal of spare time in which to philosophize, however. Furthermore, the firm was doing well financially, and so, as owner, Klee found a certain consolation in the healthy state of his firm's balance sheet.

About a year after the layout artist took another job, he dropped by to visit his former colleagues. He found Klee still filling in for him. The staff still spoke of dedication to excellence and insisted that the day when Design Inc. again became an academy was close at hand. The visitor sensed a certain hollowness in their bluff statements, however. It seemed to him that employees were less certain of their mission and less confident about the future than they let on.

The layout position was never readvertised, and no new candidates were ever interviewed. Most of the original staff are still with the firm, however, which turns a respectable profit each year.

REVIEW: SOCIOLOGICAL THEORIES

Analyzing cases sociologically begins by identifying social connections and using sociological theories to understand these connections. But without also seeing the context of a case—the background in which the case is situated—you are likely to have an incomplete picture of the situation. This chapter will help you begin to "draw" case backgrounds by examining culture. It will help, however, to first review what you learned in the previous chapter by discussing some of the different theoretical perspectives you could take on this case.

The "Perfection or Bust!" case is about Bill Klee and his graphic artists who are having difficulty finding a replacement for their top layout artist. Design Inc. seems to be undergoing changes, and the central issue is whether this organization can continue to be what its founder wanted it to be, an academy and a business.

Many social connections are evident at Design Inc.: the social relationship between the owner, Klee, and his employees; the groups with common interests, such as the staff and clients; the networks through which information flows and through which potential customers and employees hear about Design Inc.; the organization of this art studio that appears to be not very bureaucratic. The case raises questions about how new employees are socialized into Design Inc.; the multiple identities staff have as artists, as employees of Design Inc., and as family members; the centrality of Klee in the information flows; and how Klee's authority is legitimized.

The five images of connections and their corresponding sociological theories can help you read this case from multiple perspectives. This case could be read as a story of the weakening of formerly strong bonds among Klee and his employees. Initially, there is a high level of group solidarity among the graphic artists and designers. They enthusiastically support Klee's vision of a design firm that produces the very best graphic artwork. But as the former layout artist notes after visiting Design Inc., employees have become less certain about this mission and about Design Inc.'s future.

Alternatively, this case could be read as a story of a malfunctioning social system. After the departure of the lead layout artist, Klee takes over more and more functions, trying to do everything and be everywhere. It is as if there were no social connections integrating the parts into a whole. Rather, it is only the ever-present Klee who keeps things flowing smoothly. Without Klee, this organization could become a collection of disconnected parts.

Still another perspective can be obtained by thinking about the conflicts at Design Inc. The departure of the top layout artist indicates that there is a tension between the demands Klee places on his employees and their social and family lives outside work. This tension leads one to wonder who really benefits from the hard work performed by the graphic artists at Design Inc. Klee's business is profitable, and we know that his workers have forgone high salaries and bonus packages to work for Klee. Is Klee exploiting his employees?

You also can read this case as a story of exchanges among rational actors. Klee receives hard work and perfection from his graphic artists, and in exchange the artists, at least initially, receive valuable training from Klee along with monetary compensation. The artists apparently view working at Design Inc. as a net benefit even though it costs them in terms of lower salaries and less time with their families. It seems, however, that the terms of exchange are beginning to change. As Klee's employees receive less training, they are more likely to question the high costs of working at Design Inc.

Finally, the case could be read as a story of socially constructed webs. Klee creates Design Inc. and constructs it based on his vision of perfection. Over time, the form of sociation between a creative founder and his original staff is solidified through symbols. However, although at one time this web of interaction energized Design Inc., it now is constraining change. The constructed web seems to have no room for newcomers—those who do not already fit into the ethos of Design Inc. It is as if Design Inc. is caught in a rut of its own making.

Each of these perspectives yields valuable insights into the "Perfection or Bust!" case. However, each of these perspectives looks at this case from the outside, from the point of view of an observer. As an external analyst, you can gain valuable insights into this case especially, as you have seen, when you use sociological theories. But as an outsider, you always wonder whether you have missed something, something that insiders see and understand.

To gain a fuller understanding of a situation, therefore, you somehow need to see the situation from the point of view of the social actors in the case. This chapter is designed to help you become an insider, so to speak, when analyzing situations. As you will learn, seeing the situation from the point of view of the social actors requires analyzing how cultural meanings inform actions and interactions.

CULTURE

All of us at times have been outsiders. When in such situations we feel clueless, unsure of what is going on around us. Often "first days" have this quality. Can you remember a first day at some job, the first day at college, the first time you went to worship services of a religion in which you were not brought up, the first time you were in a foreign country? Feeling like a stranger in a strange land, you probably looked around for clues, possibly by paying attention to behavioral patterns indicative of social connections. Thinking you now had a better idea of what was going on, you may have gotten up the nerve to do or say something, only to find out that you guessed wrong. Embarrassed, you then probably wished you could get back to familiar territory where everything makes sense. But you couldn't. So what did you do? If you are like most people, you probably tried to find someone who was familiar with this "foreign" situation, an insider who could tell you what everything meant. What would this insider have told you about?

What insiders understand and what outsiders are clueless about is **culture,** the meanings that are shared by a collection of people and that are expressed in symbols, rituals, stories, narratives, values, and worldviews. Culture is a very important part of everyday life. Ignorance of a culture can lead to embarrassment, misexpectations, and misunderstandings. And so as people encounter new situations and new cultures, they try to become insiders by discovering the meanings people within a culture give to their social connections.

But how can you understand a culture from the point of view of insiders? There are many ways to learn about a culture. You can live in a culture, a practice advocated by cultural anthropologists (Mead [1928] 1961). You can interview those who are part of the culture, though often people take for granted their culture and are not very good at answering probing questions. But if you cannot afford the time to live in a culture, and you cannot rely on insiders to tell you what you want to know, how else can you learn about the content of a culture?

In the next part of this chapter, you will learn how to decode the content of a culture. It will help if you picture a culture as an onion (Morgan 1989). Onions have layers, and so does a culture. The outside layer of a culture consists of *symbols.* When people first enter a culture, this is what they tend to notice. When you peel off the symbolic layer, you uncover another level of culture consisting of *stories* and myths. Finally, at the core of a cultural onion rests its central assumptions, values, visions, beliefs, and *worldviews,* which give meaning to the outer aspects of a culture. You can decode a culture by beginning with its symbols, then listening to its important stories, and finally uncovering its core values and assumptions.

Symbols

Upon entering a culture, the first thing you are likely to see are **symbols,** objects or behaviors that convey a specific meaning to the people who share a culture. Symbols are all around us in our social worlds. Colors, objects, pictures, clothing, gestures, and words all can have symbolic meanings that outsiders may not understand and insiders take for granted. Schools have their mascots and school colors, companies their logos, social clubs their lapel pins and rings, gangs their colors and clothing styles, and countries their flags.

How do you know that an object or action is symbolic? Within a culture, symbolic objects are treated as special, things that are out of the ordinary. They may be prominently displayed, used on special occasions, or handled with care. Often, they are used in **rituals,** culturally meaningful patterns of behavior. Rituals are very prominent in religious settings. But rituals occur in many other social settings. The "boys' night out" playing poker, the raising of a flag, induction and graduation ceremonies, and awards banquets are all ritualistic occasions in which symbols are prominently displayed and used. Often, you can detect what objects and actions are symbolic by observing ritualistic patterns of behavior in a culture.

Another way to see symbols is to look at **language,** a set of symbols that enable people to communicate with each other. Usually when people think of language they think of spoken languages such as English, German, Japanese, and Spanish. But there are also nonverbal languages, such as body language and sign language. Languages, whether verbal or nonverbal, consist of symbols such as letters, words, characters, and gestures. These linguistic symbols are meaningful to those who know the language, and such symbols, therefore, can be used to convey information from one person to another.

Languages and their vocabularies can tell you a lot about a culture. Unfamiliar buzzwords, acronyms, abbreviations, technical terms, and catch phrases indicate that you are in another culture. For example, people into computers talk about gigs, RAM, interfaces, encryption, and firewalls. Part of learning about a culture involves learning the lingo, learning what words and phrases mean and what various technical terms represent.

Let us begin to decode the culture at Design Inc. by looking for symbols. The first symbol someone is likely to see is the hand-lettered sign in the reception area with the phrase "Perfection or Bust!" But other symbols abound. Upon being ushered into an office, you probably would notice how austere it is, with hard-backed, uncomfortable chairs. If you eavesdropped on conversations, you probably would hear phrases such as "no compromise with mediocrity" or "perfection is our only concern," which have become part of employees' everyday vocabulary. If you were to spend more time at Design Inc., you would begin to see rituals, such as the way employees spend their leisure time together or the way in which everyone is involved in the interview process. You may even begin to notice that Klee himself is sort of a symbol, exemplifying the values he wants to promote.

There are probably many more symbolic objects and behaviors at Design Inc., such as plaques hanging on the wall, award trophies on bookshelves, and maybe the wall colors and the layout of offices. What do all these symbols mean? Why is the furniture so uncomfortable? Why is that sign so prominently displayed in the reception area? What do the leisure time and interview rituals tell you about Design Inc.'s culture?

You probably have some ideas already about what all these symbols mean because the case discusses their meaning by telling us about the other crucial aspects of a culture—its stories and its core worldviews. Design Inc.'s culture stresses perfection over mediocrity, quality over quantity, excellence over hand holding. But as we shall see, Design Inc.'s culture is more complex. And if we were a first-time client, or a person going for an interview, we probably would notice some of the symbols and rituals that I identified previously, but we probably would be clueless about what they symbolized. Knowing what the symbols and rituals are is the first step. To understand what they mean, you must peel off a layer of the onion and look at a culture's stories.

Stories and Narratives

Suppose you come across an object or a behavior that you think has symbolic value. Because you have no clue about what it symbolizes, you ask someone. What do you think that person would say?

Consider, for example, the objects people hang from the rearview mirrors of their cars. If you ask a friend why she has some object dangling from her mirror, it is unlikely that she would give you a simple answer. Instead, she is likely to tell you a *story*. Maybe one day, while down on her luck, a friend stopped by to cheer her up, and gave her this object. Each time she looks at it she recalls that special moment.

Cultures are filled with stories, legends, and myths. Religions have their creation stories, countries their stories about their founding moments and pivotal events (Spillman 1997), corporations their stories about dynamic leaders, and families their stories about memorable vacations and difficult moves. What is a story? Sociologists and literary scholars talk about stories as **narratives,** accounts of events that have a beginning, middle, and end, and characters and plots (Miller 1990; Sewell 1992; Steinmetz 1992). Most stories have a main character, usually a hero or heroine, who experiences a series of events. The telling of the story occurs through the plot in which some events are highlighted and other events are ignored.

By creating a story, and telling and retelling it, storytellers do more than just pass on information about something that occurred. Narratives cast events in a certain light by signaling who are the heroes and heroines, who are the villains, and what are the driving forces moving the story toward its conclusion. So when storytellers tell stories, they are conveying meanings as much as they are conveying information. Stories convey through their action views about what is right and what is wrong, who is good and who is bad, what is important and what is irrelevant, what should be remembered and what can be forgotten. A storyteller could become a preacher and tell people what is of value by lecturing them about what they ought and ought not to do. But a story is much more real because it *shows* instead of tells you what is important.

The narrative component of culture is also evident in the sayings, mottoes, slogans, and songs that are prominent in a culture. Countries have their national anthems whose words and music conjure up images of what the country is all about. Organizations often have slogans and mottoes like the one prominently displayed at Design Inc.: "Perfection or Bust!"

One of the most important narrative components of a culture are the *scripts* people follow as they interact with others. All of us from time to time feel like we are on stage, acting out a role in a play by following some script. But unlike actors and actresses, people in scripted situations do not have a written-out script. So one thing sociologists do when trying to understand a culture is to uncover the unwritten scripts that are guiding behaviors in a situation (Goffman 1959).

Scripts, like stories, have characters and plots. But they are a special type of narrative because they are designed to *direct* and *guide* action. Although you can read a script as you would read a story, the best way to understand a script is to see it acted out. Because scripts are designed to direct action, they often have within them directives ("kisses Joan") and cues ("enters through door").

What are some of the important stories, narratives, mottoes, and scripts at Design Inc.? Obviously, the main story is Klee's story, the story of a founder of a commercial art studio who wants to do things differently. Success, the plot of the story, is brought about by Klee's actions: his constant striving for perfection, his mentoring of his employees, and his involvement in every aspect of the design process. Through the Klee character in the Klee success story, graphic artists at Design Inc. are shown what is of value in this culture.

The Klee story is evident in the numerous mottoes depicted in the case. All the mottoes highlight the perfection motif; they remind employees and clients that the driving force in this story is success through excellence.

Finally, there are the scripts that the graphic artists at Design Inc. act out. Perhaps the most scripted activity at Design Inc. is the job interview. As anyone who has been through a job interview knows, they often have a very theatrical flair. Dressed in suits (the costume) and carrying a briefcase (a prop), interviewees shake hands firmly with interviewers (a gesture), always looking them in their eyes, and speaking with a voice that conveys confidence. All this takes place on a stage with a set usually consisting of a desk, chairs, paper, and pencils. But what is most important, and what no one really sees during the performance because it already has been memorized, is the script. Interviewees, who are sometimes coached for job interviews, memorize a script by learning what to say, how to say it, and when to say it. And good interviewers prepare beforehand questions they want to ask.

The interview process at Design Inc. probably has some of these qualities, although it also seems to have its own script. Although the case does not tell us exactly how these interviews are conducted, you can imagine what goes on. Potential employees are scrutinized about their commitment to doing excellent graphic art, their willingness to sacrifice everything else, and their ability to get along with others. Interviewees are ushered from office to office, meeting and being "checked out" by everyone. Whenever a doubt is expressed by an interviewee, or an interviewer detects a problem, an eyebrow probably goes up, signaling that this is not the right person.

The stories, mottoes, and scripts at Design Inc., along with the symbols and rituals, can help you as an outsider to see things from inside Design Inc.'s culture. With your knowledge of this culture's symbols and stories, you are now in a position to peel off the final layer of this organization's culture and examine its core.

Worldviews

Lying at the core of a culture is its **worldview**, a term that comes from the German word *Weltanschauung,* which means an overall perspective through which people see and understand what goes on around them. Worldviews provide a frame of reference, a point of view. Worldviews help us develop accounts of why people do what they do, and they guide our behaviors and interactions with others. Within a worldview, you find values, beliefs, visions, and images. *Values,* the collective standards by which people make judgments, specify what is good and bad, right and wrong, desirable and undesirable. *Beliefs* or creeds, specific statements that people within a culture consider to be true, convey fundamental assumptions. *Visions,* desired future states of affairs, depict what people should strive for, and *images,* mental pictures that people use metaphorically as models or frameworks, help them develop accounts and make sense of their experiences.

How do you know what is of value in a culture? Where can you go to discover a culture's worldview, its core beliefs, visions, and images? Here are some of the strategies sociologists use to "see" a culture's core:

- *Begin with the outer layers of culture and work inward.* Look at the symbols and what they represent. What words and phrases keep coming up over and over? Listen to the stories and hear who is viewed as a hero and heroine, and who is viewed as a villain. To what documents and texts do those within a culture turn for advice?

- *Look at the decisions people make.* People employ values as evaluative criteria when deciding among alternative courses of action. So, for example, if people time and time again decide to spend their wealth on material objects, you have a clue that their culture values physical displays of wealth. If one organization continually enters new markets, and another always lowers its price by decreasing costs, you have a good indicator that these two organizations have different images of themselves and different qualities that they value.

- *Ask people what they value.* Social scientists and political pollsters do this all the time through surveys. People are asked about their *attitudes* on a wide variety of social, political, and cultural phenomena, such as abortion, physician-assisted suicide, the death penalty, and providing welfare to the poor. The problem with this strategy is that people may not always say what they really believe or value, especially if their values differ from the majority's value. As a result, you may not learn what someone values. But you may learn what they think the majority values, useful information in its own right.

- *Look at which behaviors are rewarded and which behaviors are punished.* Incentives, whether positive or negative, are designed to increase compliance with norms. For example, if a university rewards researchers who have lots of external grants with big offices and gives those who are good teachers but who do little research small offices without windows, you have an indication that at that university research is valued more than teaching.

- *Break the rules and see what happens.* If you think some form of behavior is valued and considered sacred, do not do it when you are supposed to, and see what people's reactions are. If they get upset and start acting in an unconventional manner, you know you are on to something. This is what *ethnomethodologists*— sociologists who study the ways in which people make sense of their social worlds—do when they try to discover the everyday rituals that express conventional values (Garfinkel 1967).

If you were to use these strategies on Design Inc., what do you think you would find at the core of its culture? What do its symbols symbolize? What values are conveyed through the Klee story and the mottoes? What is Klee's vision? What is his image of Design Inc.?

We already have touched on one part of Design Inc.'s worldview— perfection. From the austere furniture to the motto prominently displayed in the reception area, the value of perfection is conveyed. But this is only part of Design Inc.'s culture. Why is spending leisure time together such an important ritual? Why is the interview process so scripted? Why is Klee, the hero of the story, everywhere? The answers to these questions lead us to the second part of this culture, Klee's vision of Design Inc. as an academy with a training mission. This culture values learning, for it is through learning that better artwork can be produced. Many of the rituals and scripts can be viewed as attempts to reinforce the idea that Design Inc. is a place to learn and not just a workplace.

Case Application

Now that we have decoded Design Inc.'s culture, you are in a better position to understand what is going wrong in this organization. At first glance, this may seem to be a simple case of an entrepreneur who starts a successful business and who then is unwilling to relinquish control because he thinks that only he can do a good job. Looking at this organization's structure, the connections among employees, and the networks inside this company would lead you to conclude that Klee is always the central figure. But is this just a case of the inability of a founder to relinquish some control? Is there something about Design Inc.'s culture that is causing problems at this design studio?

It is important to realize that cultures are human creations. Klee articulates Design Inc.'s mission and conveys to others his vision. The stories, mottoes, and scripts are human creations designed to *mobilize commitment* to Klee's vision of Design Inc. as a training academy with an unswerving commitment to perfection. The rituals and symbols *institutionalize* this commitment by providing daily reminders about what is of value. Those who are part of this culture—Klee, his employees, and even his clients—have bought into this culture. They see themselves as an oasis in a business world that stresses price competition. They are different because they value perfection and they see their graphic arts studio not just as a producer of commercial art but also as a place where graphic artists learn how to make the best art.

But there are tensions within this culture. Students who are learning are not perfect; they make mistakes. Training requires working with those who do not yet have the skills to do "perfect" work. If this culture views graphic artists as students, how can it expect perfect work from them? Perfection and excellence may be the goal, but during training imperfect art will be created. The only way to resolve this tension is for the teacher, Klee, to be everywhere, making sure that his students' mistakes do not go out the door, and prodding them to do better and better. And to maintain the image of perfection in the face of mistakes and learning, this culture has to present itself as superior, as a culture that values excellence more than all of us do. The result is a culture of superiority, an elitism, in which outsiders are viewed as inferior and others are seen as unable to be part of this special culture.

Therefore, the problems at Design Inc. can be viewed as cultural problems resulting from the tension between two values: perfection and learning. Over time, the perfection motif remains, but the academy character of Design Inc. recedes into the background. This cultural change creates a problem. Why should graphic artists at Design Inc. strive for perfection when they gain little, are paid less than artists at other establishments, and are required to make sacrifices? Initially, striving for perfection is justified because it is part of the training mission. But as the learning emphasis becomes less important, what motivates perfection? The answer lies with Klee and the culture of perfection he creates. Klee, by taking on more and more responsibilities, pushes his employees to be perfect. The symbols, rituals, mottoes, and stories remind the artists that they are in fact special and better than artists working elsewhere, motivating them to strive for perfection.

As the culture evolves and the academy image fades into the background while perfection and superiority values are stressed, the critical observer begins to wonder whether the training mission was really ever that central within this culture. Could this be a case in which Klee promotes perfection with the image of an academy but what he really wants is increased effort and contributions by his staff, efforts that will increase his company's profits?

To answer questions like this, you need to go beyond describing a culture by decoding its symbols, narratives, and worldviews. You need to use theories of culture to understand what cultures do.

THEORIES OF CULTURE

Now that you have a better idea of what is in a culture, you can explore how culture and social connections are interrelated. To begin with, bear in mind that culture is not the same thing as social connections. You should not reduce culture to connections, nor should you expand the notion of culture to include everything in society including connections among people. Culture, as you have seen, refers to symbols, rituals, stories, values, and worldviews, and social connections refer to forms of social organization such as social relationships, groups, networks, and organizations.

Although culture is distinct from social connections, culture and social connections are closely related. It is very difficult to think about real social connections without thinking about symbols, narratives, and worldviews. Consider Design Inc. How could you understand the social relationships between Klee and his graphic artists without understanding that the culture values perfection? So although you should not equate culture and social connections, it is one of the important tasks in reading social situations to examine how culture and social connections are related.

To do this, you need to take a careful look at what cultures do. As you will see, cultures do many things, and this is what makes their study so interesting. The various roles culture plays can be captured with five images of culture:

- As a social glue
- As an umbrella
- As a mask
- As an underlying current
- As a tool kit

You are already familiar to some extent with each of these images because they correspond to the five sociological theories and images discussed in Chapter 2. Social glues strengthen bonds. Umbrellas create a sense of a whole among disparate parts. Masks disguise tugs-of-war. Currents propel action and exchanges. Tool kits are used to create webs. In the remainder of this chapter, I use these images of culture to explore five ways to understand the relation between culture and social connections. Together with your knowledge of a culture derived from decoding a culture, these images of culture can help you obtain an insider's perspective.

CULTURE AS A SOCIAL GLUE

Social connections, as you have seen, can be viewed as bonds that join people together. But sometimes the bonds created by social relationships, groups, organizations, and networks are weak. Why are some bonds stronger than others? What accounts for the variation in the strength of the bonds we have with other people?

One possible cause of the varying strength of social bonds is culture. According to this view, culture acts as a social glue, solidifying social connections between social actors. Without this glue, the bonds people form are likely to be fleeting and temporary. With the social glue, bonds are strengthened and likely to endure.

This view of culture has its origins in Durkheim's work. Durkheim argued that societies have a **collective conscience,** "the totality of beliefs and sentiments common to average citizens of the same society" (Durkheim [1895] 1964:49). By this term, Durkheim was not claiming that there is some "group mind" lying above and beyond the members of society that, through some mysterious process, controls what people do. Instead, he thought of a collective conscience as a social glue consisting of beliefs, norms, and values that put people on the same wavelength, so to speak. From this theoretical perspective, cultures create social cohesion and, when they are very powerful, social conformity. They create a sense of "us," increasing social solidarity and loyalty to those to whom we are connected.

When you read the Design Inc. case, it was probably this aspect of culture that first came to mind. There is such a strong sense of camaraderie and solidarity at Design Inc. that readers of the case are likely to conclude that social bonds there are quite strong. The "us" mentality is seen in the superiority felt by the graphic artists at Design Inc. vis-à-vis their colleagues elsewhere. The strong collective conscience that pervades Design Inc. is seen in its symbols, rituals, and mottoes.

Until problems start to occur at Design Inc., it appears that loyalty and commitment to this organization are extremely high. This is an organization with high morale, with an esprit de corps. At least initially, Design Inc.'s symbols, mottoes, and worldview stressing perfection act like a social glue strengthening the social bonds among the graphic artists.

 ## CULTURE AS AN UMBRELLA

Suppose that we now look at Design Inc. as a social system in which social connections integrate parts into a whole. From this perspective, the major problem is keeping all the parts together. Whether it be a group, organization, community, or even an entire society, there is always the tendency for *disorganization,* the breaking down of a whole into just a collection of parts. What molds the parts together and prevents the whole from breaking up? The answer, according to structural functionalists like Talcott Parsons, is culture. Culture acts like an *umbrella,* covering all the parts and creating a sense of a whole among disparate elements.

We see the importance of a cultural umbrella in the "Perfection or Bust!" case when Design Inc.'s culture begins to disintegrate. Without a cultural umbrella, the various people doing different tasks no longer work together. All that can hold the whole together is an ever-present director, which is what Klee becomes. In the absence of cultural values backing up his commands, Klee's authority is less likely to be seen as legitimate, and cooperation is likely to decrease. Everyone will want to be their own star, to strike out on their own. The whole disintegrates into a bunch of noncooperating parts. Although this disorganization has not yet fully overtaken Design Inc., we can see the beginnings of it in the resignation of the top graphic artist and in the changing attitudes of those who continue to work there.

From this theoretical perspective, what is important about culture is its ability to move actors from thinking about things from their perspective or the perspective of their own part to thinking about things from the perspective of the whole. How does culture lead to this shift in perspective? According to Parsons (1968), the most important part of a culture is its core values. Core values, when shared among all the parts of a social system, act as standards that can be used to evaluate everyone's activities. When there is a consensus of values, disagreements over what should be done are more easily settled. But when there is disagreement over what is of value, then it is hard to imagine how a collection of parts can really function as a whole. Values, for Parsons, are the overarching umbrella that unites different parts into a whole. Values do not obliterate differences. Within social systems, people are different and do different things. But as long as they have a common value system, these differences are held together by a culture acting as a giant umbrella.

Because values are so important for a social system's survival, the maintenance and transmission of values, what Parsons calls **latent pattern maintenance,** is the most important social function in society. The institutions that perform this function—religions, schools, and the family—are, according to Parsons, the central institutions in any society. Values legitimize the norms and rules that integrate the various activities of people within a society. Without this legitimacy, people are less likely to obey rules and follow norms.

Viewed from this perspective, the key to understanding Design Inc. is the cultural value placed on perfection. Perfection is the standard by which everything is evaluated. Although the graphic artists working at this firm do different things and work on different projects, it is the standard of perfection that makes them look at their work from the perspective of the whole. Through this culture, they are asked to put aside their personal perspectives and to think only about what they are doing from the perspective of Design Inc., the best graphic arts studio.

Because this perfection standard requires sacrifice, maintaining and transmitting this value is very important. The symbols, rituals, and mottoes are designed to keep this perfection value in the

forefront, and the interview process demonstrates the importance this organization places on finding people who have the same
values.

According to this perspective on culture as an umbrella, the major
challenge facing social systems is to devise ways of integrating new
parts into the whole. Either new parts must be socialized so that
they learn the standards through which behaviors are evaluated or
there must be some way in which only those parts that already have
those values are allowed to become a part of the whole. This is why
in organizations like Design Inc. culture is very evident in the hiring, interviewing, and training processes. Design Inc. has chosen to be
highly selective, allowing only those who accept Design Inc.'s perfection values to join their team. They are worried about the disorganization that they think will occur if someone who does not share
their values joins their staff. This is why they are unable to hire
anyone.

CULTURE AS A MASK

As the tension between the academy and the perfection values
increases, and the emphasis on Design Inc. as an academy fades, a critical reader begins to wonder who is benefiting from all the hard work
of the graphic artists. As long as Design Inc. is like an academy and
graphic artists are perfecting their skills, the lower pay and long hours
seem justified. But when the artists are gaining little and sacrificing
much, the conflict between Klee's interests (a profitable business) and
his workers' interests (good pay and interesting work) surfaces.

When connections are indicative of conflictive tugs-of-war, the
image of culture as a mask can yield valuable insights. Culture can disguise what is really going on by portraying an image of social connections as operating in one way when, in fact, they operate in another
way. As a mask, culture can mislead people by leading them to think
that they are not as bad off as they really are. When culture operates in
this manner, we speak of an **ideology,** a set of beliefs about how a

society works. Ideologies typically attempt to justify the fact that some people are better off than others or to convey the idea that the interests of the dominant social actor are everyone's interests (Mannheim [1936] 1988). The result, according to the ideology, is that people who are worse off come to believe that they deserve their misfortune, that their circumstances cannot be changed, or that they really are better off and not worse off. Therefore, ideologies and cultures, by masking social realities, can prevent people from seeking to change their situation.

This view of culture has it origins in the work of Karl Marx, who sought to understand why some workers who suffered in factories did not attempt to change their situation, whereas other workers did. Marx argued that as long as workers have a false consciousness about how capitalism works, they are unlikely to try to improve their situation. Only when workers become *class conscious,* that is, conscious of their interests and conscious of the real reasons why their interests are not being realized, will they seek to change their situation (Ollman 1976).

Although Marx used this image of culture as a mask to better understand class conflict, it has much wider applications. Advertisers often try to convince us that we need things that we do not really need. Unscrupulous salespeople attempt to sell products that do not do what they say the products can do. And demagogues can gain a following by portraying a false reality. People use culture to advance their interests because they know the power culture has and how cultural symbols, stories, and worldviews can shape behaviors and even desires.

Viewed from this perspective you cannot help but notice how central Klee is to all that goes on at Design Inc. He is the owner and the one who has the final say in who is hired. He is everywhere, checking people's work and allocating tasks. He is the one who benefits when Design Inc. does well and the one who suffers when it does not. And Klee is the one who promotes the vision of Design Inc. as an academy and demands perfection. This is Klee's show. And although he might genuinely have wanted Design Inc. to be more like a learning academy, this organization is first and foremost his business.

Klee succeeded, at least for awhile, in cultivating the ideology that Design Inc. is an academy. This image made graphic artists believe that the sacrifices they were making were worth it. But as the sacrifices became too great and the ideology of Design Inc. as an academy seemed no longer to be the reality, some of his artists began to question the perfection standard. According to this perspective, as Design Inc.'s cultural mask begins to be peeled away, conflict is likely to increase, and Klee will be pressured to change the way he runs his organization.

CULTURE AS A CURRENT

When you start thinking about social exchanges, another perspective on culture becomes apparent. Consider the exchanges occurring at Design Inc. Graphic artists work for Klee in exchange for a salary. Customers purchase artwork and services. For these exchanges to occur, there must be some reason people enter into these exchanges with Design Inc. Why do the graphic artists work for Klee? What motivates them to do good work? Why do customers come to Design Inc.?

When you look for the reasons people connect with others through exchanges, you cannot help but think about exchanges from the point of view of the social actor and the meanings they attach to their actions. As Max Weber argued, subjective meanings inform action, whether it be exchanges or other types of social action. To understand why people do what they do, you must examine their meaning systems. This is why Weber advocated using the *verstehen* (the German word that means "to understand") method when doing sociology (Weber 1949). According to this method, understanding action requires *interpreting* the subjective meanings actors have. Without this understanding, you are likely to misunderstand and misinterpret people's behaviors. From a Weberian theoretical perspective, culture is important because it is a meaning system that informs people's actions and interactions.

One way to think about culture as a meaning system is to picture culture as a *current,* like the current in a river. We do not really see currents. Rather, we see the effects of a current. When you throw a stick into the river and it gets caught in the current, it begins to move quickly downstream. The current becomes visible through its effects on the objects that are caught up in it. Similarly, we do not see meaning systems. Rather, we infer that they are at work because of their effects on people's actions and interactions. Like currents, cultural meanings also propel something—human action.

Culture works this way because many of our actions are *intentional* actions, that is, they have a purpose and are directed toward some end. These ends or intentions motivate people to act the way they do. Therefore, to understand people's actions, you have to pay attention to intentions. Furthermore, you should not assume that everyone has the same intentions and meanings. It is important to understand action from the point of view of the actor, that is, from within his or her own meaning system.

The "Perfection or Bust!" case is full of meaningful, intentional action. Early on in the case we learn that a lettering expert was impressed by Klee's presentation and accepted his job offer, as did other promising recruits. We know that, initially, the staff was very enthusiastic about working at Design Inc. and that they defended their firm when socializing with colleagues employed elsewhere. We are told that employees worked long hours, redid their work a dozen times or more following Klee's suggestions, and sacrificed their social and family lives. We also know that, for some workers, the choice of career over family was too much and they chose to leave. Finally, we are told about how the staff had a difficult time finding a new recruit.

All these actions are like leaves blowing in the wind; their direction and speed tells us about the underlying current. At Design Inc., the staff oriented their actions around perfection, around learning how to do the best possible job. Their actions were not based on maximizing income or maximizing time away from work. Nor were their actions based on devotion to Klee, even though they followed Klee's advice. Rather, those who worked for Design Inc. did so because they believed that at this firm they were being given the opportunity to learn how to become the best possible graphic artist. It is these intentions that inform their action and that lead them to stay at Design Inc. even when the sacrifices are substantial.

Therefore, we see the culture of Design Inc. both in its content (the symbols, rituals, and stories) and in its effects (the behaviors of graphic artists and customers). This is because culture, as this perspective highlights, provides meanings that motivate actions. Note, however, that as sociologists trying to understand the meanings people attach to their actions, we do not try to get inside people's heads and psychoanalyze them. Psychology provides many insights into the wide range of motivators that can cause various behaviors. As sociologists, however, we are interested in the meanings that are embedded in the social situation, in this case in the culture of Design Inc. It is a meaning system, captured by the symbols, stories, and worldviews, that provides the subjective meanings that inform individual actions.

Therefore, the problems facing Design Inc. are to be found in the culture. It is as if the swiftly flowing current that had enveloped this firm has stopped, and now its culture is more like a slow-moving, meandering stream. Those who still work for Design Inc. do so either because they recall the days when the current flowed swiftly or because they believe that those days will come again soon. From this perspective, what Design Inc. needs is a revitalized culture, for without meanings informing action, there is nothing to propel the behaviors of Klee's staff.

CULTURE AS A TOOL KIT

If you could observe what goes on at Design Inc. on a daily basis, you probably would be struck by the similarities in everyone's behavior: graphic artists consulting with Klee, redoing work many times over, discussing ideas with fellow workers, and always looking for ways to improve. You would think that if people create social connections through social interaction—an idea that comes from the perspective that views connections as webs—there would be a great deal of variety in these creations. And yet we often find similarities, and not just among people working in the same organization. For example, social workers tend to organize their social service agencies the same way. Many communities share similar zoning laws and residential patterns. If people create their social worlds, why do they end up creating similar social worlds with similar types of connections?

Of course, differences in how people connect to others do exist. You have only to think about the way things are done at Design Inc. in contrast to more conventional commercial art firms to recognize that people create different ways of connecting. How can we account for both the similarities in the webs people create and the variations?

One possibility is that people tend to create similar social connections because they have similar *tools* that they use when making social connections. Like a carpenter who uses carpentry tools when making a cabinet, people also use tools when constructing connections to others. But whereas a carpenter's tool kit contains saws, hammers, and screwdrivers, our tool kits contain symbols, stories, and worldviews. Culture is our tool kit (Swidler 1986). When people have similar cultural tools in their tool kits, they are likely to construct similar types of social connections. Conversely, when people have different cultural tools, we would expect different social constructions of reality.

All of us are to some extent familiar with cultural tool kits. I am sure you have had on occasion an idea you wanted to express but could not find the words to express it. Either you had the word somewhere in your tool kit but you could not find it or you had not yet acquired that tool. Language and other symbols are an important part of our cultural tool kits because they enable us to express ourselves and communicate with others.

Cultural tool kits are useful in other respects as well. In everyday life, people develop what sociologists of culture call **strategies of action,** persistent ways of ordering action over time (Swidler 1986). For example, take a student's study habits. Maybe her strategy in studying for a test is to read the required material using a highlighter to underline important points. Then she transfers definitions to note cards that she uses to memorize the material. Her strategy of action involves the use of a highlighter and note cards. In her "exam studying tool kit," she has the ideas "when reading material use a highlighter" and "when memorizing definitions first put them on index cards." She may have learned these "recipes" from a parent, big sister, a fellow student, a how-to book, or maybe even a course she took on studying for exams. Wherever she learned them, once acquired, these cultural tools are like a script that she can consult when constructing her exam-studying strategy.

The "Perfection or Bust!" case does not tell us very much about the strategies of action that graphic artists use at Design Inc. But if I were to conduct more research on this organization, one of the first things I would investigate is how the artists go about doing their work. I am sure that I would discover common patterns indicative of a script that is being followed. When unsure what to do, Klee's employees probably first look into their cultural tool kit, searching for a story, ritual, or symbol that can guide them. While at Design Inc., the artists have in all likelihood acquired not just skills and technical knowledge but also a repertoire of possible actions that they could draw on when solving problems and doing their work.

From this perspective, what makes Design Inc. so different from other commercial art establishments is not a core value that guides action or provides motivational meanings. Rather, Design Inc. is different because those at the company have a different cultural tool kit. Their cultural tools promote perfection, excellence, and learning by providing templates for action. As graphic artists at Design Inc. make decisions about what they are going to do, they use cultural items (symbols, stories, worldviews) to frame issues and to provide models for their actions.

It should be noted that cultural tool kits both enable and limit. Design Inc.'s culture provides recipes and scripts for attaining excellence, but it is not very helpful when it comes to figuring out how to recruit new personnel or how to delegate responsibilities. From this perspective, the problem at Design Inc. is that the tools that were helpful in starting up an innovative design firm and attracting qualified personnel are not as useful when it comes to building and maintaining this organization. The staff, including Klee, does not have at their disposal a culture that can help them meet these challenges. As long as they continue to use old tools for a new job, there will be crises. What Design Inc. needs are new strategies of action and new repertoires that can help Klee and his graphic artists think about and deal with their problems in a different way.

SOCIOLOGICAL EYE ANALYSIS GUIDE

Cultures, with their symbols, rituals, stories, and worldviews, are fascinating. As you have seen through the analysis of the "Perfection or Bust!" case, cultural knowledge enriches your understanding of social situations. For it is through culture that you as an outside observer can begin to see situations and their social connections from the point of view of those who are connected. No matter how well you understand the social connections in a case, without also understanding the meanings that these connections have for social actors you are likely to misread situations. By decoding culture and examining its symbols, stories, and worldviews, you can learn what is of value for social actors in a case. And by using various images of culture—as a social glue, as an umbrella, as a mask, as a current, and as a tool kit—you can better understand how social connections and culture are interrelated.

Understanding culture is one important way in which you can situate a case and put it in context. And situating cases is very important. All of us have a tendency from time to time to take things out of context. A situation may look strikingly similar to another situation. An event may lead you to recall a similar event.

We often want to see what is common across situations instead of what is unique about a specific situation. And although common-alities do exist and are important to notice, things can appear simi-lar on the surface when in reality they are quite different. Exam-ining the context and situating events can help you to uncover important differences and detect real similarities.

The cultural context of a case, however, is only one of the impor-tant social contexts. Understanding culture helps you to situate action, interactions, and social connections within a meaning sys-tem, a *Weltanschauung*. But you also need to be aware of another context, the context that gives people varying ability to act on their interests. As you already know, people do not enter situations on an equal footing. Inequalities exist, and they affect what people can and will do. Ignoring inequalities can lead to misreadings of situations just as much as ignoring culture can. In the next chapter, you will see how knowledge of social inequalities can lead to new insights into social situations. But for now, what is important is your ability to situate cases by understanding cultures. So use the following Analysis Guide to help you decode the cultural conflict in the "Linda Gorman" case at the end of this chapter.

Decoding Culture

❑   What objects and behaviors are symbolic in this case? What are the important rituals in which these symbols are used? Are there any special languages or vocabularies, verbal or nonverbal, that are used in this case?

❑   What stories and narratives do people tell in this case? Who are the central characters in these stories? What are the plots? What do the stories attempt to show? Are there slo-gans or mottoes that are heard over and over again? Are there scripts guiding action?

❑   What is of value in this culture? What are the important images and visions? How would you characterize this cul-ture's worldview and important beliefs?

Culture as a Social Glue

❑ Are some bonds stronger than others and, if so, which ones are stronger?
❑ What symbols, stories, and worldviews strengthen bonds?
❑ Is a strong sense of "us" evident in the case? If so, how is this sense of "us" maintained?

Culture as an Umbrella

❑ Who in this case sees things from their own perspective? Who attempts to look at things from the perspective of the whole?
❑ Are there standards according to which everyone is evaluated? If so, what are these standards and how are they used in this case?
❑ According to what criteria are newcomers selected and evaluated?

Culture as a Mask

❑ Is there a discrepancy between what people believe (or say) and what is really going on?
❑ Do those who are worse off believe that they deserve to be worse off? Do they believe that they cannot change the situation? Do they believe that they are really not disadvantaged?
❑ What ideologies lead to these views? Who articulates these ideologies?

Culture as a Current

❑ What are the behavioral patterns indicative of some underlying driving force motivating behaviors?
❑ What meanings do you think lie behind these patterns? What types of activities do these meanings motivate?

❑ How do the symbols, stories, and worldviews propel the action that is evident in this case?

Culture as a Tool Kit

❑ What are some of the similarities that are evident in the social interactions among people in this case? How do these social interactions differ from patterns you have seen elsewhere?

❑ What are the culture tools that people in this situation use as they go about constructing social connections with others? What repertoires and templates do they have at their disposal?

❑ How would you characterize their strategies of action? To what or to whom do people turn when they are trying to figure out what to do?

Decision Case: "Linda Gorman"

Sitting down and putting her feet up at the end of a long day at the Child Health Clinic at the Long Branch County Health Department, Linda Gorman, a public health nurse, silently ruminated on the hovering psychological discomfort she was experiencing. She knew she was troubled because of an encounter early in the afternoon with Mrs. Saeto, her patient's mother. "Am I just being culturally insensitive?" she wondered to herself, "or did I really miss the boat on this one?"

Mrs. Saeto had brought Marie, her youngest child, to the clinic for a well-child check and her six-month immunizations. They had been referred to Child Health Clinic by the Women, Infant, and Children (WIC) Supplemental Feeding Program when Marie was a newborn and had come for regular visits since that time. The Saeto family had emigrated from Laos, and although Marie's father worked full-time, the family had no health insurance and little money for health care. Mrs. Saeto and Linda had developed a comfortable relationship over the months that Marie had been a patient at the clinic. Linda looked forward to Mrs. Saeto's visits and had learned a lot about the Saetos' *lu Mien* culture from their conversations. Mrs. Saeto's English was excellent, and her willingness to share information about *Mien* cultural practices had permitted Linda to understand better the many *Mien* living in Long Branch County who used the clinic for some of their health care needs.

Mrs. Saeto was born in Laos, but at the end of the Vietnam War she left with friends and what remained of her family. She settled in the United States with her grandparents when she was 14. Mrs. Saeto had talked with Linda about how difficult her first year in America had

---

AUTHOR'S NOTE: This case was written by Kay Libbus and is part of the collection *Case Studies for Faculty Development* created by Rita Silverman and William M. Welty through the Center for Case Studies in Education at Pace University.

been. When she became more comfortable with her new environment, she went through what she now called a "rebellious stage." She refused to speak *Mien* except with her grandparents, and only then because they had never learned English. A part-time job provided money and independence, enabling her to feel less like an outcast in school. She told Linda that she did not really have the opportunity to enjoy her new life as an American high school student. She became pregnant before graduating and left school to take care of the baby. The father of the baby was an American high school student who quickly lost interest in the infant and finally drifted away. Mrs. Saeto had no support except for her grandparents and the *lu Mien* community, who welcomed her home without reservation.

Mrs. Saeto later married a *Mien* man. When Linda met her, they were living with his mother and their four children, one of whom was the child she had before they were married. She described herself to Linda, saying proudly, "Now I am a *Mien* woman." It seemed to Linda that she found great value in her sense of belonging. She took pride in her expanding knowledge of *Mien* traditions and beliefs. Once she sensed Linda's interest, she had eagerly discussed *Mien* beliefs regarding spirits, ceremonies, and cures during each of her daughter's clinic visits.

On this day, when Linda entered the exam room, she noted that Marie appeared to be developing normally. She smiled, vocalized, was able to sit without support, and was quite responsive to Linda. Linda plotted the weight and height measurements taken by the clinic nurse on a growth chart and showed Mrs. Saeto that Marie fell into the 65th percentile for both height and weight for her age and that her growth was proceeding normally. However, when Mrs. Saeto undressed Marie for the physical examination, Linda immediately noted five red, blistered, quarter-inch round markings on the child's abdomen.

"What are those?" she asked, concerned by what she saw.

Not hesitating, Mrs. Saeto explained that the marks were burns.

"Burns?" Linda asked, shocked by this admission.

"Yes," Mrs. Saeto told her. "This is from a *Mien* cure for pain that I used two days ago. My mother-in-law and I both suspected that Marie had a case of *Gusia mun toe.*" She went on to explain that *Gusia mun toe* is an illness seen, although infrequently, among *Mien* babies and is characterized by restlessness, agitation, constipation, and loss of appetite. "We knew that Marie had it," Mrs. Saeto continued, "because she kept throwing her head back when held. Babies who have this illness always act so," she concluded.

> The cure we used was a "string" of inner pulp from a special reed that my mother-in-law got from a *Mien* neighbor who specializes in tradi- tional cures. The pulp was dipped lightly in pork fat and then lit. My mother-in-law passed the flame quickly over the skin of Marie's abdo- men, in the area where pain seemed to be located. The flame raised a blister that popped like popcorn.

Mrs. Saeto went on, "The blisters meant that the illness was not related to spiritual causes. If blisters had not developed, we would have had to hire a shaman to conduct a spirit ritual to cure Marie."

Mrs. Saeto proceeded with enthusiasm:

> My mother-in-law said that only five burns were necessary to cure Marie. The number of burns needed depends on severity of illness and it can take three, five, seven, or even 11 burns before a person is cured. Before flame is put out, it is used to burn a spot on a wall of the room, or a block of wood, a process that transfers the pain. The person perform- ing the cure says, "The wall doesn't feel, so let the wall suffer instead of this person. Wall, let the pain go on in you forever, let the pain off this person." After this part of the cure is completed, the burns are covered with Tiger Balm, a cream that we use for many purposes.

"How did Marie respond to what you did?" Linda asked, trying to keep her revulsion at what the child had suffered out of her voice.

"Marie cried for awhile but the pain did not last very long," Mrs. Saeto said.

The pain lasts maybe for half an hour or an hour at most. With most babies the burns heal with no problems. Sometimes there are some scars, but because these are identified as the result of the cure they are not of any worry to anyone from the *Mien* culture.

"Weren't you concerned that the burns could be serious?" asked Linda.

"I know that this method of cure can be dangerous for children," Mrs. Saeto replied.

Linda said emphatically, "I couldn't agree more." However, she soon realized that their ideas about the dangerousness of burning children did not correspond.

"The cure must be done by someone skilled in burning, like my mother-in-law," continued Mrs. Saeto:

If the burn is placed too near to the line between the baby's mouth and her belly-button, the baby could become mute or even retarded. We knew that Marie's cure was successful because she soon became calm. She has been eating well, she is no longer constipated, and she is sleeping all night.

Linda completed the physical examination and was forced to conclude that, other than the burns, the baby appeared to be completely healthy. She administered Marie's six-month immunizations, noting to herself that the injections made Marie cry and, at least temporarily, affected the baby's formerly calm and cheerful disposition. She wondered to herself—and not for the first time—about the pain she routinely inflicted on children in the course of her practice. Perhaps she was neither more civilized nor more compassionate than Mrs. Saeto and her mother-in-law in her approach to health care delivery. Linda informed Mrs. Saeto of possible side effects of the immunizations, suggested that she call with any questions or problems that arose, and asked that she bring Marie back to clinic in three months for her next well-child examination.

Linda did not mention her misgivings about the practice of burning the baby to any of her colleagues. However, as the afternoon went by, she became increasingly concerned and wondered if she shouldn't have said something. "After all," Linda thought, "it is cruel and dangerous to burn babies." She admitted to herself that she didn't know much about the danger of the cure performed by an unskilled healer, but she knew well that burns cause pain, possible infection, and scarring. She also knew that most people would consider burning infants child abuse, and allowing the act would be seen as criminal neglect, regardless of the rationale. Finally, she thought about the fact that, as a licensed health professional, she was mandated to report suspected child abuse.

Linda knew that she was in the middle of a situation with no easy solutions. She couldn't dispel her uneasiness, and she noted, for the first time that day, that she was beginning to feel a bit angry. "How far am I supposed to go with this cultural sensitivity, anyway?"

CHAPTER 4

Uncovering Inequalities and Power

Decision Case: "The MPA Program at Southeastern State University: The Price of Admission"

As Alex Quill strode down the steps of the stately old administration building, his mood hardly matched the beauty of the spring day. Quill was perplexed and angry about his just-completed conversation with the provost, George Stern. He had been summoned to the provost's office to discuss what he knew was likely to be a touchy matter, but the conversation had taken an unexpectedly harsh turn. Quill had been asked to explain, and justify, a decision to reject an application for admission to Southeastern State University's Master's of Public Administration (MPA) program.

Quill, a tenured associate professor, had been at Southeastern State University for about eight years and had served as director of the MPA program throughout that period. He had graduated from a prestigious private university in the northeast and had taught there for three years

---

AUTHOR'S NOTE: This case was written by Professor Brian Fry and is reprinted by permission of the South Carolina Executive Institute in Columbia, SC.

before moving to State. The change had been something of a culture shock. Having taught some of the "best and brightest" at his previous institution, Quill had to adjust to a student body that, on the whole, was less qualified and less motivated than his previous students. Moreover, Quill had assumed the directorship of a program that resided uneasily in a political science department. The department looked somewhat askance at a program that was viewed by some of Quill's colleagues in the department as little more than occupational training. He had worked hard to establish the academic integrity of the MPA program, but it still was viewed with some suspicion. Quill had a reputation as a demanding teacher, a competent researcher, and an aggressive director of the MPA program. He had instituted a number of changes in the program, and had worked hard to establish working relationships with the state government, which was located only blocks from the university, and local governments in the area. The internal changes had produced some resentment in the department, particularly among senior faculty members who had revised the curriculum just before Quill's arrival on campus. The effort to involve state and community leaders in the operations of the program had raised doubts about Quill's dedication to academic values and standards. All of this had created a nagging uneasiness about Quill's plans for the program and suspicions about his personal ambitions.

The conversation with the provost had been precipitated by what Quill considered to be a routine action on an application to the program. The qualifications of the applicant were clearly subpar. The student had a Graduate Record Examination (GRE) score of less than 800 on the verbal and quantitative sections and a grade point average (GPA) of just above 2.0. The requirements stated in the University catalog were that, "The successful applicant is normally expected to have a GRE score of at least 1,000 and a GPA of 3.0." The applicant had no previous work experience. As required, there were two letters of recommendation. One was from a well-placed friend of the family and the other from the university's athletic director, Bob Gibbon. There was no statement of purpose with the application.

Quill had dutifully assembled the application file and circulated it to the program's admissions committee. The result was as he had expected, a unanimous recommendation that the application be rejected. The recommendation was forwarded to the graduate office, and the student was notified of the decision.

Shortly after the rejection letter went out, Quill received a call from the university president's office inquiring about the reasons for the rejection of the application. This was a bit unusual, but not unprecedented. Typically, such inquiries could be handled with a brief explanation and an offer to talk with the student to explain the decision and, if necessary, to discuss other possible courses of action. The telephone call ended without a request for further action, and Quill considered the matter closed. Within a day, Quill received the summons to the provost's office.

As Quill walked into the provost's office, he did not know what to expect other than that the provost wanted to discuss the Neville application. Quill had only infrequent contacts with the provost. The relationship was cordial, but not close. The provost was relatively new at Southeastern State, having arrived only a year earlier from a state university in the Midwest. A former naval officer with a commanding, if not intimidating, figure, the provost was also a political scientist and had been instrumental in the development of a successful MPA program at his previous institution. Stern had moved into administration at an early stage of his career, taking over the chairmanship of a troubled department while still a junior faculty member. With the support of the university administration, he had acted aggressively to deal with troublemakers in the department. His reputation as a "team player" had led to subsequent appointments and a rapid rise through the administrative ranks. He had served as associate provost before coming to Southeastern State, but this was his first service as a chief academic officer of a university. There were rumors that he had some hope of replacing the president of Southeastern University, who had been under attack for his extravagant and flamboyant lifestyle.

The conversation started with a perfunctory exchange of pleasant-ries, but the provost quickly came to the point.

"Alex," he said as he signaled Quill to take a seat, "I asked you to come over here today to discuss the Brenda Neville application."

Quill nodded in acknowledgment as he sank into a low couch across the coffee table from the wingback chair the provost had occu-pied. The sunlight behind Stern silhouetted him against the window. He continued,

> I don't know if you know it, but Brenda's father Sid is a graduate of the university and a very successful businessman in Sarasota. He was a run-ning back on the team with Coach Gibbon who, I understand, wrote a letter of recommendation for Brenda.

This was news to Quill, and a subtle change in the tone of the pro-vost's voice made him feel a bit uneasy.

> Sid has been very generous in his support of the athletic department, and we've been working on him recently to extend some of that gener-osity to the University. In fact, he is one of the primary targets in the president's new fund-raising campaign.

"I didn't know that," Quill began, "but what . . ."

Stern cut him off, "Anyway, Alex," he said, now with measured firmness, "I'm sure you can understand that Brenda's rejection comes at a very awkward time for the university."

Quill was nonplussed at what he was hearing from the provost, but he had time only to say, "I understand."

"As a matter of fact," Stern quickly went on, "Sid was so upset by your action that he flew up here last weekend to discuss the matter with me. I can tell you it wasn't a very pleasant discussion. He wanted some explanation and, frankly, I was hard pressed to give him one based on what you told the president's office."

By this time, Quill's unease was becoming defensiveness as he realized that the issue had become a personal one. The provost was talking about "your decision" and what "you told the president." Moreover, Stern was obviously distancing himself from the decision, having said he was hard pressed to give him" an explanation.

Struggling to return the discussion to more neutral ground, Quill said, "I can understand your concern, but we applied our standard criteria in making the decision, and the decision of the committee was unanimous."

Stern wasn't about to buy the policy-and-procedure approach: "Yes, yes," he said testily. "Help me with this. What is it you require?"

"You require," Quill thought, back on the hot seat.

"Well," he said, "the basic criteria are Graduate Record Examination scores and the grade point average."

"And what scores do you require?" Stern asked in what now seemed more an interrogation than an inquiry.

"We expect scores of at least 1,000 on the GRE and at least a 3.0 GPA," Quill said.

"Have you done any validation studies on the GRE?" Stern asked, becoming more aggressive as the conversation continued. Not only was Quill being asked to defend his own judgment and the program's admission criteria, but he also was being asked to validate the very concept of standardized testing. And that was a task for which he was ill-prepared.

"We did a little correlation analysis a few years ago," he replied, scrambling to muster a credible response.

"What were the results?"

"We found some relation between grades in the MPA program and GRE scores, particularly the verbal section," Quill said, now fully recognizing the game, but unable to extricate himself from it.

"Did you find any evidence that students who score below 1,000 on the GRE can't successfully complete the MPA program?" Stern asked.

"The study wasn't really designed to address that question," Quill replied lamely.

"Do you look at anything other than the verbal and quantitative scores? What about the scores on the analytical section or the political science section?"

"No, just the verbal and quantitative scores," Quill said.

"Why not?"

Quill's answers were becoming shorter as he recognized the "no-win" nature of his position. "We have just always relied on the other scores."

"That's really not a satisfactory answer," Stern shot back. "I would suggest you look into it. I think I saw something in the *Chronicle* on this recently. Have you seen that article?"

The chances of finding a copy of the *Chronicle of Higher Education* in the administration building are substantially higher than finding one floating around the political science department. Quill could only answer, "Not yet," while silently seething at what he perceived to be the unfairness of the question.

"Well," the provost said with more than a hint of sarcasm, "I would suggest you take a look at it."

"I will," Quill responded stiffly.

"How about that minimum score?" Stern asked, returning to the attack. "Have you ever admitted a student to the program with a score less than 1,000 on the GRE?"

"Yes, but only if there are other strengths in the application."

"Have any of them graduated?"

"I'm sure some have, but we really haven't tracked it."

"How about the GPA? Have you ever admitted a student with a score in the range of Ms. Neville's?" Stern's questions were coming with withering rapidity.

"Well yes, but, again, only under the most unusual circumstances."

"How did they do?"

"I'm sure some have managed to get through the program, but I'm sure the probabilities are lower."

"Have you looked into that?"

"Not systematically."

"Well," Stern said, in a look that combined the warmth of an IRS auditor and the righteousness of an adulterous preacher. "It seems to me that your admissions procedures could stand a thorough examination. These are critical decisions we are making about students' lives and we really can't be cavalier in the way we make those decisions."

Quill nodded in resignation. "I agree," he said.

Stern managed a stiff, conversation-ending smile:

> I have another appointment coming so I am going to have to cut this short. The president and I are anxious to have a successful resolution of the Neville matter. Why don't you get back to me in the next day or so and tell me what you have come up with?

Even as Quill was being ushered out of the provost's office, he was pondering how he should respond. He had just learned something about the values and priorities of the provost and the president. Now he was going to have to find out something about his own.

REVIEW: SOCIAL CONNECTIONS AND INTERESTS

As you learned in Chapter 2 with "The Towering Dilemma," people enter situations with different interests and stands on issues. Such is the situation in "The MPA Program at Southeastern State University."

Social actors, in this case Alex Quill, George Stern, and Sid Neville, have different interests, and, based on those interests, they favor different outcomes. We can map out these interests by examining their social connections and by using sociological theories to see where the social actors are coming from.

Alex Quill is director of the MPA program, a member of the political science department, and chair of the admissions committee. He has network ties to local governmental and community leaders and is in the middle of the hierarchy within a large organization, Southeastern University. His social bonds connect him to other professors and academics, even though he is also an administrator. His unit—the MPA program—performs an important graduate training function within the larger university, which has many other functions such as undergraduate education, research, and fund-raising. Quill does not appear to "own" the resources he needs to run the MPA program and, therefore, he faces tugs-of-war with higher-ups over resource allocation. He is dependent on others' support for the MPA program and is considering whether to exchange admitting Brenda for future resources. Quill is also new to the university and is still viewed by his colleagues as an outsider. His interaction with Stern takes the form of an inquisition, placing Quill on the defensive and creating a "no-win" situation for him. Quill is part of an academic culture that values *meritocracy,* a social system in which people receive rewards based on their achievements. In sum, given his social connections, his culture, and our understanding of his situation, it is clear why Quill opposes admitting Brenda. His interest is in creating a first-rate MPA program with academic integrity and in maintaining its autonomy. Admitting Brenda is inconsistent with the social connections and culture in which Quill is situated.

Sid Neville, in contrast, lives in a different world. He is a successful businessman, university alumnus, donor, and father. His social bonds connect him to his family, to business associates, and to his alma mater through a friendship tie with his old coach. As a successful businessman, he has resources the university could use, and he is the one who will decide how to distribute them. It appears that an exchange is being considered—Brenda's admittance into the MPA program in exchange for a substantial donation. Sid is viewed by others as a benefactor. Sid's culture probably stresses family, although we do not know much about his worldviews. But given his social connections, it is clear that Sid Neville wants his daughter to be admitted into the MPA program. Sid is an able but reluctant donor who is willing to give resources to others only if it serves his purposes, which are to help his friends and family members get ahead. His interest is in accumulating wealth and using it to advance the interests of those close to him.

George Stern's interests are also shaped by his connections. As provost, he runs the academic side of Southeastern University and is Quill's boss. He is one of the top academic officers, and his identity is clearly linked to this administrative group. Stern aspires to be Southwestern's president. His bonds connect him to those who manage various parts of the university, and he probably sees his job as one of balancing competing interests among the different segments within the university. He is willing to bend the rules so that Sid Neville's daughter is admitted. He is viewed as a team player, but he also seems to be a real mover and shaker. Though a member of the academic culture, Stern also has a military background in which being in charge is valued. His interests lie in advancing his own career by helping Southeastern University grow, for with that growth he will have more resources to allocate. He is willing to admit Brenda because it will build bridges with Sid, laying the foundation for future donations. His interest is in pleasing potential donors. But given his position as provost, he knows that he is constrained by the academic system. He cannot unilaterally admit her, for that could undermine his distinguished faculty whom he wants to retain so they will attract good students and external research grants. Therefore, Stern cannot order Quill to admit Brenda. Instead, he must convince Quill that doing so is in Quill's best interest.

This analysis reveals where Quill, Stern, and Neville stand on the issue of admitting Brenda Neville into the MPA program. By examining social connections, looking at this case from multiple perspectives, and thinking about the various cultures, you now should have a fairly good idea where each of these people is coming from and the reasons Quill faces a dilemma.

However, your analysis of this case would be incomplete if you stopped here. This case is not just a case about different and conflicting *interests*. It is first and foremost a case about the different *capacities* of Stern, Quill, and Neville to realize their interests. Formally, Quill, in conjunction with his admissions committee, has the ability to decide who is admitted into the MPA program. But his decisions are questioned by those with even more power, the president and the provost. The provost then attempts to use his power to convince Quill to change his mind. And the provost confronts Quill because Sid Neville has used his influence to convince the provost that admitting his daughter is in the university's best interest. Without analyzing the power of social actors and the sources of their power, you are likely to misread situations, including this case.

▨ POWER AND SOCIAL INEQUALITIES

Power, the ability to realize one's interests despite the resistance of others, is rarely distributed equally (Weber 1946). In most situations, some social actors are better able to influence decision-making outcomes and make things happen so that their interests are realized. Therefore, understanding social situations requires identifying who has power and why. Of course, you can characterize the distribution of power after the fact by seeing who wins and loses when there are conflicting interests. But, more often than not, when analyzing situations, you will want to know the *distribution* of power prior to the final outcome. To determine who has power, you will need to explore the *sources* of power.

In the final analysis, power is based on control over *strategic resources* and opportunities to obtain such resources (Lenski 1966; Pfeffer 1981). Resources such as money, land, equipment, raw materials, information, and skills are strategic when they are needed by social actors to do what they want to do. Control over strategic resources, as well as control over access to those resources

—*opportunities*—gives people power because withholding resources and curtailing opportunities can prevent others from realizing their interests.

Therefore, to understand power, you need to examine the system of **social stratification,** the processes through which resources and opportunities are distributed among various social actors. Among the many bases of social stratification, three social divisions stand out as particularly important: social class, race and ethnicity, and sex. The next three sections provide you with some tools that will sharpen your sociological eyesight and help you clearly see social class, race and ethnic, and sex-based social divisions.

SOCIAL CLASS

Most people would agree that those in the upper classes have more power than those in the lower classes. Many of us would attribute this greater power to the greater **income,** money derived from wages, salary, governmental transfers, and returns on investments that those in the upper class have. Although it is true that, with income, people can buy many things and even influence others, as you will see, classes differ in their power because of their control over three other strategic resources: *property, authority,* and *skills* (Kerbo 2000; Wright 1997).

- *Property Ownership:* All of us are to some extent owners. We own personal property such as clothes, books, automobiles, and sometimes homes. But the issue here is not ownership of personal property, but ownership of *productive assets,* that is, assets through which goods and services are produced such as factories, office buildings, businesses, corporate stock, and land. In most societies, ownership of productive assets is unequally distributed, with a relatively small number of people controlling large amounts of wealth-producing assets. Ownership is a source of power because those who own productive assets can decide how they are to be used and who will benefit financially from their use. And although there has been some dispersion of ownership with the advent of publicly owned corporations and stock trading, the important distinction is between those who have controlling ownership of productive assets and those with no or minimal ownership (Kerbo 2000; Zeitlin 1974).

■ *Authority:* The ability to make decisions and control who does what tasks is the second important dimension of social class. *Managers* make decisions about whom to hire and fire, who should do which tasks, how various types of work should be done, and how many people should work in a work unit. *Supervisors* direct, monitor, and evaluate their immediate subordinates. Within organizations, there are authority hierarchies, with presidents, chief executive officers (CEOs), and chairmen of the board at the top, vice presidents and division heads below them, followed by department heads and then lower-level supervisors, and, finally, base employees who have no authority over others.

■ *Occupational Skills:* **Occupations** are sets of jobs that involve similar activities or tasks. Occupations vary in the type and level of *skills* needed by incumbents to do the tasks that are specific to that occupation. Variation across occupations in skill type and level has important social implications. Those in occupations requiring high skill levels tend to be more autonomous in their work and to possess knowledge and information that they use to do their work (Treiman 1977; Wright 1997). In higher-skilled occupations, people tend to design the work that others in less-skilled occupations perform.

A Multidimensional Class Typology

In the early stages of capitalism, when businesses were relatively small, these three dimensions of social class—ownership, authority, and occupational skill—tended to coincide. Owners of factories and businesses also managed the business, supervised their employees, and, with their skills, designed the work that others executed. But as capitalism evolved and organizations grew in size, the ability of one person to do all these different things decreased. Owners hired managers and supervisors. They created skilled jobs into which they hired professional experts who figured out how work could be done more effectively. As a result, there emerged what we now call the *middle class*. People holding middle-class positions are, in a way, in multiple social classes; that is they are in *contradictory class locations* (Wright 1985). For example, supervisors are not owners, but neither are they ordinary employees because they have authority over others. Similarly skilled craftspeople or technicians are not owners and employers. But because of their skills, they have expertise and are not just workers.

To see the complexities of social classes, you must, therefore, go beyond a simple dichotomy between owners and nonowners. Using the three dimensions of class set out previously, you can identify five different class positions as depicted in Exhibit 4.1 (Kerbo 2000):

- *Capitalists or Owners:* Look for those who own productive assets. Although members of this class also tend to have high amounts of authority and high levels of skill, the defining feature of their class position is ownership. Capitalists will have a great deal of power because they control strategic resources that are needed to implement a decision. Threatening to withhold such resources can lead decision makers to change their objectives and make decisions that favor those who have strategic resources.

- *Managers and Corporate Executives:* Look for nonowners who have a high degree of authority because they manage an entire organization or large portions of one. Although members of this class tend to be in highly skilled occupations, the defining feature of their class position is their authority. Managers and corporate executives also will have power, but, in contrast to capitalists, their power comes from their *formal authority*—their occupancy of positions that give them the right to make impor-

Exhibit 4.1. Social Classes Defined in Terms of Ownership, Authority, and Occupational Skills

	Dimensions of Social Class		
Class Categories	Property Ownership	Authority	Occupational Skills
Capitalists/Owners	Owner	High	High
Managers/Corporate Executives	Nonowner	High	High
Experts	Nonowner	Midlevel	High
Supervisors	Nonowner	Midlevel	Midlevel to low
Workers	Nonowner	None	Low to none

tant decisions. So note who holds such high-level positions as president, vice president, CEO, or provost. Such people are authorized to make decisions, including decisions about how organizational resources are distributed. By being formally connected into decision-making channels, these people can influence what entire organizations do.

- *Experts (Professional and Technical Workers):* Look for non-owners who have high to mid-levels of skills and expertise. Members of this class usually will have some authority, especially authority over a few subordinates whom they supervise. But what distinguishes this class from others is their high level of skill and expertise. Experts have some power because they possess valuable information, knowledge, and skills that are needed to either make or implement decisions. You can identify experts by looking for those who advise people who formally make decisions as well as those whose skills are needed to bring about some outcome.

- *Supervisors:* Look for nonowners who supervise the work of subordinates. Although such employees may be in occupations requiring some skills, the defining characteristic of their class position is the supervision of other people's work. Supervisors have limited amounts of power resulting from their formal authority over their subordinates. They can influence what specific others can do, but their ability to affect larger collections of people is limited.

- *Workers:* Look for nonowners with no authority who work in occupations that require limited skills. Because workers do not control strategic resources such as productive assets, formal authority, and knowledge and skills, they have, individually, little if any power. Workers do control one important resource—their own laboring capacity. Therefore, withholding their labor can be a source of power. However, because workers usually are easily replaced, the labor that they individually control is not strategic, and, therefore, its possession does not yield much power. Instead, collectively, workers can gain power by threatening to withhold their labor.

 RACE AND ETHNICITY

Ethnic and racial diversity is a characteristic of most contemporary societies. As such, people are likely to encounter others whose skin color is different from theirs, whose ancestors came from a different country, or who speak a different language or have a different accent. These differences in skin color, country of origin, and language lead to power and social inequalities when some race and ethnic groups are treated as minorities and others are majorities (Feagin and Feagin 1993; Wirth 1945). A **minority** is a category of people who are disadvantaged and subjected to unequal treatment as a result of being dominated by a majority. A **majority** is a category of people who are privileged and have more resources because they dominate a minority. Usually, a majority is the larger group within a society, but this does not have to be the case. For example, under **apartheid,** a legal system of racial domination, whites in South Africa were the dominant majority even though numerically they were in the minority.

Minority–majority distinctions often are based on sex, race, ethnicity, age, sexual orientation, and physical handicaps. In the next section, I explore sex and gender relations and how women, who numerically are a slight majority in most industrialized societies, are often in reality a dominated minority group. In this section, I focus on race and ethnic relations, although the theoretical ideas discussed subsequently can be applied to understanding many different types of minority–majority relationships.

What is race? What is the difference between race and ethnicity? **Race** is a category of people who share a biologically transmitted trait that members of a society view as socially significant. Race, though biologically and physically based, is a *social construct*. Therefore, when identifying racial groups, do not focus on some physical trait like skin color that distinguishes one racial group from another. Instead, look for situations in which people use a physical trait as a basis for differential treatment of people.

An **ethnicity** is a category of people who share a common cultural tradition. As a cultural entity, ethnic groups are distinguished by their different symbols, stories, and worldviews. You can identify ethnic groups by looking for people who share a common language, certain types of food, common ancestors, or a religion. In the United States, many of the ethnic distinctions people make are based on country of origin, reflected in names such as Polish Americans and Mexican Americans.

For a variety of reasons, sociologists use the terms *race* and *ethnicity* interchangeably. First, both race and ethnic distinctions are based on **ascribed traits** of people, characteristics that people cannot change. People are born with a certain skin color and born into a certain ethnic group. Though born into that group, people can change their ethnic identifications during their lifetimes. Second, race and ethnicity often become intertwined as racial groups that are singled out because of a physical trait develop their own culture. Finally, both race and ethnicity are often used as bases for distinguishing minorities from majorities.

Throughout the remainder of this volume, I talk about race–ethnic groups, though it should be kept in mind that race is different from ethnicity. Ethnicity is primarily a cultural distinction, and over time, ethnic differences can change and even disappear. But because race is based on a physical trait, it is virtually impossible to hide a racial identity. Although both are social constructs, racial differences are much more visible than ethnic differences.

Race and Ethnic Relations

The power of racial and ethnic majorities over dominated racial and ethnic minorities historically has taken many different forms: genocide, expulsion, slavery, and segregation. **Genocide,** the intentional extermination of one category of people by another category of people, is the most extreme form of domination. Genocide has been used to get rid of racial and ethnic groups whom the majority considered to be inferior and the cause of society's problems. Horrendous examples include Hitler's genocide against Jews and the more recent "ethnic cleansing" of Bosnian Muslims by Serbs. **Expulsion,** the forced removal of entire categories of people from a territory by another category of people, can lead to genocide. Mass expulsions were the fate that North American native peoples suffered as white Europeans marched across the continent and forced Native Americans onto reservations.

Slavery, the ownership of one category of people by another category of people, is one of the saddest and, until recently, one of the most common forms of domination. In the ancient world, slavery was commonplace. But the most extensive period of slavery began at the end of sixteenth century as Europeans brought slaves from Africa to the Americas and the islands of the Caribbean. By the time of the U.S. Civil War, 90 percent of the four million blacks in the United States were slaves. Slaves were treated as less than human, were bought and sold like farm animals, and were denied the freedoms that white people took for granted.

The abolition of slavery in the United States and in other countries did not end the differential treatment of racial and ethnic minorities. Today, **segregation,** the physical and social separation of categories of people, is the most prevalent form of domination. Segregation can and does occur in many different arenas: in housing, education, occupations, and public facilities. After the U.S. Civil War, freed African American slaves were dominated by white majorities through **de jure segregation,** separation created by laws and enforced by the police. Known as Jim Crow laws, many continued to exist into the 1970s. These laws were a major cause of the civil rights movement of the 1950s and 1960s, which sought to end segregation in the United States. Although today *de jure* segregation is itself illegal, there still remains **de facto segregation,** segregation created by unwritten norms that guide people's behavior and that result in actual separation. Such segregation is especially evident in both residential and occupational locations (King 1992; Massey and Denton 1993; Reskin and Cassirer 1997).

Despite the fact that the most extreme forms of racial and ethnic domination—genocide, expulsion, slavery and de jure segregation— are formally outlawed and less prevalent in modern societies, ethnic and racial domination is not a thing of the past. Unfortunately, race and ethnic divisions continue to be very important bases of social stratification and power in modern societies. However, today the mechanisms through which dominant racial and ethnic majorities exercise power over dominated minorities are less visible. In prior forms of domination, a majority's power was institutionalized through procedures, rules, and laws. As a result, how dominant majorities controlled dominated minorities was relatively transparent. In contrast, the mechanisms of contemporary segregation are more hidden. Because of this opacity, people tend to ignore the systematic ways in which discrimination occurs and to view existing segregation as just the result of antiquated ideas held by a few people. Although prejudice does continue to play an important role, to see racial and ethnic divisions fully, you need to look for other ways in which racial and ethnic minorities are disadvantaged.

Prejudice and Discrimination

Prejudices are attitudes of liking or disliking that involve a strong belief about an entire category of people. **Discrimination** refers to actions and practices by members of a dominant majority group that have a harmful impact on members of a dominated minority group. Prejudiced individuals are likely to discriminate, although laws and the actions of others may prevent them from doing so.

Prejudice often leads to discrimination because prejudices are based on *stereotypes*. You will recall from the discussion of gender stereotypes in Chapter 2 that stereotypes consist of a set of characteristics that are attributed to all group members. Stereotypes such as "Irish Americans are drinkers" or "Jews are shrewd" are inherently false. Why? Because stereotypes imply that everyone in a certain category has a trait, when in fact there can be as much variety within an ethnic or racial group as there is between groups. Stereotypes lead to rigid thinking. When social interaction is based on stereotypes, people prejudge others, leading to prejudice. As a result, they are likely to treat those about whom they have stereotypes differently.

One of the most powerful and destructive forms of prejudice is **racism,** the belief that those in certain racial or ethnic categories are innately superior and those in other race–ethnic categories are innately inferior. Racism is typically based on stereotypes that claim that some purported common trait, such as intelligence, motivation, or physical ability, is hereditary. Racist ideologies have justified the most atrocious forms of majority domination, such as genocide, expulsion, and slavery. They also continue to be the basis of contemporary prejudices that majority members have about minorities.

Discrimination can and does take many forms (Feagin and Feagin 1993). When people think of discrimination, they usually think of **isolate discrimination,** harmful action taken intentionally against a member of a subordinate group by an individual who is a member of a dominant group. But there is also **small-group discrimination,** harmful action taken intentionally by a small group of dominant group members in concert against members of a subordinate group. Lynchings, beatings, and firebombings are examples of this type of discrimination, a type that poses the most serious threats to the lives of minority group members. Usually, dominant group members within a community view this form of discrimination with disdain, although they may do little about it unless forced to by others.

Finally, there is *institutional discrimination* in both its direct and indirect forms. **Direct institutional discrimination** refers to organizationally or community prescribed actions that, by intention, have a negative impact on minority group members. This type of discriminating behavior is based on the policies and rules of communities or organizations, such as the Jim Crow laws in the South, which forbade blacks from using the same facilities as whites. But community practices do not have to be enacted into laws for this type of discrimination to occur. Country clubs that have never had a non-white member and banks that rarely finance home mortgages in residential areas with high proportions of non-whites are probably engaging in institutional discrimination even if these organizations have no formal policy stating that they treat minorities differently.

The least understood form of discrimination is **indirect institutional discrimination,** practices that have a harmful impact on subordinate group members even though organizational and community-prescribed norms and policies guiding these practices were established and carried out with no intent to harm minority group members. Often, people overlook this type of discrimination because it is *not* intentional. But actions and social policies can and often do have unintended consequences that result in minority group members being worse off. Usually, this occurs because of *past-in-present discrimination,* in which some past direct institutional discrimination continues to have a negative impact even though that discrimination is no longer practiced. For example, suppose an employer had discriminated against minorities by not hiring them but no longer does so. Suppose also that the employer bases promotions solely on seniority, that is, how long a person has been working for him. The result is that few minorities hold middle-level management positions, even though the employer has not intentionally discriminated against minorities in filling management jobs.

SEX AND GENDER

Like racial differences, the social significance of **sex** differences lies not in the biological and physical differences between men and women. Rather, to understand power differences and social inequalities between the sexes, you need to examine the **sexual division of labor,** the process through which tasks are assigned to people based on their sex. The sexual division of labor is evident in virtually every arena of social life (Renzetti and Curran 1995; Reskin and Padavic 1994). Within families, women tend to do the cooking and cleaning and men mow the lawn and pay the bills. Within workplaces, men are more likely to hold the jobs with greater authority and responsibility, and women are more likely to be secretaries and salesclerks (Reskin and Hartmann 1986; Reskin and Padavic 1994).

The sexual division of labor allocates not only tasks to different sexes, but also rights, responsibilities, and authority. According to the sexual division of labor, when men are given the right to make the major decisions in their families and in the public worlds of work and governance, a patriarchal system of social organization exists in which men have power over women. **Patriarchy** is often seen in family systems in which men control decision making, and inheritance occurs through the males of the family.

Patriarchy has many forms. One form is the **doctrine of separate spheres.** This doctrine stipulates that there should be a separation between work and family life and that each sex should be responsible for a separate sphere. Men are expected to work outside the home to support their families. Women, on the other hand, are expected to stay home and create a safe haven to which their husbands can retreat after working. In fact, under this patriarchal system, a husband is viewed as a failure if his wife works for pay outside the home (Davidoff and Hall 1987; Skolnick 1991).

As this doctrine became accepted around the turn of the twentieth century, employers refused to hire women, especially married women. Although women, notably poor women whose families needed the money to survive, still sought to work outside the home, the doctrine of separate spheres made this difficult. The result was sex-based inequalities (Reskin and Padavic 1994):

- Men's social status increased as their work outside the home was visible, whereas women's work inside the home remained invisible and not rewarded.
- Discrimination in hiring women became commonplace and legitimized as "protecting" women from working.
- When employers did hire women, they felt justified in paying them less because men were supposed to be supporting them.
- Employers reorganized work on the assumption that all employees would be men who could work full-time and who had stay-at-home wives. This assumption freed workers (who were men) from domestic responsibilities.

This form of patriarchy made women economically and socially dependent on men, increasing male power over women. In the past few decades, however, the doctrine of separate spheres has begun to weaken as more and more women, especially married women, enter the labor force. Today, 75 percent of working-aged men and 60 percent of women are in the labor force, resulting in a labor force consisting of 54 percent men and 46 percent women. But even as the labor force participation of women has increased, breaking down the separate spheres, the consequences of the doctrine of separate spheres remain. Women, for the most part, continue to do unpaid work in the home. And when women work, they tend to be paid less than men and to work in lower-status "female" occupations.

Gender

The sexual division of labor, including the doctrine of separate spheres, is maintained through *gendering,* a process I discussed in Chapter 1. As you will recall, **gender** is a socially constructed classification system that exaggerates the differences between men and women. When people use gender, they distinguish between *masculine* and *feminine* traits and behaviors, a process referred to as gendering. The result of gendering is gender roles, sets of behaviors, activities, and traits that are socially linked to each sex. Therefore, when analyzing situations, you need to look at how gender roles reinforce the sexual division of labor by specifying what behaviors are appropriate for men and women and how men and women are supposed to interact.

Where do our ideas about what is masculine and what is feminine come from? *Sex stereotypes,* the characteristics people associate with each sex, play an important role. For example, according to traditional stereotypes, men are viewed as aggressive, rational, outgoing, competitive, and independent. In contrast, women are stereotyped as nurturing, emotional, timid, cooperative, and dependent. As noted previously, when people use stereotypes to guide their behavior, usually unconsciously, they characterize others based solely on the stereotype. For example, consider a man who walks into a meeting room where two other people, a man and a woman, are talking and proceeds to ask the woman for some coffee. The man has assumed that the women is the other man's secretary. He has associated her sex with other characteristics, in this case occupational characteristics.

Sex stereotypes reinforce gender differences by encouraging people to make assumptions about other people based solely on their sex (Basow 1992). Sex stereotypes make it appear that a gender difference is not a social construct but a natural consequence of sex differences. When, for example, we stereotypically associate nurturing with women, we do not think of that association as a social construct, that is, as an idea that results from the process of gendering. Instead, we think of nurturing as a trait that all women naturally possess, and the only reason all women could possess that trait is because of their sex. Similarly, when we stereotype men as aggressive, we no longer think about aggression as a gender characteristic, as something our society associates with being a man and teaches men to be. Instead, we think of aggression as a trait of all men, linked somehow to men because of their physiology and biology.

The ultimate sex stereotype is **sexism,** the belief that one sex, usually men, is innately superior to the other sex. Sexism is more than just a set of prejudicial beliefs about men and women. According to sexist ideologies, the traits associated with masculinity and femininity are *unchangeable,* and the male traits are superior to female traits. Sexism, therefore, is often used to justify discrimination against women. For example, sexist ideas were employed not that long ago to deny women the right to vote. Women were stereotyped as emotional and irrational, unable to make informed decisions about who should represent them. Men, in contrast, were viewed as superior, rational beings who could decide what is in the best interests of women. Sexist ideologies are also used to justify patriarchy and sexual divisions of labor. Sexist views claim that the assignment of different tasks to men and women and the control by men of women's lives is natural and in the best interests of both men and women. In reality, however, sexism is an ideology that is used by men to maintain a sexual division of labor that is advantageous to them in the face of resistance by women.

Case Application

Now that you have a better understanding of power and inequality, how would you read the situation that Quill faces? You know where he stands—he does not want to admit Brenda Neville into the MPA program. But given the power structure of the situation, do you think he will have to admit her? What are the important social divisions in this case that are the bases of inequalities and power?

First and foremost, this case is about social classes. Alex Quill is in a contradictory class location. He is not an owner; he does not run the university, nor is he a financial contributor to the university. But Quill is not just an employee. As a professor, he has skills and knowledge that give him the ability to teach and conduct research, two things that are valuable at a university. Furthermore, as director of the MPA program, Quill is a mid-level manager. His formal position gives him the right to make many decisions about the program, including whom to admit. In all likelihood, he also supervises staff. Taken together, Quill's class position gives him a good deal of power, probably more power than your typical college professor.

Yet Quill's power is constrained by someone who has even more power—Provost George Stern. Stern's class position is one of a corporate executive and upper-level manager. As provost, he has a great deal of authority. He makes appointments, reviews departments, and, along with other university officers, allocates resources to programs, including Quill's MPA program. Stern cannot formally make decisions that have been delegated to lower-level units, such as the decision about whom to admit into a graduate program. However, he can question the criteria that are being used to make those decisions, and he can use his formal authority to get people to reconsider their decisions.

Typically, you would think that top executives and managers would not use their formal authority and power to undermine their subordinates. As managers, they want their units and organizations to thrive. Therefore, providing resources, assistance, and support to those in lower positions so that they can do their jobs is crucial. Then why is Stern questioning Quill's decision about Brenda Neville? Provosts purportedly want their academic units to have high academic standards. In fact, Quill operates under this assumption. When he first receives an inquiry about the Neville application, he assumes that he will be supported in his decision after upper-level managers know the details. This is why Quill is surprised when he is summoned by the provost.

The fact that the provost uses his power to question Quill's decision shows, therefore, that even his power is constrained. Above him lies the university's president, whose power also rests with his formal authority. And above both of them are those who provide resources to the university—the heads of the state government and the major donors and contributors, many of whom probably hold positions on this university's board of directors.

Sid Neville falls into this upper class. He is a wealthy businessman and alumnus who has been a generous donor to the athletic department. Southeastern State University needs his strategic resources, his money, to grow. That is why he is a primary target of the president's new fund-raising campaign. His resources give him the ability to ask the president and provost to look into his daughter's case and to see what can be done to get her into the MPA program.

Therefore, there are two social actors in this case who face dilemmas because of the power situation: Stern and Quill. Stern's quandary is whether to support or question Quill's decision to not admit Brenda Neville. On the one hand, Stern should be supporting Quill, but on the other hand, he knows how important generous donations are to the university. The fact that he does Neville's bidding and questions Quill's decision reveals how the ability of managers to realize their interests is intimately bound up with the power of owners and capitalists.

Quill's quandary is different. As director of the MPA program, he knows that Brenda should not be admitted, and he has the power to not admit her. But he also knows that the future of the MPA program rests in his ability to obtain resources, many of which are allocated by the provost's and president's office. But in contrast to Stern, Quill is not as quick to side with those who have power over him and admit Brenda. More removed from the centers of power, the wealthy donors and top officers of the university, Quill is seriously considering sticking to his guns and resisting the power of others. But what could be the costs of such resistance? Could his recalcitrance on this issue in the end cost him his own power? If Quill believes that he can maintain his power and continue to direct a flourishing MPA program even with reduced university resources, then he probably will resist the power of those above him. But no matter what Quill does, he now knows about the power of dominant social classes. In the future, he will have to take into account the class structure of the university as he seeks to advance his interests and the interests of the MPA program.

This class analysis of the MPA program case shows how important it is to examine the entire picture when analyzing inequalities and power. Often, actors who have power over others also have power being exercised over them. We would seriously misread Quill's power if we ignored the power that both Stern and Neville have. This multi-layered character of power results from the multidimensional character of social inequalities. Because there are many resources that increase people's capacity to realize their interests, inequalities along a whole range of social dimensions must be considered when analyzing situations.

In this case, I have taken into account inequalities in skills and knowledge, in formal authority, and in productive assets—that is, inequalities based on the three dimensions associated with social class differences. But in other cases and situations, other inequalities may be important, and sometimes even more important, especially inequalities based on race, ethnicity, and sex. These inequalities do not appear to be relevant in this case because segregation and separation grounded in either race–ethnicity or a sexual division of labor are not highlighted. The issue of admitting Brenda into the MPA program has little to do with the fact that Brenda is a woman, and we have no idea about her racial and ethnic identity. No one argues that she should be admitted because as a woman she is a member of a minority that has historically been underrepresented in MPA programs.

Even though race and sex inequalities are not at the forefront of this case, a closer look reveals that the sexual division of labor could be playing an important role. All the central actors in this case are men: Sid Neville, George Stern, and Alex Quill. Why? Is this just a coincidence, or is this a typical pattern in academia? How would this situation have differed if Stern and/or Quill had been a woman? Because we know little about the sexual division of labor at this university, we should not speculate about its effects in this case. But a thorough analysis of this situation would require you to analyze the different roles men and women, and probably people of color as well, play within this university.

THEORIES OF INEQUALITY

So far, in analyzing inequalities in the MPA case I have focused on inequalities of power. But there is another set of inequalities in this case, the inequalities that are created by Quill's committee admitting some students and not others into the MPA program. A valued good—the opportunity to be in Southeastern's MPA program—is being distributed unequally. Some will get into the program, others will not. But what criteria should be used to decide who will and who will not receive this opportunity? For Quill, admitting Brenda Neville would change the criteria. Instead of prior accomplishments such as GPA and GRE scores, Quill is being asked to favor those students whose parents are well-connected. Quill thinks this is unfair, and that is why, in part, he is resisting Stern's pressure. Quill, like most of us, believes that some inequalities are fair, others are not, and that what determines whether they are fair is the *criteria* that are used to generate the inequalities.

Therefore, it is important in any situation to assess how valued goods—rewards, resources, and opportunities—are distributed. As you will see, there are a variety of mechanisms through which rewards, resources, and opportunities are unequally distributed. Your ability to identify the bases of inequalities in real-life situations will be enhanced, therefore, by examining various *theories* of inequalities.

Most of the bases of inequalities considered subsequently we would consider to be unfair. Why? Because the distribution criterion is an *ascriptive* trait. You will recall that such traits are characteristics that individuals through their own actions cannot change. Sex and race are among the two most important ascribed traits. When an ascribed trait is used as a criterion for distributing resources and opportunities, the result is discrimination. However, there are many ways in which inequalities are generated through discrimination. It is important, therefore, in situations in which discrimination is evident to not just note *who* is discriminated against but also to examine *how* discrimination is occurring. But before I explore theories concerning the causes of sex and race discrimination, let us first look at three general theories of inequalities.

General Theories of Inequality

Sociologists have identified three different processes through which inequalities are created: just rewards, social closure, and exploitation.

Just rewards. According to this structural–functionalist theory, inequalities are necessary to induce people to do important jobs and acquire the skills needed for those jobs (Davis and Moore 1945). Inequalities are seen as performing a valuable function—they motivate people to do important types of work. Because important jobs tend to be more difficult and to require sacrifices to obtain needed skills, people are unlikely to take these jobs unless there are sufficient inducements that compensate people for the costs of obtaining skills and working hard.

This is why, according to *human capital theory,* education and skills are positively related to earnings (Becker 1964). **Human capital,** skills and abilities that allow a person to do specific tasks, is accumulated by people making investments in themselves, investments that increase their productivity. Going to school, taking training courses, and obtaining skills through on-the-job experience are all ways in which people increase their human capital. Whether rational actors make such investments depends on the return on their investments. For example, schooling has costs, such as tuition, living expenses, and forgone earnings (the earnings people do not obtain while they are going to school). Only when the higher wages resulting from going to school are greater than the costs incurred through schooling will a rational actor invest in schooling.

Inequalities for both structural functionalists and human capital theorists are, therefore, the just rewards for individual contributions and sacrifices. If organizations and institutions did not distribute rewards unequally, people would not have an incentive to hold important jobs, to acquire skills, and to make human capital investments.

From this perspective, it is important in a situation characterized by inequalities to examine the extent to which unequal distributions are being used to induce people to do things that have significant costs associated with them. In particular, it is important to assess the extent to which observed inequalities result from the accomplishments and achievements of individuals. Both these theories focus attention on situations in which the criteria for distributing rewards are **achieved traits,** that is, individual characteristics such as education, skill level, and job experience, which people are able to change through their efforts.

In any given situation, however, it is difficult to determine how much of observed inequalities are really due to differences among people that deserve differential rewards. It is tempting to assume after the fact that unequal rewards are deserved, or even to claim that inequalities demonstrate differential contributions. However, although some inequalities may be needed as inducements, many inequalities are so large that you should question whether they are solely the result of the need for incentives. Furthermore, what are the more important jobs that must be performed (Tumin 1953)? If sanitation workers did not pick up trash and high school teachers did not teach, there would be major social problems. Yet these jobs are not compensated at a level anywhere near other important jobs such as doctors and lawyers. These cautions remind us that we should not assume that observed inequalities are just rewards; there often are other causes of inequalities.

Social closure. Another way in which inequalities are produced is by restricting who can exchange and interact with whom. Consider a labor market in which employers pay employees in exchange for work. You would expect employees to make more when there are many employers but a limited supply of employees. Therefore, to the extent that social actors can limit labor supplies by restricting access to certain lines of work, they are likely to make more than those working in jobs in which access is not restricted.

More generally, inequalities are created by **social closure**—the restriction of access to resources and opportunities to a limited set of eligible people (Parkin 1979). Social closure increases inequalities by increasing the value of the good whose access is restricted and by distributing that good to only those who are in the pool of eligible people (Sorensen and Kalleberg 1981). A classic example of social closure is the medical profession (Larson 1977). Restricting the number of doctors by restricting the number of medical school positions increases the value of being a doctor. And because not everyone can be a doctor, but only those who are admitted to and graduate from medical school, this valued good is distributed unequally. Only those who are in the eligibility pool, that is, those who have gone to medical school, can be doctors.

The social closure achieved by the medical profession is an instance of credentialing. A **credential** is a symbol given by a person, group, organization, or governmental agency to an individual to indicate that he or she can now do something that others without that credential cannot do. Course prerequisites and licenses are examples of credentials. But the most important credentials are usually educational credentials. Credentials result in inequalities to the extent that the credential significantly limits the pool of people (Berg 1970; Collins 1979). At one time, a high school diploma generated inequality. Because only a limited number of people had that educational credential and employers used it to select workers, high school diplomas were valuable. Today, however, that credential is not very valuable because it does not restrict the pool of job applicants very much. Instead, college and various professional degrees are more valuable credentials.

The implication is that credentials lead to inequalities not because of the skills and education obtained in getting the credential but because of the limited number of people who have the credential. If too many people have a credential, the credential becomes worthless, even if those with the credential have acquired useful skills.

Credentialing and social closure create inequalities by restricting opportunities. Only those who have a credential and, therefore, are in the pool of eligibles can compete for some valued position or resource. By limiting the pool of people who have the opportunity to compete, social closure increases the value of the position over which there is competition. For example, purportedly an MPA degree is a valuable credential, and that is why Sid Neville wants his daughter to have one. With an MPA, Brenda will have the opportunity to compete for jobs that only a limited number of people can have.

When analyzing a situation, it is important, therefore, to assess the extent to which inequalities are generated by restrictions of opportunities. Is the ability to use some resource or hold a position restricted? If so, what are the criteria that are used to restrict access? What credential do people have to obtain to be in the eligible pool? And what do people have to do to obtain that credential?

Exploitation. A final perspective on inequality focuses on how some people are better off because others are worse off. The classical example of this cause of inequalities is thievery. When a thief steals from a victim, the thief is better off as a result of the victim becoming worse off. With thievery, there is a transfer of value from the victim, who initially possessed and maybe even created the valued goods, to the thief. Thievery also can be a collective phenomenon, as when conquerors expropriate and colonize foreign lands.

Thievery is just one example of how inequalities are created through **exploitation,** the process through which some social actors become better off *because* other social actors become worse off (Wright 1985). Other forms of exploitation include slavery and feudalism. Under slavery, slave owners appropriate slave labor and use it to produce goods and services for their benefit. Under feudalism, lords exploit serfs by requiring them to give a set proportion of their agricultural produce to their lord.

Analyses of exploitative inequalities, therefore, focus on how value created by one class of people, the producers, is transferred to another class of people, the nonproducers, those who did not create that value. The core idea is that people, through their productive activities, can produce more than they consume, that is, they can produce surpluses. When producers control the surplus that they have created, they can do with it what they want. They can increase their standard of living by increasing consumption. They can invest it by purchasing more means of production, allowing them to be more productive, or to expand production, thereby increasing future surpluses.

The historical reality, however, is that often the producers of surpluses do not control their use. Why? Because nonproducers own something that leads to a *transfer* of the surplus from producers to nonproducers. In the case of thievery, nonproducers physically take what producers have produced or acquired, often through the use of force. In slavery, masters own slaves, entitling them to the surplus slaves produced. And in feudalism, lords own land that they allow serfs to till in exchange for transferring the surplus to their lord. This transfer usually occurs through charging serfs rent or requiring them to pay a tax. Lords can enforce this transfer because they own the land. If peasants refuse to pay, they are denied the ability to grow the crops that their families need.

According to this theory, capitalism is also a system of exploitation because there is a transfer of surpluses from producer employees to nonproducer employers. Although we usually do not think of paid employment as a form of rent as in feudalism, as economists and sociologists have shown, the wage relationship is like rent (Roemer 1982; Wright 1985). Workers work a given number of hours for their employer, in which time they produce marketable goods and services. Employers could divide all the produced goods into two piles, and give some of these goods to their workers and keep the rest for themselves as rent. Instead, most employers just pay workers wages. These wages are equivalent to the goods in the first pile, the goods an employer could have given the worker instead of giving him or her wages. The result is that the employer retains the monetary equivalent of the goods in the second pile—the surplus. Wages, according to this perspective, do not represent the full value of all that workers produce. Part of that value has been siphoned off as a hidden rent, resulting in a transfer of the surplus from workers to owners.

In any given situation, therefore, it is important to examine not just how some valued resource is *distributed* but also how things are *produced*. Through production, surpluses can and often are generated. Accordingly, it is important to examine the criterion used to distribute created surpluses.

According to this perspective on inequality, the crucial criterion for surplus distribution is *ownership*. Transfers of the surplus from producers to nonproducers and, therefore, the unequal distributions of surpluses, are generated by differential ownership of people, land, and means of production. What this means is that in situations in which there are inequalities, it is important to identify who owns and controls the assets that people use to produce the goods and services that they need to survive on a daily basis. Those who own those assets typically control the surplus, because without those assets, nonowner producers would not be able to produce those goods and services.

Of course, not all inequalities are generated by exploitation, just as not all inequalities are generated by social closure or inducement systems. But there is a tendency to overlook exploitative inequalities in social situations. People tend to think that inequalities are exploitative only when someone consciously and intentionally takes advantage of another person, such as through the use of force. But as you have seen, exploitative situations have more to do with how social actors are connected as they produce surpluses than with evil intentions. Instead of examining individual intentions to ascertain whether exploitation is occurring, you should look at whether and how resources have been transferred from those that produced them to others.

Theories of Discrimination

Discrimination occurs when unequal distributions of resources and opportunities based on ascribed characteristics such as sex and race negatively affect members of minority groups. Sometimes, discrimination results from prejudicial individuals using an ascribed trait when deciding how to treat others and distribute rewards and resources. Yet, as you have seen, not all discrimination is intentional. By examining a variety of theories of discrimination, you will be better able to analyze how discrimination is occurring in specific situations.

Prejudice and attitudes. An obvious form of discrimination is that which results from the prejudicial attitudes of dominant group members. Those who hold sexist or racist ideas tend to treat women and people of color differently. In the case of sex inequalities, sexism is evident in the traditional idea of **paternalism,** the idea that women, like children, are inferior creatures in need of protection. In the case of race and ethnic inequalities, racism is seen in cultural stereotypes that claim that racial and ethnic groups differ in their essential qualities.

When does prejudice lead to discrimination? Under what conditions are people more likely to be prejudiced? According to *scapegoat theory,* prejudiced people are more likely to discriminate when members of the majority are frustrated. Unable to vent their frustration against the real causes of their grievances, members of the dominant group seek out **scapegoats,** people or a category of people whom other people unfairly blame for their problems (Dollard et al. 1937). Often, such scapegoats are members of racial or ethnic minorities.

Another theory argues that prejudices are stronger among those with *authoritarian personalities* (Adorno et al. 1950). Such people are more conformist, submissive, insecure, and intolerant. Individuals who are socialized into roles during childhood in an authoritarian fashion are, according to this perspective, more likely to hold prejudicial views about those who are different from themselves.

Finally, social psychological research shows that contact between racial and ethnic groups can either increase or decrease prejudice (Allport 1958; Lieberson 1980). When contact is among those with equal status and involves cooperation, interaction decreases prejudice. However, when contact is among unequals and involves competition, prejudices and stereotypes are reinforced.

It is important, therefore, when examining race and sex inequalities, to first ascertain the extent to which prejudicial attitudes are producing inequalities. Are people expressing racist or sexist ideas as justifications for their actions? But it is also important to examine the social conditions that could be breeding prejudice. Are prejudicial individuals themselves aggrieved and scapegoating others? Are certain types of people exhibiting prejudicial views? What are the conditions under which majorities and minorities are interacting? Are these conditions reinforcing stereotypes or undermining them?

Systematic oppression and marginalization. Race and sex inequalities also can be the result of a *system* of discrimination that creates racial or sexual segregation. An especially egregious form of systematic discrimination is **internal colonization,** the situation in which members of a conquered minority are economically and politically controlled by a majority group (Hechter 1974). Internally colonized people are forced to reside in a society they do not choose, are excluded from becoming part of the dominant society, and encounter attempts by the dominant group to destroy their culture. The result of internal colonization is a segmented society divided into a thriving core and a marginalized periphery consisting of ethnic and racial minorities. Internal colonization often leads to a **caste system,** a stratification system in which a person's lifelong status is determined at birth based on his or her parents' ascribed characteristics. In such systems, there is no possibility for *social mobility,* for moving from a lower social status in the marginalized periphery to a higher status in the prosperous core.

Sex inequalities are also generated through systematic means that marginalize women through exclusion. The doctrine of separate spheres discussed earlier was institutionalized in the early 1900s with the *family wage system* (Hartmann 1979; Kessler-Harris 1990; King 1992). Under this system, men are paid a wage for working outside the home designed to support both the male breadwinner and his family. In exchange for this higher wage, women are excluded from the labor force or are paid much lower wages for similar types of work. Men benefit as the competition for their jobs is reduced by excluding women. And employers benefit because "free" labor at home by women means that they do not have to pay male workers as much. Women, on the other hand, are exploited. Restricted in their ability to work outside the home, they are forced to do unpaid and less valued work inside the home.

As more and more women entered the labor force after World War II, the family wage system underwent changes. Instead of exclusion from working outside the home, women today are more likely to be excluded from certain types of work and jobs. Sometimes this occurs through the creation of *split labor markets,* situations in which there are two groups of workers whose price of labor differs for the same work (Bonacich 1972). An example is waiters and waitresses. Male waiters tend to be employed in upscale restaurants, whereas women waitresses work in diners. By excluding women and decreasing competition for their jobs, men create an undersupply of labor leading to higher wages. Women, on the other hand, are pushed into jobs for which there is an oversupply of labor, resulting in lower wages.

Another way in which women are excluded from certain types of jobs is through *occupational sex segregation,* the tendency of women to be disproportionately overrepresented in some occupations and underrepresented in other occupations (Hooks 1947; Reskin and Hartmann 1986; Reskin and Padavic 1994). There are many causes of occupational sex segregation. Sometimes, women choose to enter certain occupations, viewing that type of work as more compatible with their gender. But more often than not occupational sex segregation is the result of discriminatory practices of employers who, sometimes intentionally but often unintentionally, use hiring practices that exclude women from learning about or being seriously considered for a job (Reskin and Padavic 1994).

Split labor markets and occupational segregation also occur along racial and ethnic lines (Farley and Allen 1987; King 1992). Throughout American history, white workers, most often men, have excluded people of color from jobs because they believed that their wages would be undermined by the influx of minorities: European immigrants at the turn of the twentieth century, Japanese and Chinese immigrants on the West Coast, African Americans who migrated North in the 1920s and 1930s looking for work, or most recently Mexican immigrants (Feagin and Feagin 1993; Marger 1997). The combined effects of race–ethnic and sex segregation in labor markets have created additional obstacles for women of color (Jones 1985).

Internal colonization, the family wage system, split labor markets, and occupational segregation are all ways in which economic and social class privileges are preserved through exclusionary discrimination. Under these forms of oppression, racial and sexual inequalities are the direct result of racial and sexual discrimination practiced by the dominant majority. However, as William Julius Wilson shows in the case of race, sometimes systematic discrimination that marginalizes members of a minority does not result from the exclusionary practices of those in the majority (Wilson 1978, 1987). Wilson refers to this type of discrimination as **structural discrimination,** inequalities that result from the normal and usual functioning of socioeconomic systems and not from the prejudicial attitudes or discriminatory laws and practices of the dominant social groups.

One of Wilson's examples of structural discrimination is the racial inequality resulting from the *spatial mismatch* between where jobs are located and where minority people live. Deindustrialization during the 1970s and 1980s resulted in the loss of good-paying manufacturing jobs and the economic decline of central city areas, especially in the Rust Belt (Bluestone and Harrison 1982). Although the service sector grew, its jobs tend to be located in suburban areas. The result is that those who reside in central city areas, who happen to be disproportionately African Americans, encounter substantial difficulties in finding work. These are the people who become, according to Wilson, the black underclass. This marginalized class is impoverished not because its members are black, though prejudice and discrimination still exist, but because they reside in a place where there are few jobs and opportunities.

Therefore, it is important when examining inequalities to analyze the whole range of ways in which race–ethnic minorities and women are systematically marginalized. Is marginalization the result of exclusionary practices of dominant majorities designed to secure and maintain their privileges? If so, how is such social closure maintained? Is there evidence of colonization, split labor markets, special wage systems, and/or occupational segregation? Is there any evidence that inequalities are the result of the normal functioning of social and economic systems?

Statistical discrimination. Economists argue that the costs of discrimination discourage rational actors, such as employers, from discriminating (Becker 1957). Employers who do not hire women or people of color are excluding potentially productive employees. As such, nondiscriminating employers benefit because they can employ the productive workers whom other discriminating employers refuse to hire. Because discriminators are at a competitive disadvantage, they should go out of business.

However, employers and other agents such as loan officers and realtors continue to discriminate. Why? A number of answers have been proposed. Sometimes, agents discriminate not because they are prejudiced, but because of the prejudices of customers, employees, peers, or people in their community (Merton 1949). Employers may discriminate if they fear that hiring or promoting people of color or women will drive away prejudiced customers or offend majority or male workers.

Rational actors also may practice **statistical discrimination,** the treatment of an individual on the basis of characteristics believed to be typical for the group to which the individual belongs (Arrow 1973; Bielby and Baron 1986). Why? Sometimes employers, so the argument goes, face uncertainty about whether potential employees will be productive and will remain with the employer. If, based on past experience and statistics, an employer knows that people in a certain group are on average more productive and less likely to quit, then it is rational for him to hire people from those groups.

According to this theory, statistical discrimination often disadvantages women because employers believe that women are more likely than men to leave the labor force and more likely to miss work because of household responsibilities. Although an individual woman may be just as likely to quit or miss work as an individual man, an employer does not know in advance whether a female job candidate is or is not like the "average" woman. Without more information, an employer will discriminate and hire the man over the woman. Although rational from the point of view of the employer, the result is discrimination based on membership in a specific group.

The extent to which sex and racial inequalities in employment and earnings are the result of statistical discrimination is hotly debated (Reskin and Roos 1990). The statistical discrimination argument assumes that employers and other economic agents face uncertainties and that the costs of decreasing uncertainty by acquiring more information are too high. But often there is little uncertainty or there are relatively inexpensive ways to decrease uncertainty. Nevertheless, this perspective implies that it is important when analyzing unequal situations to look at how other agents who do not directly benefit from the inequality and who themselves do not hold prejudicial attitudes may still in fact use ascribed traits as criteria for distributing resources and opportunities.

Assimilation. Race and ethnic inequalities also can be the result of **assimilation,** the process by which a minority is integrated gradually into the dominant majority culture. In contrast to the other theories that I have discussed, this theory is used only to explain race and ethnic discrimination and, in particular, the experiences of race and ethnic *immigrant* groups (Gordon 1964; Sowell 1981). Initially, because a minority group does not fit into the dominant culture, its members find it more difficult to do the things that majority members do. Language and cultural barriers impede holding jobs and getting an education. Tensions and conflicts occur between minorities and majorities because they speak different languages and are unfamiliar with each other's customs. But as assimilation proceeds, inequalities and tensions subside as minorities shed their past and become integrated into the dominant culture. According to this perspective, persisting inequalities are explained by the incomplete assimilation of a minority group.

For some minorities, incomplete assimilation is the result of their recent immigration. Still in the process of assimilating, first- and second-generation immigrants face difficulties that put them at a real disadvantage. But for third- and fourth-generation immigrants, incomplete assimilation is more likely to be the result of failed assimilation resulting from either the actions of the minority or the actions of the majority. Minorities may not want to shed their heritage and may view their traditional ways as a strength instead of a liability. Majorities, on the other hand, may block assimilation by preventing minorities from assimilating through discriminatory practices in workplaces and schools. Whatever the cause of failed assimilation, the result is a minority population whose members are unable to participate fully in the society in which they live.

There is much controversy over whether inequalities are really caused by failed assimilation. There is a tendency with this perspective to "blame the victim" by attributing inequalities to the unwillingness of nonnative peoples to change their ways (Ryan 1975). Nevertheless, this perspective does highlight the importance of examining the extent to which there have or have not been changes over time in the interconnections between majority and minority individuals. Are members of a minority now more able to speak with those in the majority? Have there been changes in the degree to which members of a minority interact with members of the dominant culture in schools, workplaces, and places of worship? Are minority group members now more likely to marry those in other racial or ethnic groups? And if there has not been much change, what is impeding social interaction?

Constrained choices. The final perspective on inequality focuses on how the constrained choices of people, especially women, can contribute to inequalities. According to human capital theory, occupational sex segregation is in part the result of the rational choices women make (Mincer and Ofek 1982; Polachek 1981). Why? The theory is that women are less likely to enter certain occupations because of the "penalties" associated with temporarily withdrawing from the labor force. In some occupations, previously acquired skills quickly become "rusty," requiring people to relearn them (at some cost) upon reentering the labor force. Accordingly, women who want to maximize lifetime earnings and who expect to leave the labor force for some period of time should choose occupations in which skills do not become rusty with nonuse and in which, therefore, the penalty for withdrawing from the labor force is less.

Although this theory seems plausible, the evidence for it is weak (England 1984; England et al. 1988). It is difficult to ascertain whether skills become rusty with nonuse. Although research has shown that women are penalized with lower earnings for leaving the labor force, it also has been shown that the penalties are the same whether a woman works in a male or female occupation. Male occupations do not have higher penalties for labor force withdrawal, and, therefore, higher penalties cannot, as human capital theory expects, be dissuading women from entering those occupations.

Although the evidence for the human capital explanation of occupational sex segregation is weak, this perspective does highlight an important factor that needs to be taken into account when examining sex inequalities. Women, in particular married women with children, face greater constraints on their labor market activities than do men. These constraints originate outside the world of work and from the unequal household division of labor, which makes women primarily responsible for child care and household tasks. These constraints affect women's behaviors, including their decisions about whether to work outside the home and whether to work full-time or part-time (Presser 1995; Reskin and Padavic 1994). Although at first glance it appears that inequalities are the result of women's choices, in reality the causes of these inequalities are the constraints that force women to make these choices.

The general point is that inequalities in one social arena can and often do create inequalities in other social arenas. Inequalities in the household division of labor affect women's choices in the world of employment. Residential segregation and housing inequalities constrain the choices people of color have about where their children go to school. Discrimination by high school counselors constrains the choices women and racial minorities have about their occupational careers. Therefore, in analyzing situations, it is important to study not just the inequalities that are evident in a situation. You also need to explore how other inequalities, either from a prior point in time or in another social arena, are currently affecting people's choices.

SOCIOLOGICAL EYE ANALYSIS GUIDE

Power differentials and inequalities are evident in many situations. As you have seen in the "MPA Program at Southeastern State University" case, recognizing social divisions can help you better understand the dilemmas people face. Often, social actors, as a result of their social connections, have an interest in some outcome but lack the capacity to realize their interests. Confronted by other social actors who have more power, they even may be forced to do things that are not in their interest. By identifying social classes, analyzing race and ethnic minority–majority relations, and examining sexual divisions of labor, you can determine who has power and why, and better understand the quandaries people face when inequalities are present.

Because social class, race–ethnic, and sex-based inequalities affect what people can do, it is important to ascertain how inequalities are produced. Theories of inequality, including both general theories and theories of discrimination, direct attention toward the *criteria* that are being used to distribute valued resources, rewards, and opportunities. By determining what those criteria are and analyzing how they are being used to generate inequalities, you can understand the social, economic, and political conditions that perpetuate and reinforce inequalities.

Analyzing power and inequalities is, therefore, another important way in which you can situate events within a larger context. As with cultural analysis, analysis of power and inequalities helps you understand the background conditions that make the actions, interactions, and social connections among social actors possible. But to understand the context fully, you also need to imagine how those background conditions could change. So far, when analyzing cases and situations, we have focused on what is and what has been. But you also need to explore what could be and what could change. In the next chapter, you will learn how to construct scenarios of the future by exploring driving forces that propel social change. But for now, what is important is your ability to see social divisions and to situate cases by analyzing power and inequalities. So use the following Sociological Eye Analysis Guide to map out who has power and to determine how and why resources, rewards, and opportunities are unequally distributed.

Interests and Power

- ❑ Who are the key actors in this situation? What are their interests? What do they want or need? What is their stand on the central issue of this case?
- ❑ Who has power? Rank order the key actors in terms of their power. What events indicate to you that there is this distribution of power?

Seeing Social Classes

- ❑ What are the important productive assets in this situation and why are these assets important? What groups or individuals have controlling ownership of these assets?

❏ Who has authority? Who is involved in making important decisions, and how are they so involved? Who is responsible for directing, monitoring, and evaluating the behavior of others?

❏ What are the important activities and tasks being performed in this situation? Are special skills needed to do these tasks? Who has these skills?

❏ Based on your analysis of ownership, authority, and skills, how would you describe the class structure of the situation? Who are the capitalists, the managers, the experts, the supervisors, and the workers? Which positions in this situation would you characterize as contradictory class locations?

Seeing Race and Ethnicity

❏ Which categories of people are a minority, and which groups are majorities? What ascribed trait is being used to distinguish minorities from majorities?

❏ How would you characterize the race and ethnic relations evident in this situation? Is there evidence of segregation and separation? If so, in what social arenas (work, family and friends, education, religion, housing, politics and government) is segregation evident? In the past, has the majority dominated the minority in other ways? If so, what were these ways?

❏ Are people expressing prejudicial views? If so, who is expressing these views, and what prejudices and stereotypes do they have?

❏ Is there evidence of discrimination? Have members of the minority group been harmed by the actions and practices of those in the majority? If so, what forms of discrimination (isolate, small-group, direct institutional, or indirect institutional) are evident in this situation? Are there any indicators of unintentional practices that nevertheless harm those in the minority?

Seeing Sex and Gender

☐ How would you characterize the sexual division of labor? Do men and women do different tasks and hold different positions? In this situation, are men more likely than women to make the important decisions?

☐ Is there any evidence of the doctrine of separate spheres? Are women more likely to be found in the private, family sphere? Are men more likely to play roles in the public spheres of work and politics?

☐ Is gendering occurring in this situation? What gender traits are being emphasized, and how would you describe the important gender roles?

☐ Are sexist attitudes evident in this situation? Who holds sexist views, and what sex stereotypes do they have?

General Theories of Inequality

☐ What valued goods—resources, rewards, opportunities— are being distributed? Who is distributing them? What criteria are people using to decide who does and does not get these goods?

Inequalities as Just Rewards

☐ Are valued goods being distributed to induce people to do things they might not otherwise do? What are the things that a group, organization, or social institution is trying to get people to do through the use of incentives? What incentives are they using?

☐ Are people making sacrifices for which they are being compensated, and, if so, what are these sacrifices?

☐ To what extent are the achieved characteristics of people being used as distribution criteria?

Inequalities as Social Closure

❏ Is there any evidence that the pool of eligible people who can receive some valued resource or opportunity is restricted? If so, how is access limited, and what criteria are being used to determine who can be in the pool? Who is excluded and who is included in the eligibility pool?

❏ Are credentials important in this situation? Who gives the credential, and what do people have to do to obtain the credential? Why is the credential needed? What things can people not do (or not gain access to) without the credential? To what extent does the credential delimit the pool of eligible people? How imbalanced is supply and demand because of the use of the credential?

Inequalities as Exploitation

❏ In this situation, are some people worse off because other people are better off? If so, which groups of people are worse off and which ones are better off?

❏ Are surpluses being generated? Who are the producers of the surplus? Do the producers control the distribution of the surplus?

❏ Is some of the surplus transferred from producers to nonproducers? Who are the nonproducers who receive some of the surpluses generated by others? What do the nonproducers own that gives them control over surplus distribution, and how does ownership of those assets give them such control?

Theories of Discrimination

Prejudice

❏ Are people expressing racist or sexist views as justifications for their behaviors or when interpreting other people's behaviors?

❏ Is there any evidence that some people are being scapegoated? Who are the scapegoats, and who is doing the scapegoating? For what problem are people being scapegoated?

❏ Are certain types of people expressing prejudicial views? What distinguishes those who are doing so from those who are not?

❏ On what basis are majority and minority group members coming into contact with each other? Is there evidence of competition or cooperation? Do those in the minority group hold similar (equal) or different (unequal) positions than those in the majority?

Oppression and Marginalization

❏ To what extent are members of race–ethnic groups or women marginal social actors in this situation? Can you identify core and peripheral segments? Are women and people of color more likely to be found in peripheral positions?

❏ Is marginalization the result of the exclusionary practices of dominant majorities? If so, what privileges are members of the majority attempting to secure and maintain for themselves through exclusion?

❏ How do those in the majority exclude minority group members? Is there any evidence of colonization? Are people receiving different rewards for the same type of work as in a split labor market? Have special compensation systems been devised that restrict what women and people of color can do? Is there any evidence of occupational segregation?

❏ To what extent are marginalization and inequalities the result of the normal and usual functioning of organizations and social institutions? What is the history of those who are marginalized? What historical events and processes created the current marginalized situation in which people now find themselves?

Statistical Discrimination

☐ Are those who do not hold prejudicial views discriminating? To what extent are the prejudices of others leading them to discriminate? Who are these other people, and how are their prejudicial views affecting the discriminating agent?

☐ To what extent does this situation involve uncertainty about people's qualities and abilities? How are those involved in distributing valued goods dealing with such uncertainties? Is there any evidence of statistical discrimination (that is, the use of a group characteristic instead of an individual characteristic as a distribution criterion because of uncertainty about which individuals have the desired individual trait)?

Assimilation

☐ Are minority group members immigrants or children of immigrants? To what extent have immigrants and their children assimilated into their new society? How well do they know the native language and customs? To what extent do minority group members interact with those in the majority in workplaces, schools, neighborhoods, and religious organizations? How much intermarriage is there between the minority and majority groups? Do immigrants think of themselves as belonging to a minority, or do they think of themselves as members of the majority?

☐ Is the immigrant group more or less assimilated today? If more, what is enhancing assimilation? If less, what is impeding it? Are minority group members resisting assimilation? Are majority group members blocking it?

Constrained Choice

☐ Are people not taking advantage of opportunities that they formally have? If so, what are the opportunities? What must people do to take advantage of these opportunities? Are there prior and/or other current situations that people face that are making it difficult for them to take advantage of these opportunities?

❑ When making choices, do those in the minority have to take into account things that those in the majority do not have to take into account? What are these things, and how are they affecting people's choices? Are the choices that are being made by minority group members in one social arena constrained by the practices in other social arenas of those in the majority?

Decision Case: "Robert Lopez"

Last summer, I got the opportunity to be a teaching assistant for an incoming group of freshman minority scholarship students in the Opportunity Program. The university designed the program as a sort of "Head Start" for college. It was a commitment not to abandon these promising minority students who had made it this far to a top research university. For me, a second-generation Mexican American, half Anglo and half Mexican, it was a real opportunity to begin to help some younger students perform better academically and to come to terms with a predominantly white culture as well as chance to face my own cultural roots in a positive way.

This was important to me because my own family history shielded me from dealing with my Mexican heritage. When my father attended the University of California, Berkeley, in the late 1940s, there was no such thing as "multiculturalism." The only perceived option for him, I suppose, was to integrate, to be like white men. Needless to say, although he worked overtime trying to, my father never achieved "white" status. It was the source of constant feelings of inadequacy for him and for us as a family, where he exercised what little power he did have. As a consequence, my mother, sister, brother, and I received the angry projections of my father's frustration with trying to fit in and be promoted at a large white multinational corporation. The company had conveniently "ghettoized" him into Third World sales.

We all were deprived, it seems to me now, of the other half of our cultural heritage. The only Spanish spoken in the house was between my father and grandfather, when my grandfather stayed with us. My brother, sister, and I grew up in white middle- and upper-middle-class

AUTHOR'S NOTE: This case was developed by Mitchell Dean Diaz. It is part of the collection *Case Studies for Faculty Development* created by Rita Silverman and William M. Welty through the Center for Case Studies in Education at Pace University.

neighborhoods, thinking we were white, with only faint reminders that there was something different about us. My basketball and football teammates in junior high referred to me affectionately, I then thought, as "Taco." My older sister and I obtained our early, formative schooling on the west and east coasts, but my brother started school in Texas. He was put in remedial education courses even though at 13 he could build radios and repair motorcycles, literally from scratch. He dropped out of school before finishing the 10th grade. My choice of sociology as a profession was a conscious one that I slowly came to after years of questing, which began after the death of my father when I was 16.

My job last summer, which required special training and weekly meetings, entailed reinforcing the content of a beginning sociology course being taken by some of the students in the Opportunity Program. I was to help them develop better study techniques as part of the overall design of the program to improve their academic skills. I was to work with these students in a special discussion section of a regular sociology course. The discussion section met twice each week, instead of once, and I was to help them with effective note taking, text reading, exam preparation, small-group discussion, time management, and so forth. It was my first real opportunity to teach and to try to act on my ideas about how education could empower minority students.

I was assigned as a special teaching assistant (TA) for an Introduction to Sociology class taught by Uma Gidwani, an Indian woman in the last stages of completing her dissertation at Southwest University. She had chosen a conflict-oriented text and expressed as one of her objectives that we would deal candidly with issues of class, race, and gender inequality. She decided that it would be better if she did not have a second TA for the rest of the class, believing that to do so might give the impression that she was advocating "separate but equal" practices in the classroom—a TA for minorities and another one for the rest of the students. We also decided that we would not inform nonminority or nonscholarship minority members in the class that the scholarship minority students had a special TA. I was to sit in class, take notes, and generally keep a low profile, volunteering only an occasional clarifying question for the benefit of students.

As the class progressed through the shortened summer term, things seemed to be going well. My Opportunity students were performing as well as I expected, and I was proud of them. As a group, they had outscored the class average by about six points on the first exam. In addition, we were beginning to get to know one another and to share our insights from our different life experiences. I especially liked Juan Cortez, a second-generation Mexican American who told how his father had struggled to provide him with a quality education. He was bright and thoughtful and had hoped to study computer science at MIT, where he had been accepted. Unfortunately, he could not get any financial aid and ultimately came to his third choice, Southwest, which provided him with a $5,000 annual scholarship. But Juan took it with grace. He was judicious and unflappable. I liked him.

One Monday, about three quarters of the way through the term, our topic was racism. I was seated in my usual place for Uma's lecture, in the back corner. Next to me that day were two fraternity types—at least every day they wore clothes with the same fraternity letters on them. They were carrying on before class about what a rough weekend of drinking and partying they had endured. They continued to cut up and crack jokes even after the class started.

Their behavior irritated me—memories of having to put up with guys like them when I was working my way through undergraduate school at Southwest as a night security guard at an expensive dormitory in the "Greek" neighborhood came back to me as I glared at them. One of them caught my glare, looked me in the eye, leaned over, and defiantly began copying my notes.

Just as defiantly, I moved my notes to the other side of my desk and suggested to him that he needed to pay attention to the lecture.

Uma was asking for examples of different types or acts of racism—individual, small-group, institutional. When she asked for an example of institutional racism, Juan raised his hand and told how his father had been placed in remedial education because he was a Mexican American and how, in spite of this and although he had to work twice as hard, his father was now not only a successful businessman in that same community but the superintendent of the very school district that had once labeled him in need of remediation.

Juan's story evoked much emotion. Never in my eight years of undergraduate and graduate classes at Southwest had I heard such public candor from a minority student. It seemed that the dynamic in this class was such that a minority student, and a male minority student at that, felt comfortable enough to share his hidden feelings. Memories of my father and brother were coursing through my head. I wished I could have shared this experience with my father.

My buoyant feelings ended abruptly as the two fraternity guys turned to each other, raised their eyebrows, smirked, and said to each other, "Yeah, right, greaser! Good example!" My memory flashed to a frat guy who drove by me several years ago and yelled, "Hey, you, fat greaser!" My blood began to boil, but I knew saying anything might reveal my position as the "minority" TA and have negative consequences for the whole Opportunity Program.

Uma had followed Juan's story with an example of small-group racism, describing an incident that had occurred last year in a segregated part of the city in which swastikas had been painted on African American churches, presumably by a small Klan or skinhead group.

I glanced over at the frat guys, who were now laughing and drawing swastikas and Klansmen all over their notes. My anger rose, but again I checked it.

Uma, oblivious to my turmoil and to the frat guys' heckling, moved on to talk about stereotypes. She shared how an Asian woman friend of hers constantly encountered surprise from people when they found out she was studying liberal arts and not math or science, and how they were further surprised to find out that her parents were not hardcore disciplinarians.

Again, the frats laughed and commented, "Those aren't stereotypes, that's how those people really are! Yeah, no shit!"

At this point, I could tolerate them no longer. I turned, looked at them, and said, "If you guys don't cut out the shit, I'm going to kick you out of here."

The student sitting next to me, surprised, crunched up his nose, puckered his lips, shook his head up and down in short, quick deliberate nods and said, "Oh, yeah, sure."

The two remained silent for the rest of the class. At the end of the period, I rose from my seat at the back of the class and turned to the two, pointed my finger at them, and said,

Listen, I want to tell you two guys something. Racism is not going to be tolerated in this class. I heard what you said all during class, I saw the pictures you drew, and I know what fraternity you're in. All I have to do is walk over to the Dean of Students Office, report this, and you'll be out of here.

"We're not in a frat," the taller of the two answered.

"Look, I don't wanna hear it!" I responded evenly, remembering as I did his drunken disrespectful type when I was a security guard, remembering the drunk frat guy yelling "Greaser," remembering another yelling "Nigger" at a black driving his truck through the white part of campus at 2:00 a.m.

"Yeah, who are you, anyway?" said the other frat guy.

"I'm on staff for this class, and I can and will have you thrown out!" I shot back, my emotions breaking through to my speech.

"Well, we were just joking," said the first.

The second chimed in, "Yeah, we were just joking."

"And, the audacity you had to do this in front of me!" Their deference seemed to make me angrier.

"Well, we're real sorry," said the first.

"Yeah, real sorry. We were just joking," chimed in the second, as they made their way out the door.

At that, our interaction ended. I was totally spent and upset with myself for overreacting and missing the opportunity to more "objectively" tell them I was disturbed by their comments, that I was on staff, and that I wanted to sit down and talk with them about it.

Feeling dejected and violated, I went to tell Uma what had happened, feeling that as an Indian woman she would be understanding. When she finished talking to a few students, I told her I was really upset and explained what had happened. She was supportive and then, as we were walking out of the classroom, she looked at me and said in what I took to be a minimizing comment, "Well, welcome to the club."

I dropped my head, walked outside, and began sobbing. I got control of myself as best I could and walked over to the Dean of Student's Office to talk to Maya Scott, the African American woman who was director of the Opportunity Program. Though usually helpful, my supervisors in the Learning Skills Center were all white, and I just didn't feel like risking another violation that day. Maya was very supportive. She took me back in her office with a friend who had worked with me with "at-risk" minority students the previous year. As I told them what had happened, I began to cry again. I felt so naïve, so stupid, so violated. I wanted to physically hurt those frat boys. I couldn't get that feeling out of my mind, despite the fact that I knew such action was totally irrational and counterproductive.

Now that I am several months away from this "event," I still feel very ambivalent about it. On the one hand, I regret the way I handled it. I missed an opportunity to challenge two young men meaningfully and positively, men who obviously needed challenging. On the other hand, I felt violated for myself, my family, and my students and felt the need to assert myself forcefully.

CHAPTER 5

Imagining Futures

Decision Case: "Where Have All the Salmon Gone?"

"SELLING THE BOAT?" Chad Wiggins let out a howl like the cry of an animal in pain. "Dad, you can't mean it. I can't believe you mean it."

Cy Wiggins turned away, unable to face his son, feeling as if his life was being crushed like so many oyster shells. Chad looked at his father's back, shoulders bent, a man in defeat and heard the words, small and soft, coming from a voice he barely knew. "I'm sorry, son, but there just aren't enough fish anymore to make the money we need to feed this family and pay all our expenses. Commercial fishing is dead in the water." Nobody laughed at the pun. Chad kicked the screen door open and burst down the steps into the backyard, leaving his father alone with the stone in his heart.

Chad Wiggins began fishing with his father on his 12th birthday. He'd been waiting for that day for a long time, waiting for the time he

---

AUTHOR'S NOTE: This case was written by Selma Wasserman and is part of a database of cases available through the Case Clearinghouse, Faculty of Education, Simon Fraser University.

would be old enough to help, old enough not to be a nuisance and in the way. His father used to tell him,

> When you are 12. That's when I'll take you. That's when it will be safe. Not before then. It can be dangerous out there. You have to be old enough to be able to look after yourself. This is not a party, you know. This is hard work and I'm responsible for the boat and for all the men on board, and for our livelihood.

It wasn't until the summer that he went out with his father for the first time that Chad knew what his father had meant. The *Rip Tide,* Cy Wiggins's 24-meter boat, cost him $350,000 new. It had nine berths, two bathrooms with showers, a spacious, well-lit galley, and a wheelhouse that contained about $75,000 in electronic equipment, a state-of-the-art drum seiner. The *Rip Tide* carried a crew of six—men who all had worked with Cy Wiggins for many years. At age 12, Chad would learn to crew. By the time he was 15, his father said that he had learned enough to merit a share of the catch. Even though the work was hard, and at times even dangerous, and even though his hands felt like leather and his face was toughened by the sun and wind, Chad could not even think of another way of life. He loved the *Rip Tide,* the crew, the business of bringing the fish back to port. His father was his hero, and all Chad ever wanted for his own future was to finish school and work with his father on the *Rip Tide,* until he was able to get a boat of his own.

That was five years ago—a time when salmon were still plentiful. Commercial fishing off the west coast of Canada was not a year-round job. Because of weather conditions, government restrictions on fishing, and seasonal fish runs, fishing was, at best, a six-month occupation, with the rest of the year spent maintaining and upgrading the boat and equipment and, if the catch was less than good, filling in with other, temporary jobs. When the salmon season was good, Cy Wiggins and his crew would pull in a catch of about 100,000 kilograms (about 250,000 pounds) of fish, worth about $100,000, in six weeks. In a good season, each crew member might earn as much as $35,000—his share of the catch. In a good season, Cy Wiggins would be able to make a net profit of about $50,000—after paying fuel bills, insurance, licensing fees, maintenance on the boat, and provincial and federal taxes, which added up to about $90,000. Running a boat was not cheap! The work was hard and sometimes dangerous, the expenses and boat maintenance costs were high, but Cy would not have traded places with any man in any other job in the country. Fishing was in his blood.

At first, Cy would not believe the reports in the newspapers that told of the decline in fish stocks. He thought that these were false alarms, ignited by radical environmentalists who cared more about fish than they did for the "little guy who has to make a buck." Almost overnight, the reports about fish-starved fisheries on the Atlantic and Pacific coasts broke out in the press like a bad case of measles. The cod fisheries in the Northern Atlantic, off the coast of Nova Scotia and Newfoundland, were going bankrupt. The cod had been fished out, they said, and season after season of poor catches and high expenses had left commercial fishing reeling from plant closures and layoffs.

In the Gulf of Mexico, the newspapers reported that those fishermen whose livelihoods had been tied to the seafood-rich bays and estuaries of the Texas coast were also in jeopardy. For several years, they had to contest with the U.S. government-set limits on their daily catch—a step intended to prevent overfishing. But now, shrimpers were faced with contamination of their catch from petrochemical plants that had state permits to dump their toxic waste material into the Gulf. Cy Wiggins could no longer believe that the fish-starved ocean was an environmental ruse. He could see from his own work, season after season of small catches and declining profits, that there had to be some truth to this appalling news. Last week, he and his crew had been lucky. But there had been 47 other boats in the sea who had not done as well, and he knew that at least 18 of them had not caught a single fish.

Cy knew that he somehow would have to break the news to his family. He knew what it would mean to Chad, whose only dream was to follow in his father's footsteps. He had planned to retire one day and leave his boat and the business to Chad. Chad had never even considered another occupation. What would he do? One evening, he tried to explain the situation to his son.

"We've got to think of the future, Chad," he said, unable to look his son in the eye, feeling, unexplainedly, as if it was somehow all his fault.

"What do you mean, Dad? I don't understand."

Well, it's this way, son. I've talked to Jim Lavaca, the chairman of our organization, and he says if we're smart, we've got to start thinking about making some plans to find other sources of income. Certain salmon species have definitely gone down, and the coho and spring have been fished out, until there's almost nothing left. Pink and sockeye are still okay, but we don't know how long they will be holding. There's herring, of course, and they are still abundant, but there's less of a demand for them, and the prices are not very good.

"So what are you saying, Dad?" Chad would not let himself comprehend the issues.

"Son, it all boils down to this. Too many boats out there, and not enough fish. Each season it's going to get harder and harder to make a buck. And our expenses will kill us."

"This is crazy, Dad. Just crazy." Chad felt his voice rising, going out of control. "How can there be no more fish? Where have all the fish gone? There have got to be jillions of fish out there. We're just not finding them. But they're out there. They've got to be out there." Chad's voice exploded with emotion and his fist thumped the table, making it bounce back in response.

I know, son. I know. At first, I thought that, too. I thought that there was an unending supply of fish in the ocean and that all we had to do was go out and catch them. Well, it turns out that that was just wishful thinking. Too many boats and high-tech equipment have badly overfished the stocks. On top of that, toxic waste dumping into the oceans has further reduced stock by contamination. It's true, son. The fish are disappearing. If I want to feed this family, I'm going to have consider other options.

No matter how Cy Wiggins tried to impress his son with the seriousness of the situation, Chad seemed to push the idea away from him. He just did not want to believe that such a thing could actually happen. Maybe next season his father would see that he, and all the other alarmists, had been dead wrong.

This season, however, in 12 weeks, they had barely caught enough to make ends meet. To make matters worse, the Deep Bay Packing Company, to which Wiggins sold his catch, went into receivership, and was unable to pay him for the fish. It was at that point that Cy Wiggins decided to pack in commercial fishing and look for employment opportunities elsewhere. But who would hire a 50-year-old man who only knew one trade—commercial fishing? To what other job would his skills be applicable? He felt defeated and saw his life washing away, like a bad undertow.

Cy Wiggins knew that Chad would take the news hard. But he had hoped that the boy would at least try to understand and to see the situation from his point of view. Selling the boat would give them a bit of a stake—a few dollars in the bank after all the bills were paid. He looked out to the garden, where Chad sat, with his back to the house and his head down, and he wondered how he had failed his son. How was it possible that fish, in such abundance, could now be in such short supply? How could we have let this happen?

 REVIEW: SOCIAL CONNECTIONS AND CHANGE

"Where Have All the Salmon Gone?" is a case about an impending change—the Wiggins family's departure from commercial fishing. But this is not the first case we have looked at that deals with change. Peter Heywood in "Separate but Safer" attempted to change the separate lunchrooms policy. In the "Towering Dilemma," changes in who could use Devils Tower were debated. Changes at Design Inc. in "Perfection or Bust!" led us to wonder whether that organization will continue to be what its founder, Bill Klee, wanted it to be, an academy and a business. And in the "MPA Program" case, Alex Quill is being asked to change the criteria that he and his committee use to decide whom to admit into the MPA program.

Although each of these cases is about change, we did not analyze them as cases about change. We did not think about what the future holds in store in each situation. We did not imagine how the current course of events could be altered by some future event. Instead, when we analyzed these cases, we focused on the existing social connections, culture, and power relationships and how they were shaping actions and interactions.

However, it is difficult in "Where Have All the Salmon Gone?" to ignore change and the future. The situation has come to a head. Declining fish stocks can no longer support a once-thriving commercial fishing industry. The future is bleak for Cy Wiggins. He must act now if he and his family are to get anything out of the investments they have made in their boat *Rip Tide*.

There was a time not that long ago when Cy Wiggins did not think very much about the future and the possibility that his whole life could change. We are told that, initially, Cy did not believe newspaper reports about declining fish stocks. Thinking they were false alarms of radical environmentalists, Cy continued to do what he had been doing for many years, fish for salmon off the west coast of Canada. If we had visited Cy and his family five years ago and analyzed their situation, we too would not have imagined the crisis facing commercial fishing today. Instead, we would have analyzed the situation by looking at the social connections within the fishing community, especially the family ties and the culture that sustained this way of life. We probably would have noted inequalities and how those engaged in fishing face financial difficulties when their costs remain fixed but the price they receive for their catch goes down. If we had just focused on the

Wiggins family and their fishing community, we would have had no idea, given the abundance of salmon, that five years down the road their whole way of life would be in turmoil. But could we or, for the matter, could Cy Wiggins have foreseen the future? Could he have known what he now knows—that overfishing and pollution would force him and many other fishing families to give up fishing for good?

It is unlikely that we can foresee the future with any degree of certainty, and we should not expect social scientists to become fortune tellers. The social worlds we live in are too complex. Many things that you do not anticipate now will happen in the future. But although you cannot predict the future with certainty, you can use sociological tools to help you imagine scenarios about the future. You will not know until time passes whether any of your imagined futures will come about. But by imagining them, you can prepare yourself for their possibility. The remainder of this chapter provides you with the tools to analyze potential social changes and construct scenarios about the future.

CONSTRUCTING SCENARIOS

Imagining futures is not easy. People have a tendency to think either that the way things currently are will continue indefinitely or that anything is possible. But rarely are changes either impossible or unlimited. So to rigorously think about the future and examine social changes, you need a tool that you can use to imagine a limited set of futures. *Scenarios,* "stories about the way the world might turn out tomorrow," are such a tool (Schwartz 1991). By constructing scenarios, you can organize in a systematic way your ideas and thoughts about what could happen.

The objective, however, is not to construct a scenario that you think has a high probability of coming to fruition. For rarely do we know which scenarios are more probable than others. Instead, you want to consider many possibilities and construct multiple scenarios. Over time, you may see that one scenario is playing itself out more than the other scenarios. But the evidence you initially bring to bear when building scenarios is designed to help you imagine multiple possibilities and not to determine which scenario will become the reality.

So the real purpose in constructing scenarios is not to predict the future but to place the current situation in a larger context so that you can see the multiple possibilities that exist in the present situation. You already have seen how important it is to place situations within their contexts. In Chapter 3, you learned how to analyze the cultural context so that you could see situations from the point of view of insiders. In Chapter 4, you learned how power and inequalities affect the ability of people and groups to act on their interests. In this chapter, you will learn how to contextualize situations in yet another way, by analyzing the *conditions* that make a situation possible.

Consider the conditions that make possible the way of life Cy Wiggins and his family had prior to the decline in fish populations. For Cy and his family to prosper, there had to be a sufficient supply of salmon; a demand by consumers for salmon; people who would buy, process, and distribute the salmon; boats and fishing equipment; a supply of people willing to work as crew members; a local community in which supplies can be purchased and people can find social support; banks to loan people money so that they could purchase boats and equipment; and governmental support such as harbor infrastructures and treaties with other countries where overfishing can occur. These larger conditions make possible the fishing way of life for the Wiggins family.

But when analyzing situations, we usually do not see these conditions. They are in the background. During normal times, they remain fairly constant and so both actors and observers take them for granted. You can think of these conditions as the terrain on which action, interaction, and the formation of social connections take place. Our attention when analyzing a case is usually directed to the foreground, to the interactions and, as you have learned through this book, the social connections among people. But to fully understand a case and, in particular, to be able to imagine possible futures, you must shift your attention to the background, to the terrain on which the action takes place.

One way you can bring the background conditions to your attention is to consider hypothetical situations by asking "what if" questions. For example, What if the salmon population was to decline? What if fishing boats from other countries were to start fishing in the same waters? What if banks were less willing to loan money for the purchase of expensive fishing boats and equipment? What if the fish processing companies went bankrupt? What if the government cut back the Coast Guard and reduced its infrastructural support for fishing? What if salmon farming became more economical? What if the children of fishing parents no longer wanted to live where they grew up? What if the courts began to uphold Native American claims to salmon that were stipulated in treaties signed many years ago? By highlighting changes that could occur, these hypothetical questions draw attention away from the foreground and to the background, allowing you to think about the conditions that make the current situation possible.

Asking what if questions is the first step in building scenarios. But in any given situation, there are an unlimited number of what if questions. Which what ifs should you seriously entertain? And how do you turn what if questions into full-fledged scenarios that allow you to map out what really could change?

The key to building scenarios is the analysis of **driving forces**, "the elements that move the plot of a scenario, that determine a story's outcome" (Schwartz 1991). In the remainder of this chapter, you will learn about three important driving forces: demographics, technology, and collective actions. You will learn how to build scenarios by

- Empirically investigating how each of these driving forces is creating the conditions that make a given situation possible
- Imagining how demographic changes, technological developments, or collective actions could alter the existing conditions

So let's examine each of these driving forces and see how you could use your understanding of them to investigate social change and imagine possible futures.

DEMOGRAPHIC FORCES

One of the most important driving forces in any society is **demographics,** the characteristics and dynamics of human populations. Demographers, social scientists who study populations, analyze demographic processes to understand and predict changes in the demographic profiles of populations. Usually, their focus is on *human populations,* consisting of people residing in a specific geographic area. But the tools of demography can be used to study other types of populations, such as members of an organization, clients of a business, students in a school, and even firms within an industry. Before beginning a demographic analysis, it is important to identify and delimit the population you are studying.

Three Demographic Processes

The most studied demographic trait is *population size,* the number of people residing in a specific place. Changes in a population's size result from a combination of three demographic processes: fertility, mortality, and migration. **Fertility** concerns the incidence of childbirth within a population, **mortality,** the extent of death, and **migration,** the movement of people into and out of a population residing in a specific territorial area. Therefore, building scenarios requires taking into account each of these three demographic forces.

Fertility. The first thing you need to do is examine changes over time in fertility levels and compare them to the levels found in other populations. To do this, you need an indicator of fertility. A measure that is often used is the **crude birth rate,** the number of live births in a given year per 1,000 people. It is a crude rate because, technically, you should only consider the number of births among those who are able to have children. Therefore, a better measure is the **general birth rate,** calculated as the number of live births in a given year per 1,000 women of childbearing age (usually 15 to 44 years old). In the United States and many other industrialized countries, this fertility rate is at or below the replacement rate of 2.1 children per woman, resulting in *zero population growth,* the level of fertility that maintains a population's size at a constant level.

The next thing you need to do is investigate the causes of variation in fertility. Why do some populations have higher fertility levels than others? Why have fertility levels changed over time? In answering these questions, consider some of the factors that demographers have identified (Weeks 1996):

- The availability of birth control leads to lower fertility.
- Delayed age of marriage tends to lower fertility rates. Women who marry at a later age have a shorter amount of time during which they can have children.
- Declines in mortality rates often lead to lower fertility rates. In societies with high mortality, especially **infant mortality**—the number of deaths of infants under 1 year of age for each thousand live births in a given year—women tend to have more children in order to have enough children to support them in their old age. But as mortality rates decline, the need for high fertility decreases.
- Women tend to have more children when children are viewed as economic assets because they work and bring resources into a household. As infant mortality rates decline and children become more economic liabilities (because of the high costs of raising children), women tend to reduce their fertility.
- Fertility tends to be lower in populations with higher levels of education. This is because women who have educational and career opportunities are more likely to choose to do other things besides have and raise children. Education also exposes women to information about birth control and family planning.

Mortality. As with fertility, you also need to map out changes in mortality levels and compare them across populations. To do this, you can use the **crude mortality rate,** the number of deaths in a given year per 1,000 people in a population. However, because mortality rates vary a great deal by age, it is often more insightful to compute *age-specific mortality rates,* such as the infant mortality rate. On the basis of mortality rates, you can compute **life expectancies,** the number of years on average a person can expect to live.

The next step is to explain the variation you have observed. Variation in mortality is primarily the result of changes in the health of people within a population. Obviously, wars, famine, and disease all tend to increase mortality. On the other hand, medical advances and public health measures, such as sanitation systems, water treatment facilities, and immunizations, decrease mortality. In preindustrial societies with poor health conditions, infant mortality rates are very high, and, therefore, life expectancies are very low. In industrial societies with low infant mortality rates, life expectancy levels have continued to increase as the result of declining mortality rates at older ages brought about by medical advances.

Migration. The final process you need to investigate when constructing scenarios about demographic change is migration, which really is two processes: immigration and emigration. **Immigration,** movement into a population, usually is measured by the in-migration rate, the number of people entering a population in a given year per 1,000 people who are already in the population. **Emigration,** movement out of a population, is measured by the out-migration rate, which is just the number of people who have left a population in a given year per 1,000 in the population. Subtracting the out-migration rate from the in-migration rate yields the **crude net migration rate,** an indicator of the extent to which a population's size is increasing (a positive number) or decreasing (a negative number) as the result of migration patterns.

Migration is harder to predict than fertility and mortality and therefore it tends to be the "wild card" in demographic analysis.

Migration rates vary for many reasons (Weeks 1996). Governmental restrictions on both in-migration and out-migration affect migration levels. Political conditions such as persecution, war, and regime changes can lead to out-migration from a country. Economic conditions are also important as people move to find work and to enjoy a better standard of living. Though attention is often focused on migration between countries, internal migration within countries also can be very important.

Population growth and decline. Because migration is less predictable, demographers initially examine changes in a population's size in terms of fertility and mortality and then bring in migration patterns to complete the picture. The most widely used measure of overall demographic change is the **natural growth rate,** computed by subtracting the crude death rate from the crude birth rate. This measure captures the extent to which a population is increasing or decreasing as a result of fertility and mortality patterns. In 1999, the U.S. population grew at an annual rate of 5.6 percent per thousand, the difference between a crude death rate of 8.7 and a crude birth rate of 14.3 (U.S. Census Bureau 2000a). Using this annual growth rate, you can compute the *doubling time of a population,* that is, the number of years it will take for a population to double, by dividing the growth rate into 70. With a 0.56 percent growth rate, the U.S. population will double in 125 years. In contrast, Mexico's population, which had an annual growth rate of about 2 percent in 1999 (in large part because of a very high birth rate, which was more than 23 live births per 1,000 people in 1999), will double in size in 35 years.

In sum, the first thing you need to do when constructing scenarios that take into account demographic forces is *decompose* possible changes in a population's size into the three contributing factors of fertility, mortality, and migration. By examining trends in each of these demographic processes and thinking about the economic, social, and political factors that could alter fertility, mortality, and migration patterns, you will be able to imagine how a population's size could change in the future.

Population Composition and Structure

Demographic forces can alter not only a population's size but also its structure and composition. The two most studied compositional variables are sex and age. *Sex ratios,* the number of men for every 100 women, tend to be less than 100 in industrialized societies because women tend to live longer than men. But, in societies in which men are valued over women, sex ratios are significantly above 100, as parents either abort female fetuses, practice infanticide of female children, or give their female children less care.

Age composition is depicted by computing the size of each age group or what demographers call **cohorts,** people who were born in the same period of time (e.g., a five-year period). Comparing the size of cohorts allows demographers to ascertain where there are bulges and contractions in the age structure of a population.

A helpful tool that is used by demographers to capture a population's structure is an age-sex pyramid (see Exhibit 5.1). This graphic representation of a population's composition has a pyramidal shape because of higher mortality rates at higher ages. Inspection of these pyramids can provide valuable insight into future trends. For example, a bulge in the pyramid indicates a large birth cohort that, as it ages, will continue to be relatively larger in size than other age groups. This is clearly seen in the U.S. pyramid (U.S. Census Bureau 2000b). Known as the baby boom of the 1950s and 1960s, this bulge resulted from higher fertility rates during that period of time. It was followed by declining fertility in the 1970s, which created much smaller cohorts among those who in 1999 were 20 to 30 years old.

Note that the size of the cohorts who in 1999 were 5 to 20 years old is bigger. Is this because fertility rates increased again in the 1980s? No. During the past couple of decades, fertility rates have remained relatively constant. What changed is the number of women of childbearing age. The big baby boom cohort began to have babies, and because there were lots of baby boomers, there were lots of babies. Demographers refer to this phenomenon as *demographic momentum,* the effects of past changes in fertility and mortality on

Exhibit 5.1 Population Pyramid of the United States, 1999

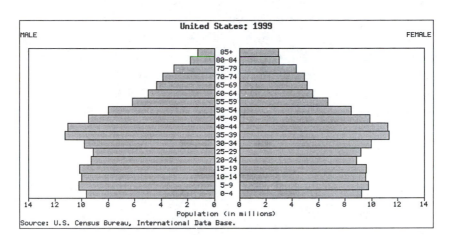

population size and composition that occur when fertility and mortality rates are fairly constant.

Another use of population pyramids is to help you see *dependency ratios,* the ratio of the dependent age population (those younger than 15 and older than 64) to those at the traditional working ages (15–64). Population pyramids that look like an hourglass with a smaller middle indicate dependency problems. In some developing societies, there are not enough adults of working age to support a growing youth population and an older population that is surviving longer. Some industrialized societies also have or will soon hav high dependency ratios because of (1) small working-age populations as a result of fertility rates below the replacement rate of 2.1 and (2) increasing life expectancies among the elderly.

In sum, the second thing you need to do when constructing demographic scenarios is to consider changes that are, so to speak, in the pipeline and that will come to fruition as people within the population age. You can do this by examining a population's current structure, especially its age–sex composition.

It should be noted that the tools of demography can be used to study a wide variety of populations, such as a company's employees, a church's membership, or the population of firms within an industry. Periods of rapid growth in an organization can lead to age bulges, whereas periods of low growth in membership can result in an aging population. Thinking demographically is an important skill that allows you to understand the composition, size, and character of populations by examining births, deaths, and flows into and out of it.

Demographic Changes

The most important demographic change in the past 100 years has been the **demographic transition,** the change within a society from a population characterized by high birth and death rates to a population with both low birth and death rates. This transition has three stages:

- *The Pretransitional Stage:* During this stage, a population's size remains relatively stable, as high mortality counterbalances high fertility.
- *The Transitional Stage:* Mortality rates decline due to medical advances, public health measures, and increased food production resulting from industrialization. But birth rates remain high and, as a result, societies experience rapid population growth.
- *Posttransitional Stage:* Birth rates decline as a result of increased education and economic opportunities. As birth rates approach the mortality rate, population size again becomes stable, although it is now much larger than it was during the pretransitional stage.

Though many societies have undergone this demographic transition, there are social forces that can impede it. Demographic momentum can slow the demographic transition as societies that had high birth rates continue to grow because of the large number of childbearing-aged women. But the biggest impediment is the vicious cycle of poverty and high fertility. Outside assistance can help a poor society move into the transitional stage by lowering death rates, especially infant mortality rates. But because poor societies have limited internal resources that must be used to feed a growing population, there is little left to do the things that would lower birth rates. As a result, investments in schools or industry are minimal. Without growing opportunities for adults, poor families continue to rely on having more children to bring in more income. The result is a vicious cycle in which poverty both prevents investments in social institutions that could lead to lower fertility and creates incentives for parents to have more children (Grant 1994).

This vicious cycle of poverty and population growth is compounded by the effects of both poverty and population growth on the environment, leading to what is called the *Poverty–Population–Environment (PPE) Spiral*. As populations grow, more and more land is cleared for agricultural production, grazing, and fuel. Overgrazing and deforestation lead to the eventual deterioration of the land, causing further poverty. Poverty in turn leads to high fertility. With more mouths to feed, overuse of the land increases. The result is a growing poor population that is destroying the environment it needs to sustain itself.

Industrialized nations do not experience the PPE spiral because of stable populations resulting from low birth rates. However, environmental degradation continues. As we see later in this chapter, some of the degradation results from technological changes. But a good deal of the degradation results from high levels of consumption (Ehrlich and Ehrlich 1987). Smaller populations with high consumption levels can wreak just as much havoc on the environment as do much larger populations, and sometimes even more havoc. The resulting environmental degradation in the form of pollution, overuse of land, and depletion of natural resources, in the long run, can undermine economic growth. These problems have led social activists to call for *sustainable development*, patterns of consumption and uses of resources that can be sustained by a population over time because they do not harm the environment.

Urbanization and Communities

Demographic forces also operate within populations as a result of **internal migration,** changes in residency that occur within a society's borders. The most important internal demographic process in the past century has been **urbanization,** the process whereby people move from rural areas to cities. Urbanization has led to the enormous growth in the size of cities, not just in industrialized societies like the United States but also in developing countries like Mexico. Combined with **suburbanization,** the process whereby people leave central cities for areas outside cities that are either adjacent to a city or within commuting distance, urbanization has changed many aspects of modern societies.

Urbanization has shaped the pattern of urban development, a process analyzed by **social ecologists,** social scientists who examine the relation between the physical and social aspects of communities. Urbanization has put strains on local city governments, which often have difficulty providing the levels of service (police, fire, roads, sanitation) that are needed for a growing population (Kasarda 1972). Suburbanization has resulted in strip mall development and the decline of central city shopping districts. It also puts financial strains on central cities, which lose tax revenues as higher-income families move to the suburbs. Finally, suburbanization, which is often caused by *white flight*—the movement of whites to suburbs in part to avoid having to send their children to schools with large populations of African Americans—has resulted in new forms of racial segregation.

Decline of community debate. Has urbanization led to a decline in community? More than a century ago, Ferdinand Tönnies argued that it had. Tönnies ([1887] 1963) contrasted what he called a *gemeinschaft,* a German word that is often translated as "community," with a *gesellschaft,* which in German means "association." He argued that *gesellschafts* were replacing *gemeinschafts* as people left small rural villages for urban areas. In *gemeinschafts,* there is personal and close interaction, whereas in *gesellschafts,* social interaction is more formal

and less personal. Rural villages have *gemeinschaft*-like qualities because they are *closed* social entities in which everyone knows everyone
else. Because people are unlikely to leave these places, they share a
common history and a common future, leading them to create *gemeinschafts* (Fischer 1977).

In contrast, according to Tönnies, in cities *gemeinschafts* are rare
but *gesellschafts* are more prevalent. People form or belong to associations (*gesellschafts*) for instrumental reasons. They voluntarily associate with others only when it is in their self-interest. The result is the
decline of community, as people leave rural areas for cities, leaving
behind *gemeinschafts* and joining *gesellschafts*.

At first, social ecologists who studied cities found evidence that
supported Tönnies's hypothesis (Wirth 1938). Combined with the
development of a mass society that was decreasing regional variation
and increasing alienation, urbanization was seen as causing major
social problems (Nisbet [1953] 1976). But other research appeared to
contradict the decline of community thesis. *Ethnic enclaves,* places
within an urban area where people from a particular ethnic group or
country reside, show strong signs of community. Some neighborhoods within cities have the traits of what Herbert Gans (1962) calls
an *urban village.*

People within cities also have intimate and close social ties through
networks just like people in small towns and rural villages (Fischer
1982). However, whereas in rural areas, networks involve kin and
people who live nearby, in urban areas, ties are to friends who are voluntarily chosen. Because cities are big and diverse, there are a larger
variety of subcultures, providing opportunities for people to form
friendship ties with those who have similar interests and tastes
(Fischer 1975). So, in contradistinction to Tönnies, there is evidence
that cities do not destroy community but instead create opportunities
for forming new and different types of communities.

This debate over the effects of urbanization reveals an important
point about driving forces: Often, they have both positive and negative consequences. Urbanization both undermined the small town,

close-knit type of community and at the same time stimulated the creation of diverse urban landscapes. Unfortunately, when thinking about the future, people tend to focus on either the positive or the negative trends. Cynics construct pessimistic scenarios highlighting the negative impacts. Optimists construct rosy pictures emphasizing the positive impacts. But because of uncertainty about the future, developing a full understanding of what could happen requires imagining the different ways in which a driving force could play itself out. By looking at both the positive and negative consequences, you can construct scenarios that take into account the different possible directions that change could take.

 ## TECHNOLOGICAL FORCES

Technology is another very important driving force in society. Unfortunately, when examining situations, people have a tendency to think narrowly about technology. People focus on major technological innovations, such as the telephone, television, and computer. But technological change can occur on a much smaller scale in workplaces, schools, homes, and even religious institutions. Furthermore, technology does not just refer to equipment and machines. Therefore, to understand this driving force, the first thing you need to do is broaden your perspective on technology so that you can characterize the wide variety of technologies that are used in different settings.

Technology refers to the tools, knowledge, and skills people use to achieve some practical purposes. So when identifying the technology in a given situation, do not just look for the physical apparatus like tools, equipment, and machines. Instead, you should pay attention to the following three things (Bijker, Hughes, and Pinch 1987; Hickson, Pugh, and Pheysey 1969):

- What tasks are being performed? Identifying the specific tasks will help you see the technological process by which some input is transformed into some output. Social scientists call this the *operations technology.*

- What materials and supplies are used when people do these tasks? By identifying the inputs, you will see what is needed to do some transformation. Social scientists call this the *materials technology.*

- What do people have to know to do tasks? By examining how people acquire knowledge and skills through schooling, training, or experience, you will have a good idea about what social scientists call the *knowledge technology.*

Once you have identified the operations, material, and knowledge aspects of a technology, you can proceed to compare and contrast it to other technologies. The typical way in which we array technologies is in terms of their *complexity.* But there are many different ways of capturing technological differences in complexity:

- *Automaticity:* The most common way to think about technological differences is in terms of **automaticity,** the degree to which energy and then information are provided by machines rather than people (Hickson et al. 1969). The simplest technologies are hand-held tools, followed by power tools that use nonhuman energy sources, and then self-guiding machines. At the highest levels, you have automated and computerized equipment that can adjust itself by processing information from sensing devices.

- *Production Continuity:* You also can characterize technological differences in terms of the degree of continuous production (Woodward 1957, 1965). In *unit* or *small batch* technologies, a small number of products are produced one at a time. Often referred to as *craft technologies,* examples include much of the construction industry and made-to-order products and services. With *mass production* or *large batch* technologies, substantial amounts of identical products are produced through a detailed division of labor. The classic example of this technological type is the assembly line used in automobile production. Finally, with *continuous process* technologies, material flows through a production process in which it is refined and combined with other materials. This type of technology tends to be highly automated, with the major tasks being the monitoring and maintenance of equipment. Oil refineries, pharmaceuticals, and alcohol distillation are examples of continuous process technologies.

- *Routinization:* A final way to capture complexity is to consider how routine a technology is (Perrow 1967, 1986). With routine technologies, the primary task is the transformation of some input into some output. When the input is relatively uniform and well understood (e.g., dirty clothes coming into a dry cleaner), there usually are standard routines for processing the material. In contrast, in nonroutine technologies, people must first figure out how to transform some input prior to actually doing the work. Because the input can vary (e.g., patients at a medical clinic) and knowledge about them and their problems is limited, problem-solving technologies are needed to figure out what to do prior to actually doing the transformation.

With these distinctions, you are now in a position to analyze the technologies that you find in a given situation. Consider the technologies that Cy Wiggins employs in his fishing business. The operations technology that he uses to catch fish includes such tasks as sailing his boat to where he thinks there are fish, using fishing equipment to catch fish, storing and delivering the fish to market, and maintaining equipment. In doing these tasks, Cy uses lots of equipment, including his boat, the expensive electronic navigating equipment, a drum seiner, and many different types of hand tools. The material technology he employs includes such inputs as netting, lines, and bait. But probably his most important material technologies are the natural resources and utilities such as air, water, and energy. Cy needs fuel to power his boat and unpolluted waters in which to catch fish.

The importance of Cy's knowledge technology is seen by considering what his son, Chad, would have to know if he were to take over his father's business. He would need to know how to operate the boat and all its equipment, manage a crew, catch fish with the equipment, and take care of the financial side of the business.

How would you compare Cy's fishing technology to other technologies? Probably, you would classify it as relatively simple. Although nonhuman energy sources are used, there are probably few automated pieces of equipment, the exception being the advanced navigating equipment. With nets, large batches of fish are caught at one time. However, each fishing expedition is a limited production, more like building a house than mass producing automobiles. Finally, commercial fishing is fairly routine. Though unforeseen events requiring quick reactions do occur, for the most part there are standard procedures for catching and processing a fairly uniform input—fish.

Although the examples so far have focused on technologies involved in doing work, technologies are used in a variety of social settings. Changes in technology have affected household cooking and cleaning tasks as well as the ways in which teachers educate students and the ways clergy convey religious meanings to lay people. Technological changes in infrastructures—such as communication and power grids, transportation systems, and waste disposal—also have had wide-ranging effects.

Technological Revolutions

It is important when developing scenarios to examine the specific technologies in a given situation and how they could change. Technological changes within workplaces, schools, governments, and households have important impacts on social connections, culture, and inequalities. But you also need to step back and examine major technological revolutions.

The first technological revolution—the Neolithic revolution—occurred about 10,000 to 12,000 years ago. Prior to this revolution, technologies were fairly primitive, as people relied on hand-held tools and simple techniques for hunting animals and gathering food from plants. With the manufacture of simple tools such as digging sticks and hoes, people began to live in permanent settlements. Gathering was replaced by *horticultural* technologies, the use of hand tool technologies to cultivate plants, and hunting gave way to *pastoral* technologies used for the raising of animals.

About 5,000 years ago, the invention of the plow and the development of irrigation systems led to a second technological revolution. Along with other inventions such as the wheel, writing, and numbers, the plow and irrigation enabled *agrarian societies* characterized by intense agricultural production to accumulate large surpluses. Often, elites used these surpluses to finance standing armies with which they created empires by conquering lands and peoples.

Until relatively recently, agriculture was the primary technology in most societies, and in some societies today it is still very important. But with the Industrial Revolution, which began in the late 1700s, a major shift away from agriculture began. The invention of the steam engine replaced humans, animals, wind, and running water as the energy source for powering machines. The resulting mechanization of work decreased the need for agricultural labor and increased the need for factory labor. In factories, commodities were mass produced and then transported with new railroad and steamship technologies. Eventually, other energy sources replaced steam, resulting in the automobile, electrification, and many other technological innovations.

These technological changes had profound impacts on social connections, culture, demography, and inequality. As you saw in Chapter 2, the first sociologists—Marx, Weber, and Durkheim—analyzed the effects of the Industrial Revolution. Technological changes led to an increasingly complex division of labor with many new occupations. They also generated large surpluses through both increased productivity and increased work effort by factory workers.

Most modern societies still exhibit many of the traits of industrialization, such as relatively large manufacturing sectors and the mass production of consumer goods and services. But a fourth technological revolution—the information technology revolution—has begun to change industrialized societies. This revolution began in the 1950s with the invention of the transistor and the integrated circuit, which eventually led to the microprocessor, a computer on a chip. Since then, computers and their ability to process information have spread throughout most societies. With computers and their software, people are now able to *act* on information by processing it, transforming it, and distributing it through networks such as the Internet (Castells 1996).

The information revolution has led to new forms of social organization and connections, as well as changes in culture. Because we are in the midst of this revolution, it is difficult to see all the implications of the technological changes we are now experiencing, although numerous scholars are currently studying this momentous change. This technological revolution has created new economic sectors involved in the production of information technologies (what some call the *new economy*), transformed existing industries as they employ information technologies, and increased the demand for information technology workers. But perhaps the most important change is the increasing importance of networks both for the flow of information and as a way in which to organize activities globally through the use of information technologies (Castells 1996).

Technological Impacts

Technological changes have major impacts on virtually every aspect of society. Subsequently, I highlight three potential impacts of technology that you should take into account when constructing scenarios: on work and jobs, on economic development, and on the environment.

Work and jobs. The first impact you should investigate is the impact on work and jobs. Technological changes often bring about the restructuring of firms, organizations, and the economy by affecting both the types of goods produced and the types of jobs that are available. The mix of **industries,** branches of activities devoted to the production of a particular good or service, changes as a result of the technological developments. Social scientists often speak of a tripartite division of the economy into three industrial sectors (Hodson and Sullivan 1995; Singleman 1978): the primary sector (agriculture and extractive industries such as mining, lumber, and fishing), the secondary sector (manufacturing), and the tertiary sector (services). In the United States, the primary sector has dramatically declined in size from more than 40 percent of the labor force in 1900 to less than 3 percent today. From 1900 to 1950, the manufacturing sector grew from 28 percent to about 36 percent of the labor force; since 1950, however, it has steadily declined in size and is now at around 20 percent. The greatest growth has been in the service sector. Today, around 77 percent of all workers are employed in jobs having to do with the delivery of some service.

Technological changes can result in more than just industrial restructuring. They also can lead to changes within industries in the mix of *occupations*. During the middle of the twentieth century, operative occupations involved with the running of machinery and equipment grew as the manufacturing sector grew. But in the last part of the century, professional and technical occupations have grown in part as the result of the increasing importance of information technologies.

Because technological changes can affect work and jobs, you need to investigate in which industries opportunities are decreasing, and in which industries they are increasing. Technological changes can affect job opportunities in two ways. First, technological changes can undermine old industries and stimulate the growth of new industries. For example, the invention of the television undermined the once-thriving radio industry. Second, when technological changes increase labor productivity, they decrease the need for labor. For example, the mechanization of agriculture led to the creation of large agribusiness, undermining the small family farm and resulting in the exodus of large numbers of people from farming.

Economic development. The second impact of technological changes that you should look for is the impact on economic development. There are two contrasting views on how technology affects economic development. *Modernization theory* argues that societies become wealthier through technological changes. In contrast, *dependency theory* argues that economic development is affected by a country's position in the world system. Technological changes are often impeded in countries that are heavily dependent on other countries.

According to modernization theories, societies go through developmental stages (Rostow 1960, 1978). Initially in poor societies, traditional cultures impede technological change. But with a weakening of tradition, technological changes are adopted and the economy grows. Often, richer countries advance this take-off stage by providing foreign aid, transferring technology, investing capital, assisting in population control, and providing educational opportunities to those in poorer countries. As an economy grows and becomes more diverse, people begin to experience the benefits of industrialization, and poverty declines. Although people regret the loss of traditional values and ways, the availability of relatively cheap commodities as the result of mass production raises living standards dramatically.

Constructing scenarios based on modernization theory requires taking into account the availability of technological advances to a society or region. The unavailability of modern technology is likely to lead to economic backwardness. Modernization theorists have an unrelenting faith in technological progress. From their perspective, the primary impediment to economic development is the failure to acquire and use technological innovations.

In contrast, dependency theory sees the world economic system as divided into three types of countries: *core* countries that are highly developed, *peripheral* countries that are underdeveloped because they are exploited by core countries, and *semiperiphery* countries that experienced some development because of their strategic position or valuable natural resources even though they are still dependent on core countries for capital (Wallerstein 1974, 1979). To construct scenarios based on dependency theory's ideas, you need to consider where a country or region stands in relation to other countries and regions.

Dependency theory grew out of analysis of *imperialism,* a social system in which core nations annex colonies from which they extract valuable raw materials and agricultural products (Frank 1975). These materials are then shipped back to the core country and used in manufacturing. After political independence, former colonies remain economically dependent because they are primarily export-oriented economies, producing a small number of exports (e.g., bananas, coffee, copper). Because of unequal exchanges, peripheral countries do not receive much for their exports, and often the capital they do receive goes to ruling elites who benefit from the export-oriented economy. As a result, these countries are unable to develop their own manufacturing base. Therefore, they become dependent on core countries for manufacturing products and capital.

Although both modernization theories and dependency theories believe that technological changes stimulate economic development, they disagree over what social forces impede technological change. For modernization theorists, technology is a driving force with a life of its own. Once unleashed, it inevitably leads to modernization. The major impediment is traditional cultures. But with education, communication, and the enjoyment of modernization's benefits, old traditions are abandoned.

In contrast, according to dependency theory, technological progress is not inevitable. Those in power have an interest in impeding those technological changes that would undermine their power. Technological change, therefore, is shaped by the interests of core countries. Because core countries benefit from the cheap raw materials and, more recently, cheap manufactured products produced for export in peripheral countries, core countries have an interest in maintaining technological underdevelopment in peripheral societies.

Although both modernization and dependency theory were developed to explain economic development (or the lack of it) in countries, these ideas can be applied to other social units. For example, when constructing specific scenarios, it may be more relevant to examine uneven development across regions within a country, across sectors of an economy, or even across organizations within an industry.

The environment. Without a doubt, technological changes have improved people's lives. Probably the most dramatic effect has been in the area of medicine and health. Technological advances such as sanitation systems and indoor plumbing increased public health, and the invention of the new drugs, vaccines, and medical procedures have saved millions of lives. Until relatively recently, the unabashed faith in technological progress had been a hallmark of Western civilization. Problems that did occur were seen as the result of **cultural lag,** a period of delay that occurs when one part of society changes but other parts have not changed accordingly (Ogburn 1964). Cultural adjustments to technological changes take time. But the problems resulting from technological change were seen as temporary ones that would be overcome as society adjusted to the changes.

In the past few decades, social scientists and the public have begun to question this overly optimistic view of technology (Schumacher 1975). Spurred by technological disasters such as the nuclear power plant accidents at Three Mile Island and Chernobyl, large oil spills onto pristine shores, the disappearance of animal species as the result of environmental pollution, and health problems in urban areas resulting from air and water pollution, people have begun to examine the costs of technological changes.

The technical term economists use for such costs is **externalities,** consequences of behavior that are unintended and therefore do not figure into the initial determination of the price of some activity or commodity. The classic example of a negative externality is automobile air pollution. An individual driver has no economic incentive to decrease the pollution caused by driving her automobile. If everyone else continues to pollute, she will not benefit from installing a costly pollution control device on her car. Furthermore, there are no immediate costs to her from polluting. Polluting does not prevent her from driving her car. The costs of pollution are external, borne by the entire society or area in which she lives as a result of many people driving cars that are polluting the air.

Recognizing externalities is facilitated by adopting an **ecological approach** to technology, in which you study the interaction between living organisms and their environment. Ecologists look at entire *ecosystems* in which living organisms interact within their natural environment. They note how technological changes can have both short-term positive benefits and long-term negative, unintended consequences that are often very difficult, if not impossible, to reverse. Among the various impacts of technological changes that you should take into account when developing scenarios are the following:

- *Population growth:* As noted earlier, technological advances have decreased mortality rates, especially infant mortality. In the absence of decreasing fertility, population growth can be extraordinary. Add to this the migration to cities brought about by technological change in agriculture, and you have large concentrated populations consuming a great deal and, through their consumption, depleting resources and increasing pollution.

- *Wasteful consumption:* Developed societies have become "disposable societies," with consumers willing to buy products that are disposed of after some use and that come with lots of packaging.

- *Pollution:* The production at high levels of many goods and services that people want to consume causes pollution. Air pollution has increased as the result of the internal combustion engine used in automobiles, the generation of electricity from the burning of coal, and the release by manufacturing plants of harmful chemicals into the atmosphere. Water pollution results from the disposal of chemical byproducts from production processes, as well as from the dumping of raw sewage and industrial accidents.

- *Depletion of natural resources such as oil, water, and even land:* The reliance on technologies such as the automobile and agricultural methods that require irrigation deplete resources that are in limited supply. Urban development and suburban sprawl consume land.

All these adverse impacts can be viewed as negative externalities. Individuals who are living now have little incentive to change the behaviors that are causing pollution and depleting resources. This is why governmental regulations and laws are used to decrease pollution and alter consumption patterns. Combined with education and cultural changes, governmental actions decrease the negative consequences of existing technologies and, at times, even spur the development of alternative technologies. But we are far from what ecologists refer to as a *sustainable ecosystem,* in which the needs of a current population are met without destroying the ability of future generations to meet their needs.

COLLECTIVE ACTIONS AND SOCIAL MOVEMENTS

A third important driving force is **collective action,** attempts by a group of people to pursue their common interests either by promoting some change or by resisting a proposed change. Collective actions are a very important driving force, because it is through them that people can change their situations.

The reality is that from time to time people find themselves in situations in which they do not want to be. Unable to change the situation through their own individual actions, people either accept the situation and make the best of it, or they attempt to leave and move into another situation that they hope will be better. Consider the case of Cy Wiggins. He now finds himself in a situation in which he cannot profitably continue to fish. When problems first began, he coped with the smaller catches and continued fishing. He tried through his individual actions to make the best of the situation. But as the situation worsened, Cy realized that he was unable to change the situation of declining fish populations and he therefore had to get out of fishing.

But although people like Cy can rarely change the situations that they find themselves in through their own actions, they can and often do join with others to engage in collective actions that could lead to such changes. Cy Wiggins, for example, could have worked with other fishermen or even with environmental groups to change the situation. Collective actions could have stopped overfishing and decreased water pollution, allowing fishermen like Cy to continue to fish. But Cy and others did not engage in collective actions, and so they now find themselves in their current predicament.

The fact that Cy could have engaged in collective actions but did not brings out an important point about collective actions—they are neither automatic nor always successful. Individuals with common interests may not get together to pursue their interests, and if they do, their collective actions may be ineffective. Therefore, when constructing scenarios about collective action, it is important to examine the conditions that give rise to such actions and the conditions that lead them to be successful.

Collective actions are often part of larger **social movements,** organized and concerted efforts to promote social change by individuals and groups, such as the civil rights movement, the labor movement, the women's movement, and the environmental movement. Throughout the remainder of this chapter, I use the terms *collective action* and *social movement* interchangeably. You should keep in mind, however, that collective actions can occur without a social movement and that within social movements there can be many different types of collective actions.

Types of Social Movements

The first step in analyzing social movements and collective action is to map out what they are about. This can be done by analyzing three aspects of a social movement: identity, adversary, and societal goals (Castells 1997; Touraine 1965, 1966).

- *Identity:* a movement's self-definition of the situation. You can obtain a good sense of a movement's identity by determining for whom it speaks and who it sees as its potential members.

- *Adversary:* a movement's enemy, that is, the people, groups, or-ganizations, or institutions that it wants to change or wants to prevent from proceeding with some change. You can obtain a good indication of the adversaries by noting the identity of the targets of collective actions.

- *Societal Goals:* the vision that those in the movement have of what an alternative situation would look like. You can identify the goals by looking at the model behaviors that activists seek to emulate and for which they strive. Sometimes, intellectuals within the movement construct utopias that convey their goals and visions.

Within broadly construed social movements, there are often submovements with different identities, adversaries, and goals. Con-sider the *environmental movement,* which includes all forms of col-lective action designed to change the destructive relations between human action and the natural environment. Within the larger envi-ronmental movement, there are the conservationists who see their constituency as nature lovers, their adversary as uncontrolled devel-opment, and their goal as preservation of wilderness areas. In con-trast, there are the "not in my backyard" groups, which see the local community as their primary constituency, target polluters, and who have as their goal quality of life and health issues. There is also the "save the planet" component of the environmental movement repre-sented by Greenpeace. Their identity is as internationalists, and their adversary is unfettered global development and the governments that support it. Their goal is to create environmental sustainability (Castells 1997).

Of course, there is a good deal of overlap between these three seg-ments of the environmental movement, and that is why they are all part of the larger environmental movement. But when it comes to

constructing scenarios based on your understanding of possible collective actions, it is important to map out the range of possible identities, adversaries, and goals of those with common interests. For
example, in "Where Have All the Salmon Gone," we could imagine
collective actions by environmentalists designed to stop salmon fishing altogether; actions that would attempt to decrease water pollution; or actions aimed at regulating large-scale, corporately organized
fishing. Each of these strategies emerges from a different identity and
has different adversaries. Most important, each would affect Cy
Wiggins and his family in a different way. Conservationists' attempts
to stop fishing would mean an end to Cy's way of life. Controlling
polluters, if it worked, could allow Cy to continue to fish, and a
Greenpeace strategy of stopping "corporate" fishing could reinvigo-
rate "family" fishing.

Logics of Collective Action

Just because collective actions could lead to positive changes in
people's situation does not mean that they will engage in those
actions. Therefore, understanding collective action requires analysis
of both the factors that make collective actions more likely and those
that can impede collective action. To facilitate such analysis, histori-
ans and social scientists have highlighted four important components
of collective action: interests, mobilization, organization, and opportunity (Tilly 1978).

Interests. The first thing you need to do when constructing scenarios
about collective action is look for people who have *grievances* and,
therefore, a common interest. For example, neighborhood residents
may be upset about a proposed school closing. People of color harmed
by racial segregation and prevented from voting had grievances that
led to the civil rights movement. Cy Wiggins and other fishermen are
aggrieved by their inability to catch large enough numbers of salmon.

By identifying the common interest and grievances, you can
delimit the population that could be mobilized to engage in a

collective action. Because those with a grievance have an interest in changing the situation (or preventing a proposed change in the situation), they are the ones who could engage in a collective action designed to further their interests.

The earliest theories of collective action tended to focus on the importance of interests and grievances. *Deprivation theory* argues that social movements are more likely when people feel deprived of what they believe they deserve. According to this perspective, it is **relative deprivation,** a person's sense that he or she is disadvantaged in comparison to others, that leads to collective actions (Merton and Rossi 1957). For example, discriminated groups often feel relatively deprived as they compare what they can do to what those in the discriminating majority are able to do.

Relative deprivation also can be felt as a result of changes over time in people's expectations. Known as the "J-curve" thesis, this perspective argues that collective action is more likely to occur during times of rising expectation (Davies 1981). During such periods, people expect their situation to improve, usually because there has already been some actual improvement. But when their situation stops improving and becomes worse, the gap between what people expect and what they are actually experiencing widens, leading to grievances.

Grievances and relative deprivation are often the result of structural strains caused by changes in social institutions (Johnson 1966; Smelser 1962). As social institutions and old ways of doing things change, people are forced to change as well. But because their expectations are based on the old system, they experience relative deprivation. This perspective tends to see collective actions as outbursts of discontent resulting from people's reactions to the strains created by larger structural changes.

Those who focus on rising expectations and social strains tend to view grievances, perceived or real, as automatically propelling people to act collectively. But the reality is that people often have grievances and fail to act to change their situation. This has led social scientists to examine other factors that contribute to collective action.

Mobilization. Grievance, although necessary for collective action, is not sufficient. Also required is **mobilization,** the marshaling of resources that are needed for a collective action to occur. Through mobilization, those who have a grievance come together and engage in activities designed to change their situation. Therefore, understanding social movements also requires analyzing how groups mobilize their members and the resources they need to engage in collective action (Oberschall 1973).

The perspective that focuses on mobilization is known as *Resource Mobilization Theory.* This theory developed out of a paradoxical insight: It is often rational for an individual who has an interest in a collective action to *not* participate in the collective action. Why is nonparticipation, also known as "free riding," rational?

The problem of free riding occurs when people are trying to procure a *public good,* a product or service whose consumption cannot be withheld from some and provided to others (Olson 1971). City parks are public goods, as is the military, which defends a population from potential attacks. Because the benefits of public goods cannot be withheld from some and provided to others, rational actors can free-ride and not contribute to the provision of the public good but still enjoy the benefits of a good that they want. However, if everyone acts rationally and free-rides, the public good will not be provided and everyone will be worse off. That is why governments usually finance public goods such as parks and the military through obligatory taxes.

Collective action can be viewed as a public good. Those with grievances want a change (or want to prevent a change). If the collective action is successful, they will benefit. But the benefits of collective action, such as civil rights legislation or keeping a neighborhood school open, cannot be given to just those who participated in the collective action. So rational actors have an incentive to not participate in a collective action even though they want what the collective action is seeking to obtain. As a result, many collective actions never get off the ground because everyone thinks that others will engage in the collective action and they will be able to reap the benefits of others' actions.

How do those with grievances overcome the free rider problem and mobilize people and other resources for a collective action? People can be induced to participate through *selective incentives,* rewards given directly to them for their participation (Olson 1971). Unions, for example, have been known to give members life insurance policies. People also can be moved to participate through the intrinsic rewards of participation. Ideologies and propaganda also can persuade people to participate, as can group loyalties and identities.

The need to induce participation to mobilize a group points to the importance of **social movement organizations,** formal organizations that work toward social movement goals. These organizations are pivotal, according to resource mobilization theory, because it is through them that people are motivated to contribute the resources—money, time, materials—needed for collective actions (McCarthy and Zald 1977; Zald and McCarthy 1987). You can even have an entire *social movement industry* consisting of competing social movement organizations that vie for the same resources, and *social movement entrepreneurs* who make their fame and fortune by facilitating resource mobilization.

Organization. Because of the need to mobilize resources, organization becomes crucial in collective action. But it is not just social movement organizations that are important. Other organizations and social networks can play a very important role. For example, studies of the civil rights movement have shown how important black churches were in mobilizing people (Oberschall 1973). So it is also important when constructing scenarios about collective action to examine the preexisting social connections among those within an aggrieved population. Two types of connections are especially important (Tilly 1978):

- *Catness:* the degree to which people belong to the same category and are, therefore, a relatively homogeneous group. A common category creates loyalty and increases the salience of an over-arching identity.

- *Netness:* the degree to which there exist social networks linking people to one another. Networks are an important means for disseminating ideas and coordinating collective actions.

Together, catness and netness organize a population and thereby increase the probability that individuals will contribute resources to collective actions.

Opportunity. Although the internal dynamics of social movements—interests, mobilization, and organization—are very important, you also need to take into account the opportunities a group has for engaging in collective action. Aggrieved populations, even with good organization and mobilization potential, are unlikely to engage in collective action if the potential costs of doing so are too high (Tilly 1978). For example, under repressive regimes that are willing to use force to maintain their power, there is less opportunity to engage in collective action. In contrast, opportunities are greater when there are political vacuums, that is, when power realignments are taking place and those vying for political power are seeking additional sources of support.

In general, when developing scenarios about collective action, you need to take into account the interests and actions of both parties that are in conflict over some social change—the aggrieved party and those who are the target of the collective action. Reaction by targets can range from outright repression to encouraging facilitation. Therefore, an important predictor of the occurrence of collective action and the forms it takes (e.g., violent vs. nonviolent, legal vs. illegal means) is the climate's conduciveness to such actions (McAdam, McCarthy, and Zald 1996). It is also important to investigate the extent to which targets attempt to co-opt social movements and their leaders by giving in to some demands but not fully redressing a group's grievances.

SOCIOLOGICAL EYE ANALYSIS GUIDE

Imagining scenarios about the future is the final step in analyzing a case or situation. After you have mapped out the social connections, examined them from multiple theoretical perspectives, explored how social actors see them through their culture, and analyzed how power differentials and inequalities affect what people can do, you need to step back and place the situation within its broader context. This requires, as you have seen, examining the social conditions that make a specific situation possible.

You can shift your attention to these background conditions by examining multiple driving forces. Analyzing *demographic forces* will help you construct scenarios about changes in the larger population in which a case is situated. Analyzing *technological forces* will help you imagine scenarios about changes in the tools, knowledge, and skills people have at their disposal and the effect of these changes on social connections and the environment. And analyses of *collective actions* and *social movements* will help you devise scenarios that take into account how people can change the situations in which they find themselves.

Of course, in any given situation, some driving forces may be more important than others. In "Where Have All the Salmon Gone?" technological changes and, potentially, collective actions appear to be important driving forces that could alter the situation in the future, whereas demographic forces seem less relevant. However, even when a driving force seems irrelevant, you should not ignore it. For example, the fact that the Wiggins live in a rural area with strong ties within their community could be important, as could the trend for children of parents who work in the primary sector (farming, fishing) to leave that sector and migrate to urban areas. There are also other driving forces that you may want to take into account, such as political forces having to do with governments and laws and economic forces that shape markets and competition.

So when you imagine how things could change by constructing scenarios, think about all the driving forces that could be at work and then select those driving forces that you think are the most relevant given the situation you are analyzing. Use the following Sociological Eye Analysis Guide to help you analyze the driving forces that you may want to take into account as you construct scenarios about social change.

Constructing Scenarios

❏ How would you describe the background conditions that make the current situation possible?

❏ What are some of the "what if" questions that you could pose about this case?

❏ If the background conditions were to change, how would such changes affect social connections and interactions?

Demographic Forces

❏ How would you describe the population in this situation? For example, are they people residing in a geographic area, or does the population consist of members of an organization, clients of a business, students in a school, or organizations within an industry?

Population Processes

❏ How big is this population? Has it been growing or declining in size?

❏ What are the birth and death rates within this population? Have these rates been going up or down? Compared to other populations, are they high or low? What factors are contributing to the observed level of births and deaths in this population? Do you expect these factors to change?

❏ Is there movement into and out of this population? If so, which movement is more prevalent? What factors are propelling (or prohibiting) exits and entries?

❏ Overall, how would you describe this population's dynamics? Would you characterize it as a high-fertility, high-mortality population; a high-fertility, low-mortality population; a low-fertility, high-mortality population; or a low-fertility, low-mortality population?

❏ Are the population and its use of resources sustainable in the current environment? Is the population caught in a vicious cycle characterized by population processes that are exacerbating problems like poverty?

Population Composition

❏ What is the sex ratio in this population? Has it been fairly constant or changing over time?

❏ Is the population's age distribution skewed toward specific age groups? Compared to other populations, are their proportionately more older people, more younger people, or more middle-aged people?

❏ Given the current age structure, are there demographic futures in the pipeline? If so, what is likely to happen and when?

❏ What is the dependency ratio in this population? Is this ratio likely to change as this population ages?

Urbanism and Community

❏ Where does this case take place? Is this place a rural, urban, or suburban area? How do you think the level of urbanization is affecting what goes on in this case?

❏ How would you characterize the extent of community in the current situation? Do people have close social ties to others? Are there ties to family members or friends? Have there been changes in the extent of community?

Technological Forces

☐ How would you describe the technologies that are used in this case? What tasks are being performed? What materials and supplies are used? What do people have to know to do the tasks?

☐ How complex is the technology? Compared to other technologies, is it more or less automated? Is it more or less routine? How would you characterize the technology in terms of production continuity (small-batch, large-batch, or continuous processing)?

☐ To what extent has the technology that is currently used been affected by the information technology revolution? How important is information in this technology, and how is information processed, transformed, and distributed? How would changes in the use of information affect the current technology?

Technological Impacts

☐ If this situation deals with work, in what sectors of the economy (primary, secondary, or tertiary) is this work located? Has the industry in which the activities take place been growing or declining? Have there been technological changes in how people do work in this sector? If so, what new occupations are on the rise, and what old occupations are in decline?

☐ How would you characterize the level of technological development of the society (or region, sector, or organization) in which this case takes place? Is it highly developed (on the cutting edge), in the process of developing, or undeveloped?

☐ Where would you place the society (region, sector, or organization) in relation to other societies (regions, sectors, or organizations). Is it in the core, the periphery, or the semi-periphery? How dependent is it on other countries (regions, sectors, or organizations)? What factors are impeding technological development?

❏ Do the currently used technologies have negative externalities, that is, costs that do not figure into the price of the technology? If so, what are these externalities? Do they involve impacts on the environment, and, if so, what are the negative impacts? Have governmental actions attempted to decrease these externalities, and, if so, how?

Collective Actions and Social Movements

❏ Are there aspects of the current situation that some people would like to change (or would like to prevent from changing), and, if so, what are these aspects?

❏ Are any social movements or recent collective actions shaping the current situation? If so, how would you describe the social movement or collective action? What is its identity? Whom does it see as its adversary? What are its goals?

Logics of Collective Action

❏ Is there an identifiable population that has a common interest and common grievances? If so what is the common interest? What are its grievances?

❏ Compared to other populations, are those in this population better off or worse off? Do those with grievances feel relatively deprived?

❏ Have there been any changes in this population's situation? Have expectations been rising? Has the ability to meet these expectations changed?

❏ What is the "good" that the social movement or collective action is trying to bring about? Will it be difficult to withhold this good from some and provide it to others?

❏ Is there any evidence of free riding, that is, cases of people who want a public good but who are not participating in the collective action? If so, how are those involved in the social movement attempting to overcome free riding? Are there social movement organizations involved in mobilizing resources and people?

❒ Within the aggrieved population, what is the extent of "catness" and "netness"? How homogeneous is the population? What networks exist within this population, and how are those networks created and maintained?

❒ How would you describe the opportunity structure? Are there significant costs of potential collective actions? Does it appear that there is or could be a political opening that could create opportunities for collective action?

Decision Case: "Deaf President Now!"

On a Sunday afternoon in early March 1988, the board of trustees of Gallaudet University met in a hotel room in downtown Washington, D.C., a few miles away from the campus, to consider three finalists for the position of president of the university. Two of the finalists were deaf men, and one was a hearing woman. Gallaudet, the world's only liberal arts college devoted exclusively to the education of deaf students, had never had a deaf president in its 124-year history. Was this when the pattern would change? It was time for the board to decide. There were many people who had been working for months promoting the view to the board and to others that it was long past time for the institution to have a deaf president. There had been dozens of articles in deaf publications and letters to the board presenting lists of qualified deaf candidates. There had even been a rally the week before in which leaders from deaf communities all over the country spoke about the need for a deaf president. What should the board do, the 17 hearing and three deaf members asked themselves? After several hours of very heated deliberations, the board made its decision.

Meanwhile, on campus, hundreds of deaf people gathered near the front entrance of the university anxiously awaiting the announcement from the university's board of trustees of whom they had selected as the new president of the university. The mood of the crowd was one of cautious optimism. After all, two of the three finalists were deaf. People milled around in the balmy, unusually warm late-afternoon sunshine. They were waiting for a representative from the board to come to Gallaudet to announce what had been decided.

But no one came from the board of trustees. Rather, someone distributed a preprinted flier from the university's public relations office

AUTHOR'S NOTE: This case was written by John Christiansen and Sharon Barnartt. A more detailed description of the events discussed in this case can be found in Christiansen and Barnartt (1995).

that stated that the board had selected as the university's seventh president Elisabeth Zinser, a hearing woman with almost no knowledge about deafness but with extensive experience in higher education administration. The crowd reacted with disbelief, incredulity, anger, hostility, and, within a few minutes, outrage at the board's decision. Many people charged onto the busy street that borders the university's front entrance. They blocked traffic, made speeches in sign language, or watched others making speeches. One of the speakers angrily vowed to make many people "pissed off" tomorrow, and another said that the decision by the board showed that they were "deaf to our demands." One speaker exhorted the crowd to demonstrate its displeasure by marching to the hotel where the board was meeting and demanding an explanation. Scores of deaf people and a few hearing supporters walked, ran, or drove several miles to the hotel to confront the board and insist that the decision be changed.

Chaos reigned at the hotel where the board was meeting, as the uproar was unexpected and unprecedented. For one thing, the board thought that most people on campus agreed with them that the hearing woman was the most qualified candidate. In fact, there had been several campus committees involved in the job search, and most of them, including the faculty senate, had endorsed Zinser. What was happening? Never before had deaf people reacted so strongly or so negatively to a decision made by their purported benefactors.

The board soon agreed to a hastily arranged meeting with a small delegation of protesters. Afterward, the chairperson of the board, Jane Bassett Spilman, was widely quoted as having said during that meeting that deaf people were not ready to function in a hearing world. (It turned out that she was misquoted, but the damage was done.)

After the meeting, Spilman came down to the hotel entrance and addressed the impatient throng. Impeccably dressed as always, austere and aristocratic, Spilman, in her sixth year as the head of the board, attempted to explain the rationale behind the board's decision to appoint someone who neither could sign nor knew very much about deafness or deaf people as the next president of the university for deaf students. In this effort, she was altogether unsuccessful. Perhaps one reason she had difficulty persuading the crowd was that she, like most of the other hearing members on the board, could not sign either. As usual, she relied on an interpreter.

Act I of what became known as "Deaf President Now" (DPN) ended late Sunday night. After the protesters attempted to vent their anger at the board's decision at the hotel, some of them trekked to the White House and then to the U.S. Capitol to continue to express their displeasure. Eventually, all of the protesters headed back to the campus about a mile northeast of the Capitol.

Meetings took place throughout the night. The board had made their decision; now, students and other members of the deaf community tried to decide how best to overturn the board's decision. After long discussions, some people decided to move a large number of cars from their customary places and park them in such a way that they blocked all but one of the gates to the campus. It was thus impossible to open those gates when faculty and staff members began arriving for work the next day; protesters monitored who could come in through the one open gate. The campus was effectively closed, and no classes could be held. Because the weather was unseasonably warm, students and other protesters stayed outside, having rallies and meeting and waving signs at cars driving by on the main street that borders the campus.

By the next afternoon, the protesters formulated a list of demands. These included the resignation of the newly appointed president and appointment of a deaf president, the resignation of the chairperson of the board of trustees, no reprisals against the protesters, and a deaf majority on the board. Words like "paternalism" and "plantation mentality" began to be used to describe the board of trustees. Meetings of members of the board and representatives of the protesters produced no changes on either side.

As the week progressed, events escalated. Four undergraduate students, three men and one woman, all the children of deaf parents and thus native users of American Sign Language, emerged as leaders of the protest, although they were not the original instigators. Deaf students in several residential schools closed their schools in sympathy protests, and many deaf people rushed to Washington to join the protest. Offers of help and statements of support came from local and national disability rights and civil rights organizations, congressional representatives, and several presidential candidates. Unsolicited donations—ultimately totaling more than $25,000—poured in. The protest was covered in newspapers from the *New York Times* to small-town papers, it received extensive coverage on national television and radio newscasts, and one of the student leaders was named "person of the week" by ABC News. Even the Gallaudet University faculty and staff voted to support the protesters against the board of trustees.

After four days of protest events, meetings, marches, and the continued closure of the university, the new president resigned. Three days later, the board of trustees agreed to all of the protesters' demands. A deaf man, King Jordan, a popular Gallaudet dean with limited experience in higher education administration (and one of the three finalists for the position), was appointed as president, and another deaf man was selected as the chair of the board of trustees when Spilman resigned. There were no reprisals against students, and a task force was established to study the composition of the board, which came to have a deaf/hard-of-hearing majority within a year after the protest.

PART II

Decision Cases

The Worth
of a Sparrow

Who sees with equal eye, as God of old,
A hero perish or a sparrow fall,
Atoms or systems into ruin hurl'd,
And now a bubble burst, and now a world.

Alexander Pope
Essay on Man, I, 3, 87ff.

As Phil Larsen drove past the university's research fields on June 6, 1991, his eyes took in the deep green patches of winter wheat laid out in squares and, beyond them, plots of stout barley and pale green oats. "A regular smorgasbord," he thought. "Just like Wharton says, one big bird feeder."

"How'd I get into this mess anyway?" he asked out loud. Phil was head of the Department of Plant Pathology at the University of Minnesota's agriculture campus in Saint Paul. He had just left a meeting of the Bird Control Committee; he was the committee chair.

Phil's "mess" had started about a year earlier, on August 1, 1990. On that day, he had been heading home for supper via this same route when he noticed a remote telecasting van for a local TV station parked

AUTHOR'S NOTE: This case was written by R. Kent Crookson, Melvin J. Stanford, and Steve Simmons. It is part of the database of cases available through the Clearinghouse for Decision Case Education at the University of Minnesota.

in the plots with people standing around one of the bird-cage traps. "I was aware of the Animal Rights Coalition's concern about the trapping of birds on campus and realized immediately what was going on," he said. With mixed feelings of responsibility and curiosity, he drove over to the site. His anxiety increased as he discovered that the crew was not just filming; it was telecasting live the lead story for KSTP's *Six-o'-Clock Evening News,* one of the Twin Cities' major news programs.

Although Phil always had known that live trapping of birds represented a public relations problem, he had never guessed it would come to this. As the prospect of serving as a live-telecast spokesperson for the university on the sensitive issue of humane treatment of animals presented itself before him, Phil became keenly aware of the burden of public accountability that went with his administrative job.

Over the past several years, the university had been the focus of a continuing barrage of negative or unflattering news stories. The stories accused the university of environmental insensitivity, harboring reprobate athletes, an inefficient physical plant, and so forth. The coverage of one 1987 story about alleged misuse of state funds had resulted in the resignation of the university president.

To his relief, Phil was not asked to speak before the cameras that night. Had the telecasters known he was head of the department responsible for bird control, he might not have been so lucky. His involvement with the Animal Rights Coalition (ARC) was certainly not over, however; it had just begun.

Phil had joined the University of Minnesota in 1985. When he first learned that his department's responsibilities included controlling birds in the campus cereal research plots, he didn't give the responsibility much thought. "I wondered how we got the job," he said. "I was simply told that Plant Path had always done it. I never did question our control procedure."

The University of Minnesota's research fields were plagued by birds that flew in from surrounding urban neighborhoods annually to feed on the ripening grain. Several control measures had been implemented with varying success depending on the crop and season. Ears of corn were individually bagged with paper as the crop approached maturity; this proved to be costly but highly effective. Birds did not attack soybeans. The small grain plots, on the other hand, had been subjected to very serious bird damage. In addition to a variety of control methods (including scarecrows, noise guns, and scare balloons), traps were placed near the most vulnerable plots.

Phil found records indicating that the traps had been used continually since 1955. In two of the years during that period, more than 10,000 birds were trapped, but the average was closer to half that number. They were "live" traps; birds were lured inside with pieces of bread where, because of the trap design, they were unable to escape. Water and shade were provided so that the birds were contained in relative tranquility until someone came to empty the traps. "Desirable" birds such as doves and song birds were set free, but "undesirable" ones such as sparrows, starlings, and grackles were stuffed into a bag and suffocated.

For many years, the suffocated birds had been discarded, but, beginning in the 1980s, they were provided another fate. In the 1970s, the university had established a raptor center, which began as a hospital for injured wild birds of prey. By 1990, the center had become very popular nationally and treated more than 500 injured birds, almost half of which were returned to the wild. It had developed into a renowned research and education center and, in 1990, had accommodated 73,000 schoolchildren, who came as curious visitors to learn about some of nature's most fascinating creatures.

Many of these raptors (kestrels, falcons, etc.) were natural bird hunters; small birds were an essential part of their diet. Therefore, it was convenient for both the cereal researchers and the raptor center researchers to get together. Beginning in the mid-1980s, the center fed all the birds trapped and not released (about 6,000 each year) to raptors in their care.

Over the years, the bird traps had been a subject of controversy. A 1981 letter from one of the university's mathematics professors to the College of Agriculture dean called for abandonment of bird trapping in the university's agricultural fields. The professor noted how disturbing it would be to one day have university bird trapping featured on the evening TV news or in the morning newspaper. The dean acknowledged the potential negative impact of the practice on public support of the university and said he would urge serious consideration of alternative methods of protecting the crops.

Faculty in Phil's own department questioned the adequacy of the bird control measures. In July 1987, one of the cereal pathology professors complained that the traps and other methods of control were not successfully protecting his research plots and requested that a committee be formed to determine effective control measures.

Phil shared the letter with a few interested staff in the department. One professor responded that the present bird management was expensive and apparently not too effective. He suggested that the research be moved out of the cities "to avoid the social and pest problems currently being experienced." The university held more than 1,000 acres of research land, of quality equal to the campus land, about 20 miles south of the campus.

Moving the research out of the cities was felt to be the "last resort" by most of the university cereal researchers, who considered the availability of extensive plot areas adjacent to their offices and laboratories to be of "inestimable value." Yet, because of their convenient in-city location, the on-campus plots were raided annually by thousands of birds that nested in the trees of the surrounding suburban yards. The university's cereal plots located out of the city were spared bird damage, apparently because of their position within a landscape of similar fields and because birds were fewer in number in the country.

For the six years prior to the summer of 1990, Phil had given little thought to the bird control issue. Other issues had kept his thoughts occupied, among them the fact that the Department of Plant Pathology had suffered very steep cuts in its education funding because of low undergraduate enrollment.

Cereal breeders in the Agronomy Department, plus virtually all of his own faculty and staff who worked in the fields, recommended that the traps and other control methods be maintained. "The traps are highly effective," said Dann Adair, the field plot supervisor who managed them.

Then, on August 1, 1990, the mathematics professor's decade-old fears were realized. Both the evening telecast and the next morning's newspaper featured bird killing at the university. On August 2, the morning after the telecast, Dan Oldre, Vice President of ARC in Minnesota, hand-delivered a letter to the dean of the College of Agriculture. ARC had conducted a surveillance and investigation and determined that the university had been killing 10,000 birds per year by trapping and then suffocating them, 400 to 500 at a time, in a bag. ARC objected to this cruel wasting of animal life, declared it ineffective in controlling the birds, and insisted that the university "immediately stop the killing of these birds." The letter was copied to several university administrators and many of the television, radio, and newspaper outlets in the Twin Cities. The KSTP telecast had preceded the letter because of a tip given to a KSTP reporter.

Both the *Minneapolis Star Tribune* and the *Saint Paul Pioneer Press* ran articles about the confrontation between the university and ARC. Phil was quoted in the August 4 *Star Tribune* as saying "We certainly do not enjoy killing birds, but I think it needs to be said that these plants are extremely valuable and will be useful in the development of high-yielding plants that will feed people worldwide." Oldre responded:

> We're not saying their experiments are not valuable, and we're not saying the birds are not a threat, but the method they are using to control the birds is cruel and extreme. . . . We want them to dismantle the cages and get them out of there and never try that again.

Dean Wharton consulted with Phil and Adair and, on August 6, responded to Oldre's letter. He promised to pursue alternative methods to control the birds and offered to meet with ARC members for a discussion.

Until the August 2 ARC letter, birds caught in university traps were suffocated. On August 7, the university's newspaper, *The Minnesota Daily*, ran an article titled "Researchers Pick CO_2 as Bird Control Choice." The article quoted Adair as saying, "This is still a form of suffocation, but it may be less stressful for the birds. We want to do the most humane thing. We'll try it out and experiment with it to see if it's a good way."

In the same *Daily* article, Guy Hodge, staff naturalist for the Humane Society in Washington, D.C., was quoted as saying, "By trapping the birds, you have only reduced the competition for ideal nesting sites. What you end up with is an increased survival rate among the [remaining] birds, thus increasing the population." The article quoted "University officials" as saying, "We have detailed records kept from 1955 saying the traps do undoubtedly make a big difference in reducing the numbers of birds."

A meeting between university and ARC representatives was held on Friday, August 10. On Monday, August 13, the *Daily* ran an article that reported that the university and ARC had agreed on the use of bird traps for the rest of the season but that the ARC would insist on more humane methods next year.

An August 13 letter to Dean Wharton from Mary Britton Clouse, an ARC representative, reviewed several of the agreements that she understood had been reached during that meeting. On August 20, Phil wrote to Dean Wharton with reactions to several of Clouse's impressions about agreements reached at the meeting. An August 22 letter from Dean Wharton to Ms. Clouse clarified the university's understandings. Dean Wharton was careful to point out that although the university would explore additional and alternative methods for controlling the birds, it had not agreed to stop trapping.

About that time, Phil began receiving some supportive comments from members of the community. A telephone message taken by his secretary read "Any time you kill a grackle or sparrow, we bird watchers really appreciate it." A woman from Saint Paul sent a $10 contribution in support of the bird control program with a note that said

"Please accept this small donation to help you smother sparrows and starlings who attack your crop next year."

A campus employee sent Phil an article that appeared in a weekly paper called *Minnesota Outdoor News.* The article was about an organization called Putting People First, a group of concerned citizens who objected to being intimidated by "animal rights activists." Accompanying the article was a petition to the U.S. Congress requesting that votes by Congress reflect the majority of American citizens, not just "a minority of vocal extremists." There was a place to sign the petition and instructions for joining the organization and/or for sending money to support it.

It was in this climate of diverse viewpoints that Phil pondered his course of action between the 1990 and 1991 growing seasons. "It seems to me that this grain is important enough to justify the sacrifice of these birds," he said to colleagues. "There are world hunger and economic implications. We have to consider our right to prioritize research of value to humans over creature life. And there's another, kinda far out issue," Phil offered. "Do plants have a right to protection? I've heard it asked several times."

On September 7, 1990, Phil met with several interested university faculty and field staff to consider the issues. Minutes from the meeting included the following statements:

> The effectiveness of our current bird control program was discussed and it was agreed that the current program was effective and needs to be continued. . . . Phil Larsen appointed a committee, for which he will serve as chairperson, to develop and establish an integrated plan for bird control on the Saint Paul plots that includes coordination of all individual projects so that everyone knows what our overall objectives are.

The first Bird Control Committee meeting was held on November 6, 1990. There was a discussion of present techniques being used for control, including trapping, use of ribbons and balloons, alternate feeding sites, and raptors (a falconer had been employed from 1982 to

1990 to visit the plots during periods of heavy bird feeding. He not only helped collect trapped birds for the raptor center but also brought live raptors with him that flew over the plots to scare the birds). Following a discussion of the merits and shortcomings of current approaches, committee members were assigned to check out other control options, including hawk-shaped balloons, recorded distress calls, and applications of hot pepper oils to the grain.

The next Bird Control Committee meeting was held on December 10, 1990. Progress reports were given on assignments from the previous meeting, and there was a discussion about sending representatives to the upcoming Great Plains Animal Damage Control meetings to be held in Nebraska.

At the March 1991 Bird Control Committee meeting, an update on alternative control methods suggested several promising options. John Arent (the falconer) and colleagues reported on a study they had initiated to evaluate various sprayed repellents. Phil reported on a meeting with Mary Britton Clouse during which Mary provided additional bird control information and informed him that the Humane Society of the United States provided small grants (approximately $3,000 to $5,000) for research. The College of Agriculture's public relations officer attended and discussed proper handling of public interactions.

At an April 25, 1991, meeting of the committee, Adair and Arent gave a report on the Animal Control Conference they had attended in Lincoln. They indicated that there were lots of ideas that "someone said" worked, but nothing of particular promise. The group recognized the need for a statement for the media in anticipation of objections to the bird control program for the 1991 season. It was agreed that Phil and Adair would prepare a one-page document providing an overview of the college's bird control program to be posted on the bird traps and anywhere else that might be appropriate for the purposes of communicating the issues.

What to do in the case of a hostile confrontation was discussed during the April 25 meeting. Phil observed, "Both Dann and John know that this is a potentially very delicate issue, and that they will be under intense scrutiny." This led to the question of abandoning trapping, but "capitulation" was felt to be out of the question by most of the committee. The possibility of trapping and re-releasing the birds was suggested (re-releasing at night or at some distant location) but was considered impractical. Toward the end of the meeting, one of the cereal breeders said, "Right now let's not confuse the process. Let's go forward; follow the KISS principle." Phil knew this meant "Keep It Simple, Stupid."

On May 29, 1991, the committee met again to make specific decisions for implementing a bird control program for the coming year. It was decided to employ traps as early as June 15 to protect the winter wheat that would be forming grain. Various assignments were made, including an evaluation of sprayed grape juice concentrates (reported to repel birds), sprayed hot pepper sauce, balloons, ribbons, and loudspeakers with distress calls. The plan was to vary the approach throughout the season to prevent birds from becoming accustomed to any one control tactic. A June 6 meeting was planned for all faculty and technicians from participating projects to inform them about, and to solicit their participation in, the control program.

There was a small crowd at the June 6 meeting. Larry Hood, assistant director of the Law Enforcement Division of the U.S. Fish and Wildlife Service, was there. Phil distributed a handout containing information about the bird damage management program for the 1991 season. It noted that birds would be trapped if necessary.

A few questions were asked, the history of the university/ARC interactions was briefly reviewed, and then Larry Hood initiated an interesting dialogue.

"Think about how this looks folks," he began.

If you don't let the momma bird go back to her nest, the young back in the nest will suffer. The "humaneiacs" will nail you if they find one dead robin, bluebird, or dove in your traps. And you will be extremely vulnerable. You will have violated the migratory bird laws. Those laws have been here since 1918.

"You gotta realize that they're on us," Larry continued. "They ask me: 'Why are you not enforcing the law?'"

"If one protected bird is in your trap, you're in violation," Larry warned. "Could be a $20,000 penalty, maybe a hundred thousand. The problem with trapping is, you attract them. Mourning doves will give you fits."

"What's to stop them from planting a protected bird in our traps?" asked one professor. "How can we avoid being framed?"

"You can't," answered Larry.

"So why don't we stop trapping?" asked the college's public relations officer.

Adair's response came quickly: "It's clearly valuable to trap."

"How do we know that?" asked another professor. "Does trapping really help, or is it a matter of revenge? Isn't it possible the baited traps actually attract birds? Do we have any data on the effect of traps and actual damage to the grain?"

"Tell us how to conduct the study and we'll do it," responded Adair.

Phil was as confused and concerned as any in the group by what he was hearing. It was obvious that some felt the trapping should be stopped. He looked at his watch. It was time to leave for an off-campus meeting. He asked Adair to field any remaining questions and excused himself.

And so it was that on the morning of June 6, 1991, Phil was again driving past the cereal plots asking out loud, "How'd I get into this mess anyway?" A colleague was with Phil in the car; he also had been in attendance at the June 6 meeting. Phil did most of the talking.

"We wouldn't be into this if it wasn't for ARC," he said.

But I've got to give them credit. We're all a lot more conscious and sensitive about the way we view the life of a creature. We've done a lot of things to get our act together, things we would never have tried on our own. But I'd like to get us to a place where we say "Enough is enough." We need to be ethically responsible, but we can't go overboard. They have taken the issue and exploited the media to influence public opinion in their favor. Will we really serve the public if we give in to them?

"And there's another thing about all this," Phil continued. "I'm concerned about vandalism. I've heard that animal rights activists have the potential to act as terrorists. I've never feared for my life, but I've definitely been concerned about vandalism of the plots."

Phil looked at this colleague. "What's the right thing to do?" he asked.

Conflict at Riverside

Steve Williams and Rod Jessop find themselves in a new and interesting situation. They recently have become brothers-in-law. After years of viewing and dealing with each other from a distance—Steve is a senior manager and Rod a prominent trade unionist with a local engineering company—they now find themselves meeting socially on a regular basis. Given free choice, neither would seek the other's company. But because the Jessop family is a close-knit bunch that believes in doing things together, they have little choice. Anne, who is Steve's wife and Rod's sister, quietly insists that they try to get along "for the sake of the family." Both are good-natured fellows, and they resolve to do their best.

One Friday evening, they find themselves feeling very mellow. They have had a good meal and just enough beer and wine to fall into excellent conversation. After awhile, they find themselves alone, breaking an implicit taboo; they are talking about work. Both are in fine spirits, however, and are happy to continue. They are savvy operators and know that they will be able to steer clear of trouble. And who knows? They might just learn something useful from each other.

After some friendly jousting over the latest company gossip, Steve feels that the time may be right to find out where Rod stands on contract negotiations at the company's Riverside plant. The plant had been selected recently for major redesign of production operations.

AUTHOR'S NOTE: This case appears in G. Morgan, *Creative Organizational Theory*, pp. 335-337, copyright 1989 by Sage Publications. Reprinted by permission of the publisher.

Whereas the old design used fairly traditional systems of manufacture, new proposals had been developed to move toward a highly automated system involving a form of "group technology." Employees would work in teams responsible for major sections of the production process rather than as individuals working on separate and narrowly defined jobs. Many traditional tasks would disappear as computers and robots took over some of the routine functions, leaving the employees to perform the work requiring a higher degree of discretion and skill. The nature of the raw material being processed in the plant is such that this human element is still necessary. Thus, the management of the company had designed a plan to retrain employees for their new roles and to guarantee that all would have a place in the new system. The project is being heralded by senior managers within the firm as a "cutting edge" development that will help the company hold its competitive edge in the industry. However, the plan has been greeted with considerable skepticism among many employees and their union representatives.

Steve began, "You know, I'm having a really hard time in understanding what's happened at Riverside. By all accounts we have an ace production system that's absolutely essential if we are to keep abreast of new developments and remain competitive. The development department and the group handling the project seem to have worked out a scheme that will keep everyone happy. Better wages. No layoffs. A better quality product, and jobs that seem a darn sight cleaner and more interesting than those we have at present. It only makes sense that the contract should go through as soon as possible. It's the only way to secure the company's future. And we all win."

"Well, that's a matter of debate," replied Rod. "Sure, it looks like a great technology with a lot of advantages. But there's talk at the plant that this is the beginning of the end. Sure, it looks rosy up front, especially for you guys at head office. But many of the guys at Riverside and elsewhere have their doubts."

"What do you mean?" asked Steve. "How can there be doubts? Retraining, more money, and everyone has a job. No layoffs! What more can one ask for? Progress demands change, and this seems a change where everyone is being looked after. What do you mean this is the beginning of the end? It's the beginning of a new future for the company."

"For the company maybe," replied Rod. "But a lot of people on the shop floor think the writing is on the wall. Computers and robots are already replacing some of the jobs. The workforce will decline by at least 20 percent over the next five years. I know that's being handled through retirements and general turnover, and there will be no layoffs now. But what about after the honeymoon? It stands to reason that the workforce is going to decline as the system takes hold. Most of us may have no role in the company of the future. So why should we get excited? Sure, there's a sweetener. We are going to get a little more in the pocket in the short run, and for many of us a change in work would be nice.

"But what about five years from now? How many jobs will be left then? And what about promotions? These changes are going to eliminate most of the supervisory jobs, so there will be no obvious path from the plant into management. We're going to find ourselves in a dead end as far as a career is concerned. And a lot of the guys feel that Riverside is just the thin edge of the wedge. If the pilot scheme goes through here, then the other plants will follow. There's no guarantee that they will get the same privileges; there's nothing in the contract beyond Riverside. If the Riverside deal goes through, then everything may be lost. The new system of work breaks old job patterns, and teamwork often ends up as a way of busting the unions. We may be giving up everything we've fought for."

"Ah, now we're getting down to it," said Steve. "The union is worried about how it's going to work out for you guys who are holding all the power. When it comes down to the guts of the issue, it's the old "us" and "them" mentality. You can't hold progress back. Riverside is the way of the future. If we don't go that way, we're all going to be dead in our tracks."

Rod responded, "Right. We may end up dead in our tracks. But what's worrying many of the guys at present is that as far as the company is concerned *we're* going to be dead anyway, especially the guys in the other plants. There are absolutely no guarantees that they're going to get the same treatment as Riverside. If the company is allowed to go its own way and make Riverside a success, there'll be jungle warfare. People in the other plants will know that the writing is on the wall for a fair number of jobs and will probably scramble like hell to make sure that they come out OK.

"We've seen it happen so many times elsewhere. A company declares it's going to reduce its workforce: Certain people are in; certain people are out. Obviously those who are in are going to support the scheme; solidarity breaks down. It's the old principle of divide and rule! We're not stupid. The record of employee relations in our company is not great. We've had to fight tooth and nail for what we've got. And we're not going to give it away. It's not that the guys want to fight, or that the strong unionists want to hang onto their power. This company may be looking after you guys at the head office. But it's certainly not looking after us. We weren't born yesterday. The Riverside deal does look good. But we may be crazy to accept it as it stands. It could mean the end of work for so many of our members elsewhere."

"Well, I guess we'll have to differ," sighed Steve. "I know that the people at head office are trying to take a fair and open view. I don't think that the Riverside plant is a danger to other plants. It's progress, man. We can't hang onto the same jobs forever. We've got to change with the times. I know there have been bad feelings in the company, especially since the big strike some years ago. But I think that's a thing of the past. The company learned from that. We have a new president and, by all accounts, among the best development engineering and organizational development departments in the industry. Many of the staff are locals, and I'm sure they have the interests of everyone at heart. I'm sure you're going to find you're off target on this one, Rod."

"Well," came the reply, "I guess we'll have to wait and see."

Tossin' and Turnin'

The upbeat tempo of *Tossin' and Turnin'* echoed through the car as Susana raced down Highway 14 en route to work. Ironically, the tune exactly matched her sentiment at the moment. As her eyes darted ferociously to and from the clock display, Susana strained to keep her focus on the road. She felt frustrated and disturbed, not to mention physically drained. Her thoughts were consumed with the day's camp experience. "Why did I agree to take this job anyway?" was the only thought that continued to reverberate through her mind.

Susana's job as a camp counselor for special needs children had taken a precipitous turn recently, trapping her in a web of uncertainty. When she initially accepted the position, Susana never imagined how difficult her task would be or the extent to which she would get involved. Now, she was grappling with both factors helplessly. In the process of struggling to manage four radically different young boys with a wide range of needs, Susana had become emotionally attached to her campers, especially the youngest boy, Dustin. Now she questioned that involvement. Dustin's troubled face continued to flash before Susana. "Was she overreacting to the recent things Dustin had told her?" Dustin was a young boy; Susana realized how fragile he was. His negative references toward home had startled Susana. Could Dustin's mother be neglecting him or, worse, subjecting him to emotional abuse? The thought frightened Susana terribly. "Do I have the right to intercede in this family's affairs?" she pondered.

AUTHOR'S NOTE: This case was written by Christine Hahn.

Super Summer Fun day camp lasted a total of six weeks, running Monday through Thursday from 11:00 until 4:00, from the start of June to mid-July. Susana Nielson, an up-and-coming senior in high school, discovered the program through her prior volunteer involvement with State Special Recreation Association (SSRA). As a teenager preoccupied with making money and paying for college, Susana initially questioned accepting the counselor position because of the low wage. Relying heavily on volunteer support, SSRA had to deal with strained financial resources. Therefore, Susana, trying both to continue her participation with SSRA and to fill her pocketbook, accepted the counselor position as well as a second job as a busgirl in a local restaurant. Her past experiences with SSRA had been incredible; the extra burden seemed well worth it. Plus, Susana would be able to work with kids for a change. In the past, her volunteer work had dealt mainly with adults. This new prospect excited her.

A two-day orientation provided a brief overview of the weeks to come, outlining the schedule of events and safety precautions and rules as well as conveying ideas for camp activities. The counselor's job involved planning and coordinating group activities each day, ranging from craft-building to baking cookies to hiking on the site's nature trails. Susana had been assigned a lively group of four boys, ranging in age from 7 to 12. Over a short period of time, Susana quickly discovered that the differences within the group extended far beyond the age factor. Their abilities and interests varied a great deal, and each boy had his unique strengths.

Marshall, at 12, was the oldest of the four. Quiet, reserved, but highly intelligent, Marshall easily stood out as the leader of the pack. His respectful obedience and maturity always came as a welcome relief. His creativity and artistic ability made him sparkle, inspiring admiration and often times jealousy. He joined the camp as a result of his unstable family condition. Camp was intended to introduce him to a fresh setting full of positive experiences.

Grant stood next in line at age 11. He lacked the mental competency to compete with Marshall. Grant was inhibited by a learning disorder coupled with attention deficit disorder, making him a particularly difficult child with whom to deal. He thrived for attention and made his opinions and desires known to all. His heart was golden; nonetheless, he was a handful, inflexible and unruly.

Daniel, at 9 years old, had a delightful charm unparalleled by the rest. Although restrained by a slight mental deficiency and restricted flexibility of motion, Daniel participated in each activity with an open mind and infectious enthusiasm. His infallible spirit never failed to bring a smile to Susana's face.

Dustin exceeded all the others in energy at the young age of 7. His rambunctiousness peaked throughout the day, causing a constant challenge to authority. Like Marshall, Dustin participated in the camp as a result of unstable home conditions. Standing shorter than the rest of the boys and slightly overweight, Dustin often felt inferior and discouraged. Therefore, he often detached himself from activities to avoid embarrassment. Because Dustin's detachment and depression severely affected his participation, Susana always kept a special eye on him.

Susana felt exhausted after the first week. She asked, "How will I manage five more weeks?" The orientation had been helpful; nonetheless, the magnitude of the task that lay ahead felt overwhelming. The outlines of activities that she planned each day rarely mapped the day's flow. Distractions seemed to arise endlessly, throwing everything off balance. She hated feeling out of control. Susana deeply cared for her campers; she wanted their experiences to be fun and exciting. Each day after camp, however, she felt disappointed and unfulfilled.

Susana tried to choose flexible activities, but each time problems occurred. A simple craft activity created considerable conflict. One project included gathering sticks and pieces of bark to construct basic marionettes. When the time came to begin building, crises erupted. Susana's clarity of directions proved to be of little help. Marshall quickly understood the task at hand and progressed rapidly, adding his own creative flair to the puppet's construction. Daniel had a sense of what needed to be done and immediately plugged away, his tongue curled outside his lip in determination. Grant, however, expressed his discontent with the choice of activity, folding his arms across his chest and assuming a disgusted stare. Dustin, meanwhile, started the project but abandoned it after a few minutes because he couldn't loop the string correctly around the wood. As Susana struggled to remotivate Grant to participate, Dustin's short fuse expired, and the stick was projected across the room in frustration. Glancing at Daniel, she noticed he was struggling to tie a knot. Marshall leaned back in his chair and rolled his eyes; he had easily completed the activity and awaited further instruction. After a few strained reprimands, the activity was officially brought to a close. "What activity can I set up next for failure?" Susana grumbled sarcastically.

Susana tried to manage her frustration as she continued to struggle at day camp; the days crawled by. At the start of the fourth week, however, Susana reached the peak of crisis. Over time, the relationships Susana shared with her four boys had strengthened. The boys freely talked with her now about things outside camp, and Susana enjoyed sharing her experiences with them, too. Dustin outpaced the rest with his handfuls of stories. He came to look forward to seeing Susana in the morning because then was the time that he could relate all the previous day's happenings. Their growing intimacy, however, unveiled disturbing news.

On Monday afternoon during an intense floor hockey game, Dustin's temper got the best of him as he struggled to control the puck. He immediately dropped his stick and found refuge in the corner of the gym. Susana did not scold him, for she had learned from experience that this only exacerbated the problem; instead, she calmly followed and sat beside him.

"Dustin, what's wrong?" Susana prodded. Dustin only turned his glance to a different point on the wall. "Hey, don't worry if a goal seems impossible. Believe me, it's a tough skill. Those in the big leagues have to practice for years to master it."

"I don't care," he mumbled. After a long period of silence, Dustin's eyes met Susana's glance, and he murmured, "I'm not good at anything. Everyone in school makes fun of me. They say I'm fat and they tease me when I can't do something. Nobody cares about me."

Susana searched to find the right words to console and reassure him. In her response, she confirmed her faith in him. She also stressed his mom's love for him. Immediately, she regretted this comment.

"My mom doesn't care about me. She's never around. She'd be happier if I was dead." His words were interrupted by the shrill sound of Grant's voice arguing over who deserves the puck. Susana was forced to end their talk in order to resolve the heated quarrel. Susana's thoughts, though, never drifted from her discussion with Dustin.

In fact, all she could think about was Dustin. The next day, Susana scrutinized his every move and carefully monitored their brief talks. She often sensed hesitation in Dustin's voice whenever the conversation drifted toward his family or friends. However, Dustin did not mention anything further about his mother. Nonetheless, his discomfort made Susana uneasy. She worried about Dustin and his fragile confidence, leading her to wonder if a harmful family situation might be making his state worse. All Susana knew was that Dustin's registration for the day camp had been based on an unstable family background. As a counselor, however, she didn't have access to any private or more thorough information to relieve her burning uncertainty.

Susana felt that she needed to talk to someone about her concerns. Her first inclination would have been to visit Barbara Walker, the camp site director. However, based on Susana's past experiences with her, she decided against it. She could remember the first incident clearly in her head. After her first troubling week of trying to adapt to the hectic, unpredictable flow of camp, she had decided to meet with Barbara for some advice on how to be a more effective counselor. She hoped Barbara could offer her some guidelines or at least some insight due to her experience. As Susana had approached the door to her office, raising her hand in the motion of a knock, Barbara burst from behind the door, nearly stampeding over her.

"Oh, Barbara, sorry to bother you but . . ." was all Susana could manage to utter.

"Susana, hi," Barbara interrupted. "I didn't quite hear what you said but unfortunately I must run. So much to do. Let's talk sometime tomorrow."

Before Susana could mumble a response, Barbara had escaped around the corner. In the weeks following, Susana continued to have trouble communicating with Barbara. During camp, Barbara raced around in a wild frenzy, distributing medicine, coordinating upcoming special events, and overseeing the camp's flow. After hours were consumed trying to organize cleanup and taking care of endless lists of phone calls and paperwork. Susana felt unwelcome to ask questions, causing her much frustration. She wondered, "How can Barbara offer me advice on how to be a better counselor when she can't even handle her job?"

As Susana strolled down the hall after camp on Tuesday afternoon, her mind whirled. "Was she overreacting to Dustin's comments?" Susana wondered. If so, how was she to deal with Dustin's despondent behavior at camp? At the same time, Susana wondered about the consequences that would result if she continued with her focus on Dustin. Her job required a balancing act to fulfill each of the boy's needs. The recent turn of events had thrown everything in Dustin's favor. If things continued this way, the other boys would suffer from inattention. Susana loved them all; she didn't want this job to become more difficult than it already was! Glancing at her watch, Susana quickly gathered her things and darted out to her car. She was late for work!

"And I was tossin' and turnin' . . ." The melody continued its lively beat as Susana's car weaved in and out of traffic. She let out a distressed sigh. Susana was a jumble of questions. Could she afford to investigate Dustin's situation further within her role as a counselor? Had she already stepped too far beyond her "limits"? How should she proceed?

Lucy Allman

Lucy Allman tapped on the door and prepared to enter Exam Room 2 of the Clark County Health Department Primary Care Clinic. Even before she entered the room, Lucy, a recently certified family nurse practitioner, recognized the strong odor of dirty clothing, soiled diapers, and unwashed children. She peeked around the door and said, "Hi, Mrs. Bradshaw. I'm Lucy Allman, a nurse practitioner. How can I help you today?"

Entering the room, Lucy noted a young woman with three children. Mrs. Bradshaw was seated, and a small, pale girl, whom Lucy estimated to be about 14 months old, sat fretfully on her lap. The other two children, boys who both appeared to be preschool age, sat quietly on the floor at the end of the room. Mrs. Bradshaw and her children all wore grimy clothing, and the children had a pungent smell. As Lucy approached Mrs. Bradshaw, she detected the underlying scent of cigarette smoke in the mix of odors.

Mrs. Bradshaw looked at the floor and replied, "We come over here from the emergency room—they sent us over here because we don't have no health insurance, and the baby is sick. The nurse at the emergency room said you all would see to us even if we don't have no money."

AUTHOR'S NOTE: This case was written by Kay Libbus and is part of the collection *Case Studies for Faculty Development* created by Rita Silverman and William M. Welty through the Center for Case Studies in Education at Pace University.

"Tell me what's been going on," said Lucy as she took a seat opposite Mrs. Bradshaw.

We just come here last week from El Dorado County with my boyfriend. We're staying with his brother, but we've got to find another place to live because there isn't enough room. A couple of days ago Melissa, that's the baby's name, started in being real irritable, and she feels hot. She didn't sleep at all last night and kept us all awake. My boyfriend got really pissed and told me I'd better do something about her. Kids drive him crazy. Anyway, it seemed like she was pulling on her ear. She had the same thing about a month ago, and we got some medicine from the nurse where we lived before and it got better. Can you give me some medicine?

"What was wrong with Melissa when the nurse saw her? What kind of medicine did she get?" Lucy asked, attempting to maneuver herself into a position where she would be able to make eye contact with Mrs. Bradshaw.

Mrs. Bradshaw gazed at the ceiling as she answered:

The nurse said her ear was infected and gave her some kind of medicine for the infection and the fever. I gave her the medicine until she felt better. I lost the rest of the bottle when we were getting ready to move or I could have given her the rest of that. I've really got to do something to keep her quiet—she's driving my boyfriend crazy.

The larger of the two children sitting on the floor whined, "I'm hungry."

Mrs. Bradshaw quickly turned toward him and yelled, "I told you to be quiet. . . . You shut up now before I smack you."

Lucy took a deep breath. "I'll want to examine Melissa to see if we can find out what the problem is. However, since we have not seen you or your family in our clinic before, I'd like to get some history on both you and the children."

Mrs. Bradshaw told Lucy that Melissa, the youngest, was 18 months old. The other two children, Travis and John, were three and five, respectively. Mrs. Bradshaw was 19. She had finished high school but was married at 15 when she found herself pregnant with John. She was at home with the children, and her husband had been supporting the family with his earnings from two part-time jobs. About six weeks ago, her husband abandoned her and the children, and his current location is unknown. Mr. Bradshaw had not believed in welfare and had never let Mrs. Bradshaw apply for welfare, Medicaid, or food stamps. After Mr. Bradshaw left, however, she managed to get some emergency food from a church and was thinking about applying for welfare. Instead, she met her current boyfriend, Houston, about three weeks ago and they decided to come to Clark County to see if they could find work. On further questioning, Lucy noted that neither Mrs. Bradshaw nor Houston seemed to have much in the way of job skills.

Mrs. Bradshaw continued, "The boys have been pretty healthy but this one—she has been nothing but trouble from the very beginning."

Lucy probed, "Nothing but trouble?"

Mrs. Bradshaw continued:

Yeah, I was raised by my grandma and she told me girls was a lot more trouble than boys and was she ever right! I didn't plan on having *any* of these kids, but I was taking the pill when I got pregnant with Melissa. I sure don't want to have any more, and Houston, he can't *stand* kids!

"Yes . . ." said Lucy, but Mrs. Bradshaw had stopped talking and stared at a spot on the wall over Lucy's right shoulder. Hoping that Mrs. Bradshaw would volunteer more information, Lucy silently checked the intake notes and found that Melissa had an axillary temperature of 102 °F. She also noted that Melissa's height and weight had been plotted on a growth chart. Her measurements were below the 50th percentile for height and below the 10th percentile for weight.

After a silence that felt like hours but was probably no longer than 30 seconds, Lucy said brightly, "Well, let me look at Melissa and see if we can't figure out what is going on with her." With minimal help from Mrs. Bradshaw, Lucy performed a quick but thorough pediatric examination. She noted that Melissa had extremely pale skin and mucous membranes, that the child appeared to be underweight, and that she had the remains of a diaper rash. Because Mrs. Bradshaw seemed uncomfortable trying to restrain Melissa, Lucy inquired, "Would you like me to get somebody else in here to help hold her for the ear examination?" Mrs. Bradshaw nodded, almost imperceptibly, so Lucy called in one of the clinic aides to help her hold Melissa for the otoscopic examination. Her left tympanic membrane appeared normal, but the right was red and bulging with absent landmarks and a diffuse light reflex. While Melissa was restrained, Lucy also did a quick capillary finger-stick to check Melissa's hematocrit.

The aide returned Melissa to Mrs. Bradshaw. Lucy said, "It looks to me as if Melissa has an ear infection on the right side. I also want to go out and check her blood and see if she could be anemic. You wait right here. I should be back in a jiffy."

Lucy left the examining room and walked down the hall to spin down the blood specimen. She walked by the aide who rolled her eyes and whispered, "I wonder where these people come from!" Lucy blushed but really didn't reply. She had been thinking along the same lines but felt like a snob and was really not comfortable verbalizing the idea. Melissa's hematocrit was 35 percent.

When Lucy returned to the exam room, Mrs. Bradshaw was no longer there. Wondering what had become of her, Lucy walked through the waiting room and saw through the glass double-door that Mrs. Bradshaw was sitting outside on the steps smoking a cigarette and talking to a man who was also smoking. On closer examination, Lucy noted that the man appeared to be considerably older than Mrs. Bradshaw, maybe in his early 40s. Lucy knocked on the glass door to get Mrs. Bradshaw's attention and motioned her inside. Mrs. Bradshaw and her companion both extinguished their cigarettes and followed Lucy back to Exam Room 2.

When everybody was seated in the exam room, Lucy looked at the man and said, "You must be Houston." He nodded but did not reply.

Lucy turned her attention to Mrs. Bradshaw:

Melissa has an ear infection and is also anemic. I'll give you a prescription for some medicine for the ear infection, and I suggest you buy her some children's vitamins with iron for her to take. I'd also like to talk to you about getting her enrolled in WIC. Because she is anemic, she would probably qualify, and they would give you food vouchers and work with you to make sure Melissa and the boys get the right kind of food. I also will need for you to bring Melissa back to the clinic in a week so we can make sure the medication for her ear infection is working.

Nobody seemed to be paying any attention to what Lucy was saying. Melissa was whimpering and trying to climb up on Mrs. Bradshaw's lap, and Mrs. Bradshaw was trying to direct her to go back and sit with John. Lucy went on:

I'd also like to talk to you about the possibility of bringing all the children back to the clinic for a well-child examination. You probably will want to enroll John in kindergarten for the next term so we need to check and see if his immunizations are up to date.

Lucy was feeling a bit desperate and was afraid that she was starting to babble.

Finally, Houston spoke up. With a tone that could have been interpreted as mildly hostile, he turned to Lucy and said:

We don't have no money to buy medicine. The nurse at the hospital said that the health department had to give us the medicine for free. So why don't you just go get it so we can get out of here. This place is making me feel real nervous.

Lucy was at a loss for words. She nodded and hurriedly left the room. The clinic kept a small supply of antibiotics and other basic medicines. However, these medications were earmarked for "regular" clinic patients who had been certified by the social worker as being unable to pay for their medicine. As Lucy pondered her dilemma, she also thought, "Ampicillin is cheap. About three packages of cigarettes."

But Lucy was afraid that if she did not give Mrs. Bradshaw the medications, Melissa would not be treated, and the family would not return to Clark County Primary Care Clinic. Lucy also knew that handing over the medication was not a guarantee that these children would be brought back to the clinic for WIC. It was obvious to Lucy that the problems of this family went well beyond Melissa's ear infection and anemia.

She thought, "Well, graduate school taught me how to deal with an ear infection—but what do I do about the rest of this stuff?"

In the Eye of the Beholder:
The Case of the
Minnetonka Lawn Ordinance

Bill Hise fought his way through the downtown Minneapolis rush hour traffic, avoiding the potholes of April as best he could, but he hardly noticed. He was concentrating on another potential battle coming that evening. Bill was a member of the Minnetonka City Council, which was in the process of reviewing a proposed revision of the lawn and nuisance weed ordinance. A situation with a local resident had sparked a great deal of controversy over the existing ordinance and led to the proposal the council would be considering tonight. Looking back, Bill thought that no single issue in his 11 years of tenure had taken as much staff and council time. Tonight, after a year and a half of work, the council would review the second draft of the ordinance in an open work session and would decide if it was ready to send it forward for an official council vote. "What additional issues will be raised?" he wondered. "What have we missed?"

Bill knew that Minnetonka had first struggled with a lawn and nuisance weed ordinance in 1987 in response to citizen concerns about neglected yards. Residents wanted the city to take action against grass that was unmowed. There was an apparent increase in the number of

---

AUTHOR'S NOTE: This case was written by Anne M. Hanchek and appeared in *HortTechnology* (1994) 4:304-310. Reprinted by permission.

houses going through foreclosure, with homes left unoccupied and untended. Some believed that the unkempt appearance decreased the value of their nearby property and the enjoyment of their neighborhoods. Generally, the ordinance had been effective in answering those concerns. For example, in 1991, the Community Development Department responded to and resolved almost 50 complaints about yard neglect. (Enforcement was only in response to written complaints filed by neighbors directly affected; areas were never sought out and cited by inspectors. This method of "enforcement on demand" had been upheld in court as a just means of allocating city resources that otherwise would have to be spent on a full-time inspection program.) The Minnetonka City Council in 1991 governed a city with a rich variety of landscapes and land use patterns that presented almost every possible situation, from natural area to city park to farmland to manicured suburbia. In fact, many people in Minnetonka still kept horses, pastured within the city limits. The Minnetonka Horsemen's Association was a well-organized group that promoted owning horses as companion animals.

In July 1991, however, one situation raised significant controversy and demanded official attention, when a landowner was cited after complaints from her neighbors. Marjie Kline appeared before the council on July 15, 1991, and stated that she was developing her yard as a natural area for wildlife by letting the natural vegetation come back while removing noxious weeds. Her method was to leave parts of the entire yard unmowed to allow maple seedlings and other plants to grow. She wanted to retain her yard in a semiwild condition, in keeping with the woods and natural areas near her home. But Bill had driven by Marjie's property several times in advance of the hearing, as had most of the council, and noted that most of the neighborhood front yards were mowed. It seemed a clear case of respecting the overall neighborhood character, and most council members felt strongly their obligation to respond to neighborhood complaints. After discussion, however, the council voted to table action until the next meeting on July 22, when every council member would be present.

It was at that second meeting that Bill realized how complex this issue could become. Marjie even had brought an instructor from the University of Minnesota's landscape architecture program to speak on her behalf. Bonnie Harper Lore urged the council to respect new naturalizing trends in landscape design. Bill listened as his fellow council members spoke out on various aspects. One was concerned that property values in the neighborhood were decreasing and wondered if the lack of maintenance meant more nuisance animals. Another mentioned that she herself was also trying to return a portion of her property to a natural state, but she made sure neighbors were buffered from the area. After hearing evidence for and against natural landscaping, Bill summed up his ambivalent feelings by saying, "It's hard for us as a council to sit in judgment on issues like this, but it is our ultimate responsibility to make decisions in the best interest of the city as a whole." The council voted to enforce the ordinance at Marjie's property and instructed staff to get to work reviewing the ordinance in light of future similar situations.

The local media had been covering the story from the beginning. On July 24, 1991, the *Minnetonka Sun-Sailor* ran a front-page story titled "Wild Lawn is a Nuisance, According to Council" that brought the public to attention. The larger metropolitan news agencies became interested, and Bill found himself the subject of a WCCO radio interview. In mid-August, Marjie's lawyer obtained a temporary restraining order, and the council decided to postpone another hearing until the ordinance had been reviewed fully by staff. The *Sun-Sailor* reported in front-page news, "Wild Lawn Debate Now Heading to Court." Pressure from the media was just part of the job, Bill felt, but he wondered how it seemed to other council members who were up for reelection in the fall.

City staff members, headed by City Attorney Desyl Peterson and Community Development Director Ron Rankin, began an intensive study of the potential problems and issues. They realized as they worked that Minnetonka was becoming a test case on this question. There were no existing ordinances that seemed to address all the issues. In fact, other municipalities were waiting to see the finished product, hoping for a "metro model" of a lawn ordinance. City staff attended a seminar on lawn ordinances sponsored by the National Wildflower Research Center, met with Edina and Bloomington city staffs who were studying the same problem, held public information meetings, and contacted many additional experts and special interest groups, including the Minnesota Department of Natural Resources, the Minnesota Extension Service, the Minnesota Nursery and Land-scape Association, and the University of Minnesota Department of Horticultural Science. At times, City Attorney Peterson remarked that the biological and ecological facts on landscape management and res-toration seemed as uncertain as the legal issues.

Bill was very impressed by the staff's thoroughness when they pre-sented their report and first draft at the February 10, 1992, council work session, but, again, the discussion raised new questions. Peter-son noted that the existing ordinance had enforcement problems and hoped the new ordinance would address that, but City Manager James Miller remarked that it would be impossible to control this issue entirely through legislation. Several council members stated that they were pleased with the direction the new ordinance was taking, but one also felt that encouraging diversity in landscape types opened the door to possible abuse. He suggested posting areas of natural vegeta-tion based on more precise definitions. "What about requiring a resi-dent to file a restoration plan for the site?" he asked. "Then neighbors could be notified and discuss it at public hearings." Another wanted an ordinance that could be enforced if the neighbors were concerned about the way a yard looked. The effect on property values was brought up again.

In the midst of staff and council member discussion, some citizens had spoken out as well. Bill knew Marjie, of course, and she offered her ecological concerns on high-maintenance landscapes requiring too much water and chemical inputs. On the other hand, another resident spoke out against allowing what she viewed as obnoxious weeds. A Chanhassen resident also offered his case: He planned to purchase land in Minnetonka and develop a natural landscape, but he wondered how the ordinance would affect his property. "How will you separate situations that are aesthetically pleasing to some but not to others?" he asked the Council. Bill wondered the same thing.

The council decided late that evening that this first draft was too complicated. They asked the staff to continue working on a second draft, consulting experts and holding public hearings to get citizen input. This revised version of the new ordinance, which would cover the majority of situations, would come before the council for a vote of confidence at the April 13, 1992, work session. It was this meeting that Bill was pondering as he drove home. Would they have all the necessary background information? Had they thought out the future far enough? Would this ordinance last, or would they be rewriting it again next year? He had a copy of the second draft in his briefcase (see Exhibit 5.1). If they were asked to vote on adopting this version of the ordinance tonight, could he approve it, confident that the council had discharged its public duty?

Exhibit 5.1. **Second Draft of Proposed New Lawn and Nuisance Weed Ordinance, Presented to the Minnetonka City Council on April 13, 1992**

PREAMBLE. The City Council finds that there are a variety of landscapes in the City, which adds diversity and a richness to the quality of life. There are certain expectations and standards regarding the proper maintenance of these areas, which, if not met, may decrease the value of adjacent properties and may threaten public safety. In addition, if vegetation is not properly maintained or is allowed to go wild, there may be the following adverse impacts on public health, safety, and welfare:

a. Invasive vegetation such as buckthorn and tatarian honeysuckle may develop and threaten to supplant other vegetation that is an integral part of the State's plant communities, and

b. Vegetation that causes allergic reactions, such as ragweed, may develop.

The City Council also finds that it is in the public's best interest to allow the restoration of native vegetation that is more drought-resistant, places a lower demand on the public water supply, and provides a natural habitat for wildlife. The City Council enacts this ordinance to balance the public need to ensure proper maintenance of that vegetation.

MAINTENANCE STANDARD

The maintenance standard in this section applies to property which has been developed with a structure as defined in the Building Code, including vacant property combined with developed property for tax purposes, and property which has received development approval(s) from the city:

1. All turf grasses and weeds must not exceed a height of ten inches, measured from the base at ground level to the tip of each stalk, stem, blade, or leaf.

2. This requirement does not apply to the following:

   A. A wild area, and

   B. An area being restored with native prairie vegetation if:

      i.   The area is completely reseeded with native prairie vegetation,

      ii. The area is cut at least once per year to a height less than 12 inches until the native prairie vegetation covers at least 75% of the area being restored, and

      iii. A sign is posted on the property in a location likely to be seen by the public, advising that the area is undergoing a prairie restoration. This sign shall be in addition to any sign permitted by the sign ordinance but shall be no larger than six square feet and no higher than six feet tall. The sign is no longer required when the native prairie vegetation has covered at least 75% of the area being restored.

Off to College

They'd known each other since kindergarten, when a common enemy brought them together. As a result of the local bully picking on "Matt the Fat," two things were now certain: The three boys were the best of friends, and no one ever called Matthew Sachinski "Matt the Fat" again, at least not without a fight.

Small towns have a way of throwing everyone together sooner or later, even before diversity became fashionable. Rich kids, poor kids, black kids, white kids, all attend one school when it's the only one around. And so it was for Brian, Jason, and Matthew. They, like their parents, were as different as night and day.

Brian was the oldest, and, although it was only by a few months, he never let Jason and Matthew forget it. His dad was the town veterinarian, the only thing Brian could ever remember wanting to be. There never was any doubt in his mind or in his parents' that he, like his younger sister, would go to college. He was a good student, and with his cavalier grin, nonchalant ways, and little-boy good looks, he was popular with the girls. And being popular with the girls made him popular with his classmates. Nothing succeeds like success. At 18, the world was at Brian Thomas's feet.

AUTHOR'S NOTE: This case was written by Linda Mooney, Department of Sociology, East Carolina University.

Jason was one of Brian's fans, not just because Brian was deserving of his respect, but because Brian helped Jason get work after school doing odd jobs around the Thomas Animal Clinic. Jason was an only child. When she was sober, his mother worked as a cleaning woman at the local bed-and-breakfast, but everyone knew they were on welfare. No one was quite sure what happened to Jason's dad, least of all Jason. He would have been proud of his son, though, well over six feet at 14 and now, although not an academic giant, the recipient of a basketball scholarship to State University. Jason was quiet, lacking the self-confidence of class, but with an inner strength often mistaken for indifference.

And then there was "Matt the Fat." Overweight, yes, but with a personality that obscured his politically incorrect body and round freckled face. Working all through high school in the town's only pizza shop didn't help his physique or the name calling. In characteristic good humor, Matthew liked to say it was his secret to success, football success, that is. He was a defensive lineman (some said he was the defensive line) on his high school team. "After all," he would say, "it takes a lot of work to keep your weight up, and a lot of weight to keep your work up."

Matthew was the oldest of five children and knew with the birth of each subsequent brother and sister that his chances of going to college were, unlike himself, getting slimmer and slimmer. But with the strength of a strong family, his afterschool and summer jobs, and a little help from a Pell Grant, he, like Brian and Jason, would be starting State U. in the fall.

And so on Wednesday morning, as Brian's red Jeep pulled onto the freeway for the three-hour drive to State, the boys were in rare form. Matthew in the passenger seat singing loud and off-key to the latest Blues Traveler's hit and Jason's long legs spilling over the Cherokee front seat into Brian's back. "Get your legs out of my back!" screamed Brian over Matthew's squealing and attempts at mimicking a harmonica player.

"OK, OK," said Jason, wondering if he'd ever have his own car. They talked of high school, of girls, of college, and of the upcoming football season. For the first time in any of their short lives, there'd be no Cleveland Browns to cheer on.

They pulled into campus just in time to register. The first day was spent getting organized—orientation, IDs, schedules, room assignments, meal tickets, and the like. They already knew they'd be rooming together for the three-day orientation. It's what they each wanted for the school year but knew was impossible. Brian would be in a dormitory until he moved to the frat house—he was certain to be Phi Kappa Tau. His father, father's father, and father's father's father were onetime chapter presidents.

Jason would be staying at the University housing set aside for athletes, and Matthew had already found a room in a boarding house near his weekend job at a pizza shop. With his work experience, he would start as night manager. There had been lots of jobs from which to choose. After all, college towns are little more than pizza shops, bars, clothing boutiques, CD stores, and restaurant-lined streets, all desperately in need of and dependent on student labor. But night managers are paid more, and, although it meant he had to work until 3:00 a.m. Friday, Saturday, and Sunday, he had scheduled all his classes on Tuesdays and Thursdays.

The days progressed rather uneventfully. Speeches, lectures, tours, lots and lots of paperwork and forms. They met with deans and assistant deans and had a tour of the library and the computer center. They met with their respective advisors, and Jason with his coach. Two of the evenings had scheduled entertainment: a movie on Wednesday night and a concert on Thursday night. But tonight was their night, Friday night, and they were going to celebrate it in style.

"Anything but pizza," shouted Matthew in anticipation of the evening's dinner. "How about burgers, fries, and a shake?"

"OK by me," added Brian and, with a quick nod from Jason, they were off to Burger Boy, the local equivalent of Shoney's.

As they walked down the tree-lined streets in front of campus, each wrapped in their own thoughts and dreams, a young woman approached them from a side street. Tanned from the long summer months, thin, and blond, she wore a State U. T-shirt and very, very short white shorts.

"Hey, where you guys going?" she asked with a smile.

"Going downtown," said Matthew enthusiastically, but knowing immediately it was a stupid thing to say. Where else would they be headed?

"Obviously," she said, the smile now somehow strangely absent, her attention turning to Brian and Jason. "And for you, free admission to the Cove and all the beer you can drink."

"We're not 21," said Matthew, again realizing it was the wrong thing to say but increasingly getting irritated with the delay.

"All you need is a University orientation card and this coupon," she said handing one to Jason, one to Brian, and one to Matthew. "And I get a bonus for everyone I give a card to who shows up! You are going to go, aren't you?"

"No problem," replied Brian, Jason, and Matthew, recognizing the transition immediately. "Wouldn't miss it for the world," said Brian, slipping into his best W. C. Fields with his arms around Ms. Coed's shoulders.

"Parting is such sweet sorrow," yelled Brian, throwing air kisses as the three walked away and continued downtown on Waters Street, one of the two main arteries of the college town. As they approached Burger Boy, Alanis Morisette's *Isn't it Ironic* was booming from the jukebox.

"I don't think we should go," said Matthew, turning his head to order a double cheeseburger, fries, and a chocolate shake.

"Why not?" said Brian:

It's not like we'd be doing anything wrong. That's what college is all about. You think the cops care? You think the University cares? If it weren't for student money, this town would be dead. If those bars aren't for people *under* 21, then who are they for? Hell, you graduate and leave when you're 21. Give me a break.

"Just the same," said Matthew, fearing he sounded a little too much like his parents, "it's illegal and we haven't even gone away to college yet. I don't want to get thrown out before I even get here."

"So what you're saying is that the four, or five, or six years in your case . . ."

"Very funny."

". . . you're in college, you're not going to drink?"

Matthew, beginning to weaken and to lose interest, turned his attention to the recently arrived food. Jason, as always, said very little. What would happen to his scholarship? Hadn't the coach warned him and the others about underage drinking? And what about the fact that he was only 17 and shouldn't even be in a bar? "Isn't it ironic?," the song continued, "like a free ride when you've already paid." The three finished their dinner with little more than the sounds of 107.3 FM keeping them company.

It was clear that in the final weeks of August, summer school having ended, most everyone roaming the downtown streets that night was there from S.U. orientation. Nonetheless, the five or six downtown bars were filled to capacity, each advertising a nightly drink special and homegrown talent.

The boys stood and watched as student orientation cards repeatedly were checked in place of the more accepted driver's license. Eyeing Ms. Coed and the Cove, Brian turned, and, with his usual warmth and charm, said "Shall we, gentlemen?" With Matthew behind him and Jason a few steps in tow, Brian soon disappeared into the darkness of the Cove, seemingly swallowed by Hootie and the Blowfish and billows of smoke.

Matthew flashed his student orientation ID, stepped into the darkness, and then turned to see Jason lingering under the Cove's outdoor spotlights. As Jason approached the entrance, a uniformed doorman smiled and, looking at him closely, asked, "How old are you, young man?"

What's So Scary About the Truth?

It was 7:45 a.m. Monday, and Thomas Hoffman was on his way to school. As he rounded the familiar corner of Maple Drive, he switched off the droning news that had been cackling out of his old radio. It was a typical rainy morning in early April, and the slip-slapping of the wipers had a hypnotic effect. Thomas was lost in idle contemplation, considering the events that the day would bring, and he wondered, for the umpteenth time, how he would break the news to Lauren and the others. If only he could be sure of his decision. He had been unable to sleep last night, turning the situation over and over, weighing the pros and cons. Just as he thought he'd made up his mind, a tiny voice somewhere in the back of his head would point him in another direction. Either way, he knew that at exactly 1:45 that afternoon, the last period of the day, he would be facing his Grade 12 journalism class—23 pairs of expectant eyes would be fixed on him. And, of course, he had to be accountable.

He snapped back to reality as he leaned forward to wipe the coffee steam off the windshield with the sleeve of his coat and gunned the old Volkswagen up the final hill toward Bellevue Secondary school. The houses, shops, and churches on either side of the tree-lined street

AUTHOR'S NOTE: This case was written by Rachael Froese and is part of a database of cases available through the Case Clearinghouse, Faculty of Education, Simon Frasier University.

were familiar to him. For nine years, he had endured the 45-minute drive from the city to the suburbs to teach English and literature, his first love.

Bellevue had been the first position offered to Tom after he'd completed his university teacher-training program, and in nine years, he had grown to love the school and all its quirks. He valued the relationships he had built with the students and their families over the years, not to mention his fellow teachers.

This was precisely the reason Tom was dreading the decision he faced that day. If the class decided to publish the results of the survey of sexual activities of Bellevue students in the senior magazine, it would not go over very well with their parents, to put it mildly. A part of a largely Christian community, these parents did not want their children to have anything to do with sex, let alone read about it in the school newspaper. Printing this article in *Generic Youth* would not win him any popularity contests. On the other hand, what was he afraid of? The Grade 12 journalism students had identified teenage sex and its ramifications as an important issue at the school and were attempting to promote awareness in one of the few outlets available to them—a student-generated news magazine. Why, then, was Tom so worried about how their parents would react?

He eyed the neat, symmetrical rooflines of the brick and stucco homes that led up to the school, with their immaculate yards and shiny, wet, late-model sedans parked in the driveways. "What a place to grow up," he thought to himself, half good-naturedly, half anxiously. The good citizens of Bellevue Estates were upper-middle-class; but politically correct Tom thought of them as lacking in racial, cultural, and religious diversity. The students came from traditional homes with traditional values. More often than not, they had a parent who was always on hand to pick them up from school and take them to their violin or tennis lessons. The parents believed that hard work should be rewarded, and saw no reason why their children's lives should be anything less than storybook quality. And if the parents worked so hard to create such an ideal environment for their children, then the least the teachers could do would be to uphold their standards.

For the most part, the parents of the community were actively involved in their children's lives. The support they gave the school came not only from their deep pockets but also from their personal commitments. Bellevue parents, on the whole, liked to be on top of their children's education. They wanted to know what was going on inside the classrooms and weren't afraid to make their opinions known. Although their support was invaluable, the school also had experienced its fair share of difficulties stemming from this close, personal involvement. When parents felt as though their wishes weren't being addressed, they weren't timid about pulling strings with the school board. Many of the teachers believed it was for this reason that the last two principals at the school had been transferred out after fewer than two years on the job. In addition, the parents' advisory council had submitted a list to the board containing six books they wanted taken off the library shelves only last year—a gesture that went against every bone in Tom's free-thinking body.

Unfortunately, book banning was just the tip of the iceberg. Earlier that same year, after an epidemic of teenage pregnancies in the district, there had been a district-wide, student-led movement to install condom machines in the high schools. The student proposal was brought to a staff meeting of the high school faculty, which debated the issue. Tom remembered one of the many staff meetings he had sat through during the discussions on this issue. "Reading, writing, and arithmetic is what the taxpayers of this district want us to teach. Leave the values and morals to the parents," proclaimed one teacher. But the new principal, Dorothy Massingham, argued, "How can you argue with numbers? STDs [sexually transmitted diseases] and teenage pregnancy are on the rise like never before in this district, and the students themselves are asking for protection!"

After intense and lengthy discussion, the teachers finally reached a compromise. "So, as I understand it," Dorothy summarized,

> This is what will happen. We will put the matter up to a vote, and students, parents, and teachers will have the opportunity to cast anonymous ballots that respond, with a simple "yes" or "no," to a question regarding the condom machines.

Everyone agreed that this seemed the most democratic way to solve the problem and avoid conflict at the same time.

When the voting had concluded, the result was an overwhelmingly positive response in favor of the condom machines, with 70 percent of the respondents in favor. "Well, that settles that!" remarked Dorothy. Unfortunately, she was wrong.

Two weeks later, Dorothy called another staff meeting. "I'm afraid I have some rather disturbing news," said the principal. "I have here a letter from the board vetoing our decision to install the condom machines." Dorothy passed a white sheet of paper down the long table in the library for the teachers to scrutinize. "It seems that the parents' advisory council and the board are in accord, and there are clearly some influential individuals out there who don't like this idea one bit."

Breaking the news to the students had been terrible. There had been considerable protest and confusion, but the students soon realized that there was nowhere they could go with this. They had been checkmated. Their anger slowly diminished, and everyday activities at Bellevue Secondary school had resumed.

Tom sighed to himself as he reflected on these past events. He pulled into his usual parking spot and switched off the ignition. Sitting in silence for a moment, he stretched his cramped legs and pushed his thoughts to the back of his mind. "Here goes nothing," he said to himself, as he gathered his papers and lunch up from the back seat, and shifted his weight out of the small car. He locked the door, straightened up to his full six foot, three inches, and took a deep breath, wishing that his height would somehow cover up his feelings of doubt and inadequacy. As he set off across the parking lot, Tom was aware that this morning's walk past the office would bring the inevitable encounter with his principal.

"Morning, Tom," called out Dorothy from her office door. Tom froze in midstride and forced himself to turn around.

"Good morning, Dorothy," he said.

"Uh, oh. I can see that someone had a tough weekend."

"You're not kidding," smiled Tom weakly, brushing wet hair out from behind his foggy glasses. "This just feels like such a lose-lose situation. No matter what decision I make, someone is going to be unhappy."

"Then I gather you haven't yet made up your mind," the principal said as she peered at him over her bifocals. Tom shook his head.

She went on:

Well, I know this probably won't make matters any easier, but I've already had two phone calls from the head of the parents' advisory council this morning, and another three from individual parents. Now, I'm not trying to make your decision for you, Tom. You know that I support you and I trust your professional judgment. I just wanted to let you know the type of situation that we'll have on our hands if you decide to go ahead and publish the results of the survey in the magazine.

Tom did know it. He knew it all too well. Why didn't he suspect that something like this might happen when he took on that journalism class? It was the first time such a course had been offered at Bellevue. It had been a part of a new curriculum package sent down from the Ministry for Grade 12 students. What had excited Tom so much was the open-ended style of the curriculum. Getting students to write about current events in the world—this was a course that really could have an impact! Tom wanted the students to feel inspired by current events, to be able to voice their opinions on some of the issues that, as adolescents, they were facing. He decided that the course would focus on writing for journalism, and the culmination would be a student-written magazine. The fact that it would be completely student-run was challenging but only added to Tom's enthusiasm.

The class had intense debates about what issues would be published in their "baby." During one of these debates, Lauren Fielding, the assistant editor, presented the idea of a student sex survey. "I just don't think it's right that they trashed the whole idea of the condom machines without even finding out the real needs of the students," argued Lauren. Tom couldn't deny this, although his skin prickled at the thought of opening this can of worms.

"I don't care what they've decided. We can't stick our heads in the sand," argued Lauren. "It's up to us to let them know what the students of Bellevue need, not what they think we need!"

Tom's first instinct had been to grab his coat and run. What had he gotten himself into? Still, his better judgment told him that this would be teaching the students valuable lessons in democracy, in censorship, about power positions, and about getting the facts straight. He decided to proceed with caution.

Lauren was to mastermind the survey with some input from the rest of the class. Together, they tried to identify the most important questions to be asked and their relevance to the banning of the condom machines. How many people were sexually active at each grade level? At what age did they become sexually active? How many partners had they had? What form of birth control had they used, if any? Had they ever contracted an STD? Were they informed about family planning and the options available to them? This was the nature of the questions being asked.

Lauren decided to survey two homeroom classes at each grade level, 8 to 12. The survey was to be optional and anonymous. Fearing the inevitable reaction, Tom suggested that Lauren send notices home to parents of the students and to inform all the other teachers, stating the purpose and the date of survey.

As was to be expected, several parents called the school saying that they did not want their child to take part. One teacher refused to allow her students to participate. When the results finally came in, the data were quite startling for Tom, not to mention the students. More than 60 percent of Grade 12 students said they were sexually active. Even the Grade 8 students responded at the 20 percent level.

No sooner had school been dismissed on the day of the survey when the phone calls began to flood the office. Parents who didn't feel the survey was appropriate left messages with the school secretaries. "They're saying they don't want the kids to be reading pornography at school," said Dorothy to Tom. "The parents' advisory council will have plenty to say about this, no doubt."

Tom hadn't said anything. What could he say? He had tried to teach the class that as journalists it was their responsibility to be fair and to treat each story in an informed, factual, and unbiased manner, but by whose standards? How could he teach his class to be independent thinkers if he had to force them to comply with an imposed moral code? Tom opened his mouth to speak and closed it again. He had been so frustrated, he hadn't known what to say to Dorothy. Finally, he spluttered:

> The students aren't going to learn anything if we put their minds in a vise. I can't understand why these parents are so scared of the truth! These students have worked so hard to deal with this issue fairly and intelligently. They deserve praise, not a slap on the wrists!

The decision to publish the issue with the sex survey in *Generic Youth* lay in his hands. Tom knew that publishing the magazine would mean putting in jeopardy the long-standing relationship that he had built with many of the families in the community. He would be treading on very thin ice, upsetting the precarious balance that existed between parents and teachers. If he decided not to publish the survey, what would he be teaching his students? The majority of the class felt that the survey was acceptable news, yet all seemed to fear the unwritten rule that such a survey would not fly in a high school news magazine. How was it that 23 people could create and approve but were held back by one unspoken barrier that blocked their path? Many of

Tom's students were already 18. They were planning futures as adults, selecting universities, making travel plans. "As voters and taxpayers, are we not also members of society?" demanded Lauren. "Why do they get to tell us what we can and can't read or write? This is a free country, not a dictatorship!"

The first three periods of the day felt as if they would never end. Tom had never felt so mechanical in his teaching in his entire career. During lunch, he didn't go down to the staff room. He knew that Dorothy and the other faculty would have a million questions. He wanted to answer them but he just wasn't ready. But he was running out of time. The first period of the afternoon, Grade 9 English, was a nightmare. The students seemed to have consumed copious amounts of sugar, or caffeine, or both over lunch and Tom spent most of the hour trying to quiet them and keep their attention. He felt like a brand new teacher all over again. Before he knew it, the bell signaled the last period. Tom collapsed wearily in his chair as the Grade 12s shuffled in. Tom looked up from his desk to see the class, not sitting down in their seats but gathered around him, their concerned eyes peering down. Lauren Fielding stepped forward and leaned her hands on his desk.

"Well, Mr. Hoffman," she said quietly, "what's it gonna be?"

People Like You

Connie spoke, the anger rising in her throat, her face turning redder by the moment:

> Listen to me, Ted. I know what I promised, but I can't do anything about it. I didn't know this was going to happen. It's not fair to blame me. You've always blamed me for everything that went wrong in your life. It's just not fair.

Ted couldn't believe what he was hearing. She had promised. How could she do this? It was yet one more setback in more than two years of setbacks. He didn't know if he could take any more. It was one thing for society as a whole to ignore his needs, but for his family to be acting like this too was a real shock.

Only three short years ago, life for Ted was looking pretty rosy. His old girlfriend, Dorothy, had called him from Alberta and invited him to visit for a few days. The days stretched to almost a year, and in that time Ted and Dorothy cemented their relationship. Dorothy became pregnant, and a child, Ramona, was born. Soon after, Ted found a job as a delivery person for a local business. It didn't pay much but it provided the new family with just enough to put food on the table and shelter over their heads. Ted and Dorothy knew that, although neither of them was highly educated, they had each other and they had Ramona.

AUTHOR'S NOTE: This case was written by Steve Macdonald and is part of a database of cases available through the Case Clearinghouse, Faculty of Education, Simon Frasier University.

It wouldn't be long before Ted would find a better-paying job, Ramona would be old enough for preschool, and Dorothy would then find work. After that, the sky was the limit.

Ted could remember Dorothy telling him for the hundredth time,

> You know, we're pretty lucky, when you think about it. You're working and we have this beautiful child. And we live in the most wonderful country in the world. Let's talk again about what we'll do when we win the lottery.

And they would make their plans.

All these expectations and dreams came to an end not long after Ted's first year in Alberta. Although she was only in her early 20s, Dorothy suddenly became seriously ill, was hospitalized, and before he could even understand the nature of the illness, she passed away. With no one to take care of Ramona while he worked and not being able to afford day care, Ted was forced to quit his job and collect welfare. His life, and that of his young daughter, had taken a turn he had never imagined.

Ted spent the next two years collecting checks from the Alberta government, but this also came to an end. His case worker, a sympathetic older man, informed him one day, "Ted, the new government here in Alberta has decided to force people like you off welfare. You're going to have to find a job."

> What do you mean "people like me"? You mean people whose spouses have died or left them, leaving them alone to care for an infant? You mean people who can barely afford to feed their children and themselves, let alone being able to afford day care so they can look for a job? Is that what you mean by "people like me"?

As a man, Ted was not about to display his true emotions in front of this person, but he suddenly realized that tears were welling up in his eyes, then streaming down his cheek, making it difficult to focus on the face of this man who was sentencing him to such an uncertain future.

Walking slowly out of the office, Ted realized what his next move— really, the only choice he had—was going to be: He would go to Vancouver. There, he knew, the people had a more kindly attitude toward "people like him." He could begin immediately collecting welfare checks. Even more important, he could stay with his older sister, Connie. He had always gotten along well with Connie and her husband, Rick. Although Rick owned and operated a small business, Connie didn't work and might be willing to take care of Ramona. That would free Ted to look for a job.

"I can't wait to see you, Ted," Connie had said on the phone, "and Rick and I really want to help any way we can. We know things have been very difficult, so you just get yourself to Vancouver, and let us take care of everything else."

Ted didn't waste any time. He was tired of all the "welfare bashing" he had been reading and hearing about and recently experiencing in Alberta. He knew things would be different in Vancouver. So he took the next bus west, and all the while he was making plans for his future and that of his daughter.

Turning to Ramona, sitting quietly next to him on the bus, he whispered, "Maybe your mom will be right: We'll win the lottery and live happily ever after." Ramona was still too young to understand, but she giggled anyway.

Upon arriving in Vancouver, Ted noticed how busy everything seemed. People were rushing about, on foot and in speeding cars, as though they had somewhere to go, someone to see. For the first time in a long time, he felt hope and excitement about his prospects. He might not have a lot of skills, he might not have an advanced education, but he was young and strong, and he knew he was smart.

One week later, some of Ted's hope was beginning to wane. It turned out that Rick's business had been experiencing some difficult times over the past months, and the income he and Connie received from his business was shrinking. As a business owner, Rick had always worked long, hard hours and paid his fair share of taxes. With Rick's business in trouble, he found himself working just as hard with fewer and fewer rewards. He was getting anxious.

"How can I keep this up? I'm working my butt off every day—not just five days a week, but every day—and I'm getting further and further behind," Rick said over the dinner table.

"I'm sorry to hear about this, Rick," replied Ted, "and I wish there was something I could do."

"I'll tell you what you can do, Ted." Rick's voice rose quickly to a high pitch:

> You can get off our backs and get a job. For a week now, you've been wandering around here waiting to pick up your welfare check while pretending to look for a job. You know, it's people like you that really ruin it for the rest of us.

There it was again, thought Ted: "people like you." He felt sorry for Rick, but he couldn't just sit there and say nothing:

> Rick, I really appreciate everything you two are doing for Ramona and me, but I'm trying as hard as I can. There are just no jobs available. At least none that will pay as much as the welfare I'll soon be receiving.

Ted knew he wasn't sounding very convincing, but what else could he say?

His comment resulted in a heated dialogue that continued for the rest of the evening. In his anger and frustration, Rick repeated his verbal attack on Ted and complained bitterly about how so much of the income he had made as a business person was being taxed to pay for government services. Ted countered by trying to explain how there just weren't any meaningful jobs for someone with his level of education and training. He repeated that he just needed more time to find the kind of job that would allow him and Ramona to be independent. For her part, Connie remained silent, not knowing whose side to take— her brother's or her husband's.

Two days later, Ted read in the newspaper that the B.C. government had changed the way in which it was going to fund social services. From now on, the article said, people coming to B.C. from other parts of Canada would have to wait at least three months before receiving social assistance; furthermore, this new policy would apply to all those people who had entered B.C. from one month ago and from that time on. Ted was one of those people. He was about to lose his opportunity to receive government assistance because the policy was to take effect immediately.

The article went on to describe other changes in government policy, but Ted could read no further. He suddenly felt as though there were a gigantic weight sitting on his chest. He couldn't move and could barely breathe. If he hadn't been sitting at that moment, he would have collapsed on the floor.

Just then, he heard Connie entering the house. She had Ramona with her and was talking in a low voice so that Ted wasn't able to tell what was being said. As she entered the living room, she saw Ted sitting on the sofa.

"Oh, hello, Ted. I'm glad you're home because I need to talk to you about something that's come up," Connie said, her eyes avoiding Ted's. She sat on a chair across the room from Ted as Ramona plopped to the floor to play with a few toys that were scattered there.

Connie hadn't noticed the look on Ted's face, and Ted hadn't recovered from his shock to the point where he could do anything other than just stare first at Connie, then at Ramona, then back at Connie. At first, Connie sat on the edge of her chair looking down at the floor without speaking. She had her scarf in her hands, and she was nervously turning it over and over with her fingers. Finally, she lifted her head slowly and looked into Ted's eyes. "Ted, I . . . ," she began.

Before she could continue, Ted anticipated what she was going to tell him and interrupted, "I know, Connie. I just read it in the newspaper, so you don't have to tell me what the government is planning."

Connie looked confused and replied, "What are you talking about, Ted? What is the government planning? I haven't seen the paper today. What's going on?"

Ted realized she had wanted to tell him something else. "Never mind, Connie. What were you going to say?"

Connie dropped her eyes again, forgetting for a moment what Ted had been referring to, and said:

Ted, you know Rick's having a lot of trouble keeping his business going. So I've decided to take an office job downtown. In fact, I start next Monday. Ted, I'm sorry, but I don't have any choice. You're going to have to arrange something else for Ramona. As much as I've loved being with her and want to help you, I can't.

Ted was devastated by this news. He couldn't believe that he was hearing this. He pleaded with Connie, but her mind was made up.

Later that evening, as he lay awake in his bed, the same questions kept running through his mind. What was he going to do now? How could he take care of Ramona and look for work at the same time? Even if he could find someplace for Ramona to stay, how could he afford to feed, clothe, and shelter the two of them while he looked for a job? And what kind of job, if there were any to be found, would pay him enough to provide his daughter with the kind of future that he and Dorothy had envisioned?

It was a long night, but he knew there would be many long nights like this in the days to come.

Lisa's Hidden Identity

Lisa stared at the black italic words that seemed to jump off the page. She wondered if she was doing the right thing. Was she even the military type? She tried to reassure herself that she was doing this for her education. Without the scholarship she received from the Navy ROTC, she would be sitting at some lousy nine-to-five job for the rest of her life—and she knew she didn't want to live like her mother, uneducated and miserable because she could have done something with her life. But there was something that she just didn't feel right about, and it came from those little black words . . . .

Lisa was always a little "different." As a young girl, she was the one who was made fun of because she played with the boys and was actually better at sports than most of them. As she grew older and her athleticism was more respected, she was known as the girl who could take on any boy in a game of one-on-one and win. She always knew that she was a tomboy, but it wasn't until her junior year of high school that she realized she was physically attracted to those of the same sex—in simpler terms, Lisa was a lesbian.

She was very open about her homosexuality. Not in the least embarrassed or afraid, she came right out and told her parents, who were shocked at first but liberal enough to accept her sexual preference. In attending a large public high school, it was not difficult for

AUTHOR'S NOTE: This case was written by Courtney K. Howlett.

Lisa to find others who were like her, and they too were not afraid to express their sexuality—they were proud to be who they were.

Being different did not affect Lisa's grades in the least. In fact, with her good grades, she had her pick of colleges that would gladly accept her. She wanted more than anything, however, to go to Private University, but it was expensive. It was no secret that she had dreamed of attending this school all her life, but with her mother constantly unemployed, and her father barely making ends meet, she knew that she would have to carry most of the financial weight. She was determined to go to Private University, but where would she get $30,000 a year? Sure, she worked a part-time job during the school year, and she would certainly have a full-time job over the summer, but it would be impossible for her to pay for her tuition without taking out numerous loans, and the last thing she wanted to do was spend the rest of her life paying back college loans. However, she had received literature about a ROTC program offered at the university. This program would give her a four-year full scholarship as long as she was willing to commit herself to four years in the military following graduation. "Anything but loans," she thought to herself as she anxiously filled out the enclosed application.

Two months later, Lisa was thrilled to learn that she had won the scholarship for which she had applied. "So what if the military is not for me," she said to herself. "At least they're paying for my education." She quickly mailed her affirmative reply back to the university—excited as she was, she was also a little nervous, for she had no idea what to expect. She was prepared to be challenged academically at the university, and she was prepared to be challenged physically in the ROTC program, but nothing and no one could have prepared her for the challenges she would encounter on this one particular sheet of paper:

> I swear by my signature that I am not a homosexual. If at any time during my military involvement I experience thoughts comparable to those associated with homosexuality, I will not acknowledge them physically nor speak of them verbally. If at any time in my military

involvement I discover that I am a homosexual, I realize that if I am on a ROTC scholarship that it may be revoked, or if I am active duty or the reserves, I prove to be ineligible to continue service in the military.

Lisa fumbled with the pen that she was holding in her hand. The words that so many of the other students shirked off or barely read seemed to cut like a knife to Lisa. She had to sign the statement. It was necessary for the activation of her scholarship. And the scholarship was necessary for her to remain at the university. She tried not to think about it too much and signed the ugly statement anyway, trying to forget that she had just promised not to be exactly what she was and knew she always would be.

School would start in three days, and Lisa was anxious to meet all the new freshmen. She had met a handful at her ROTC orientation, but the rest of the first-year students had yet to arrive. She would be happy when she was among different kinds of people where she could be herself and forget about ROTC for a little while.

The next day, the other first-year students arrived to move into their dorms. Lisa, having been there almost a week already, had already settled into her room, so it was exciting for her to simply watch all the newcomers arrive. The girls on her floor were nice enough, but as she met each girl, a consistent thought ran through her mind—"I wonder if they can tell that I am a lesbian . . . and I wonder if they care." Of course, there was no way that she could be able to tell if they knew or if they cared, but it was a new experience for her to be completely unknown by those around her, especially about her sexuality. With ROTC, she figured it would be a good idea to keep her sexual preference a secret because her scholarship would obviously be jeopardized if it were discovered that she was a lesbian. But she was not used to the secrecy, and it didn't feel right to hide something about herself, especially something that was so much a part of her.

As time passed, Lisa found it harder and harder to keep her sexual preference a secret. She had found others who felt like her, but she was constantly worried that someone who knew that she was in ROTC would turn her in on the realization that she was a lesbian. She didn't like having to look always behind her back, and she continued to question her reasons for staying with the program. "They are paying for your education," she constantly told herself. But it didn't seem to be reason enough anymore. She wondered what would happen if she found someone whom she truly loved. How could she be secretive about that? She wouldn't want to be, and maybe she shouldn't have to be.

One night, Lisa was studying in the library and was approached by a woman whom she had seen only a few times before. Lisa was shocked when the woman knew her by name. "She is beautiful," Lisa thought to herself as she twisted nervously in her seat wondering why this woman had come up to her. "I was wondering," said the woman, "if you'd ever like to do something with me, like maybe go to a movie or something?" Lisa was taken aback. This woman, who didn't seem the lesbian type at all, was asking her out! Lisa blurted out a "Sure!" and, before she knew it, they were laughing together and exchanging phone numbers, and Lisa was excited to think that this could be the start of her first college relationship.

The next night, Lisa talked on the phone with Jenny for two hours. They talked about everything and nothing, and they had set a date for the upcoming Friday. They seemed to be hitting it off so well. Lisa didn't even think about ROTC and the statement that had caused her so much worry. Her relationship with Jenny was perfect. Their schedules always conflicted during the week, so they never really saw each other, and they were going off-campus for their date. Lisa didn't like feeling as though she had to hide her relationship, but because it just happened to be a rather discreet relationship, it couldn't have worked out better.

Friday came, and Lisa was nervous. It had been so long since she had had a real date, and she knew that she really liked Jenny. She could tell by the way Jenny looked at her that Jenny really liked her, too.

The movie was good, but the ride home was even better. To Lisa's good fortune, Jenny hinted at another date:

> There is a basketball game this weekend that my brother asked me to go to with some of his friends. I'd love for you to come with me. It will be fun. They're a great group of guys. Especially Jason. He's my brother. He goes to school here.

"He goes to school here?" Lisa asked. "How come you've never pointed him out to me before?"

"I wish I could have, but I never really see him. You see, he's always busy with ROTC stuff, so he spends most of his time in the ROTC building."

"He's in ROTC?" Lisa shifted in her seat uneasily, feeling as though she was about to be sick.

"Yeah. Hey, are you okay? You look sick," Jenny asked Lisa.

"I have to go home now, Jenny. I am sorry."

GLOSSARY

Achieved Trait   An individual characteristic, such as education, skill level, and job experience, that people are able to change through their efforts.

Anomie   A condition of normlessness in a society or in a group.

Apartheid   A legal system of racial domination that existed in South Africa in which whites were the dominant group.

Ascribed Trait   A characteristic that people cannot change.

Assimilation   The process by which a minority is gradually integrated into the dominant majority culture.

Automaticity   The degree to which energy and then information are provided by machines rather than people.

Capitalism   A mode of production in which means of production, such as land, tools, equipment, factories, and knowledge and information, are privately owned.

Caste System   A stratification system in which a person's lifelong status is determined at birth based on his or her parents' ascribed characteristics.

Cohort   People who are born in the same period of time (e.g., a five-year period).

Collective Action   Attempts by a group of people to pursue their common interests by either promoting some change or resisting a proposed change.

Collective Conscience The totality of beliefs and sentiments common to average citizens of a society.

Credential A symbol given by a person, group, organization, or governmental agency to an individual to indicate that he or she now can do something that others without that credential cannot do.

Crude Birth Rate The number of live births in a given year per 1,000 people in a population.

Crude Mortality Rate The number of deaths in a given year per 1,000 people in a population.

Crude Net Migration Rate An indicator of the extent to which a population's size is increasing (a positive number) or decreasing (a negative number) as a result of migration patterns.

Cultural Lag A period of delay that occurs when one part of society changes but other parts have not changed accordingly.

Culture The meanings that are shared by a collection of people and that are expressed in symbols, rituals, stories, narratives, values, and worldviews.

De Facto Segregation Segregation created by unwritten norms that guide people's behavior and result in the actual separation of categories of people.

De Jure Segregation Segregation created by laws and enforced by the police.

Demographic Transition The change within a society from a population characterized by high birth and death rates to a population with low birth and death rates.

Demographics The characteristics and dynamics of human populations.

Direct Institutional Discrimination Organizationally or community-prescribed actions that by intention have a negative impact on minority group members.

Discrimination Actions and practices by members of a dominant majority group that have a harmful impact on members of a dominated minority group.

Doctrine of Separate Spheres The doctrine that stipulates that there should be a separation between work and family life and that each sex should be responsible for a separate sphere.

Driving Force An element that moves the plot of a scenario and determines a story's outcome.

Ecological Approach Research that focuses on the interaction between living organisms and their environment.

Emigration Movement out of a population.

Equilibrium A state of balance among the parts of a whole.

Ethnicity A category of people who share a common cultural tradition.

Exploitation The process through which some social actors become better off because other social actors become worse off.

Expulsion The forced removal of entire categories of people from a territory by another category of people.

Externality A consequence of an action that is unintended and therefore does not figure into the initial determination of the price of some activity or commodity.

Fertility The incidence of childbirth within a population.

Gender A socially constructed classification system that exaggerates the differences between males and females.

Gender Identity A person's sense of his or her self as either masculine or feminine.

Gender Role The expected behaviors that are socially linked to each sex.

Gendering The process of differentiating the sexes based on traits and activities that people believe are associated with either men or women.

General Birth Rate The number of live births in a given year per 1,000 women of childbearing age (usually ages 15–44).

Genocide The intentional extermination of one category of people by another category of people.

Human Capital The skills and abilities that allow a person to do specific tasks and that are accumulated by people making investments in themselves that increase their productivity.

Hypothesis An unverified statement about the causes of some phenomena.

Ideology A set of beliefs about how a society works.

Immigration Movement into a population.

Income Money derived from wages, salary, governmental transfers, and returns on investments.

Indirect Institutional Discrimination Practices that have a harmful impact on subordinate group members even though organizational and community-prescribed norms and policies guiding these practices were established and carried out with no intent to harm minority group members.

Industry A branch of activities devoted to the production of a particular good or service.

Infant Mortality The number of deaths of infants under 1 year of age for each 1,000 live births in a given year.

Internal Colonization The situation in which members of a conquered minority are economically and politically controlled by a majority group.

Internal Migration Changes in residency that occur within a society's borders.

Isolate Discrimination Harmful action taken intentionally against a member of a subordinate group by an individual who is a member of a dominant group.

Language A set of symbols that enable people to communicate with each other.

Latent Pattern Maintenance The process through which a society maintains and transmits values.

Life Expectancy The number of years a person can expect to live on average.

Looking-Glass Self The sense of self derived from how a person thinks that others view him or her.

Majority A category of people who are privileged and have more resources because they dominate a minority.

Means of Production Resources such as people, land, tools and equipment, factories and buildings, and knowledge and skills that people use to produce useful things and services.

Mechanical Solidarity Social bonds among persons based on shared moral sentiments.

Migration The movement of people into and out of a population residing in a specific territorial area.

Minority A category of people who are disadvantaged and subjected to unequal treatment as a result of being dominated by a majority.

Mobilization   The marshaling of resources that are needed for a collective action to occur.

Mode of Production   The economic system through which people produce useful goods and services.

Mortality   The extent of death within a population.

Narrative   An account of events that has a beginning, middle, end, characters, and plots.

Natural Growth Rate   The extent to which a population is increasing or decreasing as a result of fertility and mortality patterns.

Norms   Shared rules and expectations that guide behavior.

Occupations   Sets of jobs that involve similar activities or tasks.

Organic Solidarity   Social bonds based on a complex division of labor that connects members of industrialized societies.

Organization   A social entity in which people are connected by a coordinated division of labor designed to attain a goal or set of goals.

Paternalism   The idea that women, like children, are inferior creatures in need of protection.

Patriarchy   A system of social organization in which men have power over women.

Power   The ability to realize one's interests despite the resistance of others.

Prejudice   An attitude of liking or disliking that involves a strong belief about an entire category of people.

Race   A category of people who share a biologically transmitted trait that members of a society view as socially significant.

Racism The belief that those in certain racial or ethnic categories are innately superior and those in other race–ethnic categories are innately inferior.

Rational Action Behavior based on the weighing of the costs and benefits of alternative courses of action.

Reference Group A social group that serves as a point of reference for a person's decisions and judgments.

Relative Deprivation A person's sense that he or she is disadvantaged in comparison to others.

Ritual A culturally meaningful pattern of behavior.

Role The behaviors expected of someone when he or she occupies a particular status.

Role Conflict The incompatibility between two or more different roles that a person occupies.

Role Expectations The behaviors expected according to a role's norms.

Salience The likelihood that a person will enact an identity.

Scapegoats People or a category of people whom other people unfairly blame for their problems.

Segregation The physical and social separation of categories of people.

Sex The distinction between men and women that is based on their biological and physical differences.

Sexism The belief that one sex, usually men, is innately superior to the other sex.

Sexual Division of Labor The process through which tasks are assigned to people based on their sex.

Slavery   The ownership of one category of people by another category of people.

Small-Group Discrimination   Harmful action taken intentionally by a small group of dominant group members in concert against members of a subordinate group.

Social Closure   The restriction of access to resources and opportunities to a limited set of eligible people.

Social Connections   Forms of social organization that shape human actions and interactions.

Social Construction of Reality   The process through which people create their social worlds through social interaction.

Social Ecologist   A social scientist who examines the relation between the physical and social aspects of communities.

Social Function   An activity that is necessary for the survival of an entire society or social entity.

Social Group   A social entity consisting of two or more social actors who have in common some trait that connects them together and provides the basis for their interaction.

Social Movement   An organized and concerted effort to promote social change by individuals and groups.

Social Movement Organization   A formal organization that works toward social movement goals.

Social Network   A set of social ties among social actors.

Social Relationship   An enduring social interaction between two or more social actors.

Social Stratification   The processes through which resources and opportunities are distributed among social actors.

Social Structure The organizing principle of a social system that generates relatively stable patterns of behavior.

Socialization The process of learning how to behave in expected ways within roles.

Sociation Patterns and forms of social associations and interaction.

Sociology The study of social connections and the social interactions that occur in society.

Statistical Discrimination Inequalities resulting from the treatment of an individual on the basis of characteristics believed to be typical for the group to which the individual belongs.

Status A position that is connected through a social relationship.

Stereotype A set of characteristics that are attributed to all members of some specific group or social category of people.

Strategy of Action A persistent way of ordering action over time.

Structural Discrimination Inequalities that result from the normal and usual functioning of socioeconomic systems and not from the prejudicial attitudes or discriminatory laws and practices of the dominant social group.

Structural Functionalism The theoretical framework that examines how social entities survive through the functioning of their parts.

Suburbanization The process whereby people leave central cities for areas outside cities that are either adjacent to a city or within commuting distance.

Symbol An object or behavior that conveys a specific meaning to the people who share a culture.

Technology The tools, knowledge, and skills people use to achieve some practical purposes.

Theory A set of concepts and propositions that people use to develop explanations of observable phenomena.

Traditions Customs and beliefs that are passed down from generation to generation.

Urbanization The process whereby people move from rural areas to cities.

Worldview An overall perspective through which people see and understand what goes on around them.

REFERENCES

Adorno, Theodor W., Else Frenkel-Brunswick, Daniel J. Levinson, and R. N. Sanford. 1950. *Authoritarian Personality.* New York: Harper & Row.

Albrow, Martin. 1970. *Bureaucracy.* New York: Praeger.

Allport, Gordon. 1958. *The Nature of Prejudice.* Garden City, NY: Doubleday.

Arrow, Kenneth. 1973. "The Theory of Discrimination." Pp. 3-42 in *Discrimination in Labor Markets,* edited by O. Ashenfelter and A. Rees. Princeton, NJ: Princeton University Press.

Basow, Susan. 1992. *Gender, Sex Stereotypes and Roles.* Pacific Grove, CA: Brooks/Cole.

Becker, Gary S. 1957. *The Economics of Discrimination.* Chicago: University of Chicago Press.

———. 1964. *Human Capital: A Theoretical and Empirical Analysis with Special Reference to Education.* New York: National Bureau of Economic Research.

Berg, Ivar. 1970. *Education and Jobs: The Great Training Robbery.* New York: Praeger.

Berger, Peter L. and Thomas Luckmann. [1966] 1990. *The Social Construction of Reality: A Treatise in the Sociology of Knowledge.* Reprint, New York: Anchor.

Best, Raphaela. 1983. *We've All Got Scars: What Boys and Girls Learn in Elementary School.* Bloomington: Indiana University Press.

Biddle, Bruce J. 1979. *Role Theory: Expectations, Identities, and Behaviors.* San Diego, CA: Academic Press.

Bielby, William T. and James N. Baron. 1986. "Men and Women at Work: Sex Segregation and Statistical Discrimination." *American Journal of Sociology* 91:759–99.

Bijker, Wiebe E., Thomas P. Hughes, and Trevor Pinch, eds. 1987. *The Social Construction of Technological Systems.* Cambridge, MA: MIT Press.

Blau, Peter M. and Marshall W. Meyer. 1987. *Bureaucracy in Modern Society.* 3rd ed. New York: Random House.

Bluestone, Barry and Bennet Harrison. 1982. *The Deindustrialization of America.* New York: Basic Books.

Bonacich, Edna. 1972. "A Theory of Ethnic Antagonism: The Split Labor Market." *American Sociological Review* 37:547–59.

Burt, Ronald. 1992. *Structural Holes.* Cambridge, MA: Harvard University Press.

Bush, Diane and Roberta Simmons. 1990. "Socialization Processes over the Life Course." Pp. 133–64 in *Social Psychology: Sociological Perspectives,* edited by M. Rosenberg and R. H. Turner. New Brunswick, NJ: Transaction Publishing.

Castells, Manuel. 1996. *The Rise of the Network Society.* Cambridge, MA: Blackwell.

———. 1997. *The Power of Identity.* Cambridge, MA: Blackwell.

Christiansen, John and Sharon Barnartt. 1995. *Deaf President Now! The 1988 Revolution at Gallaudet University.* Washington, DC: Gallaudet University Press.

Coleman, James S. and Thomas J. Fararo, eds. 1992. *Rational Choice Theory: Advocacy and Critique.* Newbury Park, CA: Sage.

Collins, Randall. 1979. *The Credentialed Society: An Historical Sociology of Education and Stratification.* San Diego, CA: Academic Press.

———. 1998. "The Sociological Eye and Its Blinders." *Contemporary Sociology* 27(1):2–7.

Cook, Karen S. and Joseph M. Whitmeyer. 1992. "Two Approaches to Social Structure: Exchange Theory and Network Analysis." *Annual Review of Sociology* 18:109–27.

Cooley, Charles H. [1902] 1964. *Human Nature and the Social Order.* Reprint, New York: Schocken.

———. [1909] 1962. *Social Organization.* Reprint, New York: Schocken.

Davidoff, Leonore and Catherine Hall. 1987. *Family Fortunes: Men and Women of the English Middle Class, 1780–1850.* London: Hutchinson.

Davies, James C. 1981. "Toward a Theory of Revolution." *American Sociological Review* 27:363–87.

Davis, Kingsley and Wilbert Moore. 1945. "Some Principles of Stratification." *American Sociological Review* 10:242–49.

Dollard, John, Neal E. Miller, Leonard W. Doob, O. H. Mowrer, and Robert R. Sears. 1937. *Frustration and Aggression.* New Haven, CT: Yale University Press.

Dunphy, D. 1972. *The Primary Group.* Norwalk, CT: Appleton-Century-Crofts.

Durkheim, Emile. [1895] 1964. *The Division of Labor in Society.* Reprint, New York: Free Press.

———. [1897] 1966. *Suicide.* Reprint, New York: Free Press.

Ehrlich, Anne H. and Paul R. Ehrlich. 1987. *Earth.* London: Thames Methuen.

England, Paula. 1984. "Wage Appreciation and Depreciation: A Test of Neo-Classical Economic Explanations of Occupational Sex Segregation." *Social Forces* 62:726–49.

England, Paula, George Farkas, Barbara S. Kilbourne, and Thomas Dou. 1988. "Explaining Occupational Sex Segregation and Wages: Findings from a Model with Fixed Effects." *American Sociological Review* 53:544–58.

Fagot, B. I. 1985. "Beyond the Reinforcement Principle: Another Step Toward Understanding Sex Role Development." *Developmental Psychology* 21:1097–104.

Farley, Reynolds and Walter R. Allen. 1987. *The Color Line and the Quality of Life in America.* New York: Russell Sage Foundation.

Feagin, Joe R. and Clairece B. Feagin. 1993. *Racial and Ethnic Relations.* Englewood Cliffs, NJ: Prentice Hall.

Fischer, Claude. 1975. "Toward a Subculture Theory of Urbanism." *American Journal of Sociology* 80:1319–41.

———. 1977. "Perspectives on Community and Personal Relations." Pp. 1–18 in *Networks and Places: Social Relations in the Urban Setting,* edited by C. Fischer, R. Jackson, C. Stueve, K. Gerson, L. Jones, and M. Baldassare. New York: Free Press.

———. 1982. *To Dwell Among Friends: Personal Networks in Town and City.* Chicago: University of Chicago Press.

Frank, André G. 1975. *On Capitalist Underdevelopment.* New York: Oxford University Press.

Galaskiewicz, Joseph and Stanley Wasserman. 1981. "A Dynamic Study of Change in a Regional Corporate Network." *American Sociological Review* 46:475–84.

Gans, Herbert. 1962. *The Urban Villagers: Group and Class in the Life of Italian-Americans.* New York: Free Press.

Garfinkel, Harold. 1967. *Studies in Ethnomethodology.* Cambridge, MA: Polity.

Goffman, Erving. 1959. *The Presentation of Self in Everyday Life.* Garden City, NY: Doubleday.

Gordon, Milton M. 1964. *Assimilation in American Life: The Role of Race, Religion and National Origins.* New York: Oxford University Press.

Gouldner, Alvin. 1954. *Patterns of Industrial Bureaucracy.* New York: Free Press.

Granovetter, Mark S. 1995. *Getting a Job.* 2nd ed. Chicago: University of Chicago Press.

Grant, James P. 1994. *The State of the World's Children.* New York: Oxford University Press.

Hartmann, Heidi. 1979. "The Unhappy Marriage of Marxism and Feminism: Towards a More Progressive Union." *Capital and Class* 8:1–33.

Hechter, Michael. 1974. *Internal Colonialism: The Celtic Fringe in British National Development.* Berkeley: University of California Press.

Hickson, David J., Derek S. Pugh, and Diana C. Pheysey. 1969. "Operations Technology and Organization Structure: An Empirical Reappraisal." *Administrative Science Quarterly* 4:378–97.

Hobsbawm, E. J. 1975. *The Age of Capital, 1848–1875.* New York: Scribner.

Hodson, Randy and Teresa A. Sullivan. 1995. *The Social Organization of Work.* 2nd ed. Belmont, CA: Wadsworth.

Hooks, Janet M. 1947. *Women's Occupations Through Seven Decades: Women's Bureau Bulletin #218.* Washington, DC: Government Printing Office.

Johnson, Chalmers. 1966. *Revolutionary Change.* Boston: Little, Brown.

Jones, Jacquelyn. 1985. *Labor of Love, Labor of Sorrow.* New York: Vintage.

Kasarda, John D. 1972. "The Impact of Suburban Population Growth on Central City Service Functions." *American Journal of Sociology* 77:1111–24.

Kerbo, Harold R. 2000. *Social Stratification and Inequality.* 4th ed. New York: McGraw-Hill.

Kessler-Harris, Alice. 1990. *A Woman's Wage: Historical Meanings and Social Consequences.* Lexington: University of Kentucky Press.

King, Mary. 1992. "Occupational Segregation by Race and Gender, 1940–1989." *Monthly Labor Review* 15:30–37.

Knoke, David and James H. Kuklinski. 1982. *Network Analysis.* Beverly Hills, CA: Sage.

Larson, Magali S. 1977. *The Rise of Professionalism: A Sociological Analysis.* Berkeley: University of California Press.

Lenski, Gerhard. 1966. *Power and Privilege: A Theory of Social Stratification.* New York: McGraw-Hill.

Lieberson, Stanley. 1980. *A Piece of the Pie: Blacks and White Immigrants Since 1880.* Berkeley: University of California Press.

Maccoby, E. E. and C. N. Jacklin. 1987. "Gender Segregation in Childhood." Pp. 239–87 in *Advances in Child Development,* edited by E. H. Reese. San Diego, CA: Academic Press.

Malinowski, Bronislaw. 1966. *Crime and Custom in Savage Society.* Paterson, NJ: Littlefield, Adams.

Mannheim, Karl. [1936] 1988. *Ideology and Utopia: An Introduction to the Sociology of Knowledge.* Reprint, Orlando, FL: Harcourt Brace.

Marger, Martin N. 1997. *Race and Ethnic Relations: American and Global Perspectives.* 4th ed. Belmont, CA: Wadsworth.

Marks, Nadine and Sarah McLanahan. 1993. "Gender, Family Structure, and Social Support Among Parents." *Journal of Marriage and the Family* 55:481–93.

Marx, Karl. [1867] 1967. *Capital: A Critique of Political Economy.* Reprint, New York: International.

Marx, Karl and Frederick Engels. [1847] 1972. "Manifesto of the Communist Party." Pp. 331–62 in *The Marx–Engels Reader,* edited by Robert C. Tucker. Reprint, New York: Norton.

Massey, Douglas S. and Nancy A. Denton. 1993. *American Apartheid: Segregation and the Making of the Underclass.* Cambridge, MA: Harvard University Press.

McAdam, Doug, John D. McCarthy, and Mayer N. Zald, eds. 1996. *Comparative Perspectives on Social Movements: Political Opportunities, Mobilizing Structures, and Cultural Framings* Cambridge, UK: Cambridge University Press.

McCall, George J. and J. L. Simmons. 1978. *Identities and Interactions.* New York: Free Press.

McCarthy, John D. and Mayer N. Zald. 1977. "Resource Mobilization and Social Movements: A Partial Theory." *American Journal of Sociology* 82:1212–41.

Mead, George H. [1934] 1962. *Mind, Self and Society*. Edited by C. W. Morris. Reprint, Chicago: University of Chicago Press.

Mead, Margaret. 1961. *Coming of Age in Samoa*. New York: Dell. (Original work published 1928)

Merton, Robert K. 1949. "Discrimination and the American Creed." Pp. 99–126 in *Discrimination and National Welfare*, edited by R. M. MacIver. New York: Harper & Row.

———. 1968. *Social Theory and Social Structure*. New York: Free Press.

Merton, Robert K. and Alice S. Rossi. 1957. "Contributions to the Theory of Reference Group Behavior." Pp. 225–80 in *Social Theory and Social Structure*, edited by R. K. Merton. New York: Free Press.

Michels, Robert. 1949. *Political Parties*. New York: Free Press. (Original work published 1911)

Michener, Andrew H. and John D. DeLamanter. 1994. *Social Psychology*. 3rd ed. Orlando, FL: Harcourt Brace.

Miller, J. H. 1990. "Narrative." Pp. 66–79 in *Critical Terms for Literary Study*, edited by Frank Lentricchia and Thomas McLaughlin. Chicago: University of Chicago Press.

Mincer, Jacob and Haim Ofek. 1982. "Interrupted Work Careers." *Journal of Human Resources* 17:3–24.

Morgan, Gareth. 1980. "Paradigms, Metaphors and Puzzle Solving in Organization Theory." *Administrative Science Quarterly* 25:605–22.

———. 1989. "Corporate Culture and Core Values." Pp. 157–8 in *Creative Organizational Theory*, edited by Gareth Morgan. Newbury Park, CA: Sage.

Nisbet, Robert. 1976. *The Quest for Community*. New York: Basic Books. (Original work published 1953)

Oberschall, Anthony. 1973. *Social Conflict and Social Movements*. Englewood Cliffs, NJ: Prentice Hall.

Ogburn, William F. 1964. *On Culture and Social Change*. Chicago: University of Chicago Press.

Ollman, Bertell. 1976. *Alienation: Marx's Conception of Man in Capitalist Society*. 2nd ed. New York: Cambridge University Press.

Olson, Mancur. 1971. *The Logic of Collective Action: Public Goods and the Theory of Groups*. Cambridge, MA: Harvard University Press.

Parkin, Frank. 1979. *Marxism and Class Theory: A Bourgeois Critique*. New York: Columbia University Press.

Parsons, Talcott. 1966. *Societies: Evolutionary and Comparative Perspectives*. Englewood Cliffs, NJ: Prentice Hall.

———. 1968. *The Structure of Social Action*. New York: Free Press.

Perrow, Charles. 1967. "A Framework for the Comparative Analysis of Organizations." *American Sociological Review* 32:194–208.

———. 1986. *Complex Organizations: A Critical Essay*. 3rd ed. New York: McGraw-Hill.

Pfeffer, Jeffrey. 1981. *Power in Organizations*. Marshfield, MA: Pitman.

Polachek, Solomon W. 1981. "Occupational Self-Selection: A Human Capital Approach to Sex Differences in Occupational Structure." *Review of Economics and Statistics* 63:60–69.

Presser, Harriet B. 1995. "Job, Family, and Gender: Determinants of Nonstandard Work Schedules among Employed Americans in 1991." *Demography* 32:577–98.

Radcliffe-Brown, Alfred R. 1964. *The Andaman Islanders*. New York: Free Press.

Renzetti, Claire M. and Daniel J. Curran. 1995. *Women, Men, and Society*. Boston: Allyn & Bacon.

Reskin, Barbara F. and Naomi R. Cassirer. 1997. "Occupational Segregation by Gender, Race and Ethnicity." *Sociological Focus* 29:231–43.

Reskin, Barbara F. and Heidi Hartmann. 1986. *Women's Work, Men's Work: Sex Segregation on the Job*. Washington, DC: National Academy Press.

Reskin, Barbara and Irene Padavic. 1994. *Women and Men at Work*. Thousand Oaks, CA: Pine Forge Press.

Reskin, Barbara F. and Patricia A. Roos. 1990. *Job Queues, Gender Queues: Explaining Women's Inroads into Male Occupations.* Philadelphia, PA: Temple University Press.

Rheingold, Harriet L. and Kaye V. Cook. 1985. "The Content of Boys' and Girls' Rooms as an Index of Parents' Behavior." *Child Development* 46:459–63.

Roemer, John. 1982. *A General Theory of Exploitation and Class.* Cambridge, MA: Harvard University Press.

Rostow, Walt W. 1960. *The Stages of Economic Growth: A Non-Communist Manifesto.* New York: Cambridge University Press.

———. 1978. *The World Economy: History and Prospect.* Austin: University of Texas Press.

Ryan, William. 1975. *Blaming the Victim.* Rev. ed. New York: Vintage.

Schumacher, Ernst F. 1975. *Small Is Beautiful: Economics as if People Mattered.* New York: Harper & Row.

Schwartz, Peter. 1991. *The Art of the Long View.* Garden City, NY: Doubleday.

Sewell, William H., Jr. 1992. "Introduction: Narratives and Social Identities." *Social Science History* 16:479–89.

Sherif, Muzafer, O. J. Harvey, B. Jack White, William R. Hood, and Carolyn W. Sherif. 1961. "Intergroup Conflict and Cooperation: The Robber's Cave Experiment." A publication of the Institute for Group Relations, University of Oklahoma, Norman.

Simmel, Georg. 1955. *Conflict and the Web of Group Affiliations.* New York: Free Press.

———. 1971. *On Individual and Social Form.* Edited by D. N. Levine. Chicago: University of Chicago Press.

Singleman, Joachim. 1978. *The Transformation of Industry: From Agriculture to Service Employment.* Beverly Hills, CA: Sage.

Skolnick, Arlene. 1991. *Embattled Paradise: The American Family in an Age of Uncertainty.* New York: Basic Books.

Smelser, Neil J. 1962. *Theory of Collective Behavior.* New York: Free Press.

Sorensen, Aage B. and Arne L. Kalleberg. 1981. "An Outline of a Theory of the Matching of Persons to Jobs." Pp. 49–74 in *Sociological Perspectives on Labor Markets,* edited by I. Berg. San Diego, CA: Academic Press.

Sowell, Thomas. 1981. *Ethnic America: A History.* New York: Basic Books.

Spillman, Lynette P. 1997. *Nation and Commemoration: Creating National Identities in the United States and Australia.* New York: Cambridge University Press.

Steinmetz, George. 1992. "Reflections on the Role of Social Narratives in Working Class Formation: Narrative Theories in the Social Sciences." *Social Science History* 16:489–516.

Stryker, Sheldon. 1980. *Symbolic Interactions: A Social Structural Version.* Redwood City, CA: Benjamin-Cummings.

Stryker, Sheldon and Richard Serpe. 1981. "Commitment, Identity Salience and Role Behavior: Theory and Research Example." Pp. 199–218 in *Personality, Roles and Social Behavior,* edited by W. Ickes and E. Knowles. New York/Berlin: Springer-Verlag.

Swidler, Ann. 1986. "Culture in Action: Symbols and Strategies." *American Sociological Review* 51:273–86.

Thorne, Barrie. 1986. "Girls and Boys Together . . . But Mostly Apart: Gender Arrangements in Elementary Schools." Pp. 167–94 in *Relationships and Development,* edited by W. W. Hartup and Z. Rubin. White Plains, NY: Longman.

———. 1993. *Gender Play: Girls and Boys in School.* New Brunswick, NJ: Rutgers University Press.

Tilly, Charles. 1978. *From Mobilization to Revolution.* Reading, MA: Addison-Wesley.

Tönnies, Ferdinand. [1887] 1963. *Community and Society.* Translated by C. P. Loomis. Reprint, New York: Harper & Row.

Touraine, Alain. 1965. *Sociologie De L'Action* (Sociology of Action). Paris: Seuil.

———. 1966. *La Conscience Ouvrière* (Working-Class Consciousness). Paris: Seuil.

Treiman, Donald J. 1977. *Occupational Prestige in Comparative Perspective.* San Diego, CA: Academic Press.

Tumin, Melvin M. 1953. "Some Principle of Stratification: A Critical Analysis." *American Sociological Review* 18:387–93.

Turner, Ralph H. 1990. "Role Change." *Annual Review of Sociology* 16:87–110.

U.S. Census Bureau. 2000a. "International Data Base" [On-line]. Available: http://www.census.gov/ipc/www/idbacc.html

U.S. Census Bureau. 2000b. "International Data Base Population Pyramids" [On-line]. Available: http://www.census.gov/ipc/www/idbpyr.html

Wallerstein, Immanuel. 1974. *The Modern World-System: Capitalist Agriculture and the Origins of the European World-Economy in the Sixteenth Century.* San Diego, CA: Academic Press.

———. 1979. *The Capitalist World Economy.* New York: Cambridge University Press.

Wasserman, Selma. 1993. *Getting Down to Cases: Learning to Teach with Case Studies.* New York: Teachers College Press.

Wasserman, Stanley and Katherin Faust. 1994. *Social Network Analysis: Methods and Applications.* Cambridge, UK: Cambridge University Press.

Waters, Mary C. 1990. *Ethnic Options: Choosing Identities in America.* Berkeley: University of California Press.

Weber, Max. 1946. "Class, Status, Party." Pp. 180–95 in *Max Weber: Essays in Sociology.* Translated by H. H. Gerth and C. W. Mills. New York: Oxford University Press.

———. 1947. *The Theory of Social and Economic Organization.* Translated by A. M. Henderson and T. Parsons. New York: Oxford University Press.

———. 1949. *Max Weber on the Methodology of the Social Sciences.* New York: Free Press.

———. 1958. *The Protestant Ethic and the Spirit of Capitalism.* Translated by T. Parsons. New York: Scribner. (Original work published 1904-5)

Weeks, John R. 1996. *Population: An Introduction to Concepts and Issues.* 6th ed. Belmont, CA: Wadsworth.

Wellman, Barry. 1983. "Network Analysis: Some Basic Principles." Pp. 155–200 in *Sociologist Theory 1983,* edited by R. Collins. San Francisco: Jossey-Bass.

Wilson, William J. 1978. *The Declining Significance of Race.* Chicago: University of Chicago Press.

———. 1987. *The Truly Disadvantaged: The Inner City, the Underclass, and Public Policy.* Chicago: University of Chicago Press.

Wirth, Louis. 1938. "Urbanism as a Way of Life." *American Journal of Sociology* 44:1–24.

———. 1945. "The Problem of Minority Groups." Pp. 347–72 in *The Science of Man in the World Crisis,* edited by R. Linton. New York: Columbia University Press.

Wolf, Naomi. 1990. *The Beauty Myth: How Images of Beauty Are Used Against Women.* New York: William Morrow.

Woodward, Joan. 1957. *Management and Technology.* London: HMSO.

———. 1965. *Industrial Organizations: Theory and Practice.* New York: Oxford University Press.

Wright, Erik O. 1985. *Classes.* London: Verso.

———. 1997. *Class Counts.* Cambridge, UK: Cambridge University Press.

Zald, Mayer N. and John D. McCarthy. 1987. *Social Movements in an Organizational Society.* New Brunswick, NJ: Transaction Publishing.

Zeitlin, Maurice. 1974. "Corporate Ownership and Control: The Large Corporation and the Capitalist Class." *American Journal of Sociology* 79:1073–119.

INDEX